Keith Hill is a New Zealand writer whose work explores the ways that spirituality intersects with culture, history, science, religion, mysticism and psychology. His books include *Striving To Be Human*, *The God Revolution* and *Practical Spirituality*, each of which won the Ashton Wylie Award, New Zealand's premiere prize for spiritual writing. His most recent book is *The New Mysticism* (2017).

BY KEITH HILL

NON-FICTION

The New Mysticism

Striving to Be Human

Experimental Spirituality

What is Really Going On?

FICTION

The Ecstasy of Cabeza de Vaca

Puck of the Starways

Blue Kisses

MYSTICAL POETRY

The Bhagavad Gita: A New Poetic Version

Walking Without Feet:
Selected Poetry of Mirabai and Kabir

Psalms of Exile and Return

WITH PETER CALVERT

The Matapaua Conversations

The Kosmic Web

THE GOD REVOLUTION

How Ideas About God Radically
Changed During The Modern Era

Keith Hill

attar books

Copyright © Keith Hill 2011
ISBN 978-0-47318763-7
Cover designed by Abigail Kerr

First edition Attar Books 2011

All rights reserved. Except for fair dealing or brief passages quoted in a newspaper, magazine, radio, television or internet review, no part of this book may be reproduced in any form or by any means, electronic or mechanical, including photocopying, recording, or by any information storage and retrieval system, without permission in writing from the Publisher.

Attar Books
Auckland, New Zealand
www.attarbooks.com

CONTENTS

INTRODUCTION   7

PART 1
THE DEATH OF GOD

1	An Impertinent Proposal	13
2	The Challenge of Science	17
2	The Bible, Critically Examined	34
4	Let's Compare Gods	43
5	Signs of the Times	56
6	Doubts of the Philosophers	65
7	The Fork in the Road	79

PART 2
GOD'S RESURRECTION

8	World War and its Discontents	93
9	God-Talk is a Human Invention	103
10	Beyond the Mythological God	110
11	Pantheism: Everything is God	121
12	Panentheism: Everything in God	136
13	Are Spiritual Experiences Real?	157
14	God After Metaphysics	178

PART 3
GOD FOR TODAY

15	The Post-God God	201
16	A Pertinent Proposal?	206
17	God as Quest	212

BIBLIOGRAPHY	215
REFERENCES	219
INDEX	224

Introduction

The last four hundred years of life in the West have been full of social, cultural, intellectual, economic, and religious turmoil and change. Throughout this period, which runs from the early 1600s to today and is broadly defined as the modern era, long established concepts about reality, mostly grounded in traditional religious beliefs, were questioned, adjusted, overturned, or discarded completely.

Key cultural shifts included the Protestant Reformation, the dismantling of medieval feudal hierarchies and their replacement with the ideal of egalitarianism, the separation of state and church, the replacement of mythological explanations of what happens in the world with scientific materialist explanations, the rise of secularism, the Industrial Revolution, and the expansion of liberal freedoms into all aspects of our lives on the assumption that we are each autonomous moral, sexual, emotional, and intellectual beings.

These revolutions in thinking and living have not only profoundly changed the West's physical and social environments, but just as significantly have radically reshaped the way we view and relate to the world today. In fact, the transfiguration of the Western worldview has been so wide-ranging that we do not – we cannot – look at the world in the same ways that our ancestors did. The modern outlook, which is predominantly rational and secular, has made a comprehensive break with the mythological and religious sensibility that previously held sway. And, as would be expected, modern thinkers have also explored radical new ways of thinking about God.

For example, the fifteenth century Spanish mystic, Teresa of Avila, assumed that God is a supernatural being and that her soul personally merged with this being. Today there is a widespread rejection of the idea that God is a supernatural being with whom we may personally merge. Other approaches are preferred.

William Blake, the Romantic English poet, described God as a repressive, vindictive, logic-driven rule-maker. Blake placed his criticism in the context of the sciences developed by Isaac Newton. Today's thinkers have extended his critique by questioning the ways that institutional and hierarchical religious structures suppress free thinking and provide cover for sociopathic individuals to do their worst in their local communities.

A third example is that the sciences are widely characterized as antithetical to religions and to thinking about God. In fact, historically the relationship between the sciences and religions has been much more complex than this. A Catholic priest, Gregor Mendel, developed Darwin's theory of evolution by proposing that genes are the biological mechanism that enables life to evolve by natural selection, while physicist Stephen Hawking has suggested that the tools of mathematics may one day enable scientists to penetrate the mind of God. And Albert Einstein famously asserted that God doesn't play dice. Where the ancient prophets of Judaism made their oracular statements in relation to animal sacrifices and the morality of sleeping with one's siblings, Einstein, a modern day Jewish prophet of a very different kind, offered his oracle about God in relation to probability functions as they operate in quantum physics.

All this means that just as the modern era has revolutionized how we conceive of and live in the world, so during the same period long-standing ideas about God were overturned, and then replaced. This has resulted in what I am calling the God revolution.

This book documents how critiques of the personal God of Christian theism, along with explorations of pantheism, panentheism, and postmodern approaches to God, have created a range of propositions that collectively add up to a revolution in thinking about God.

However, this is not actually the first time in history that a revolution in thinking about God has occurred. The religions that dominate the world today, including the post-Vedic Indian religions, Buddhism, Judaism, Taoism, and Christianity, all came into existence as a result of new concepts of God developed by religious revolutionaries who lived between 800 BCE and 200 CE.

The principal difference between those ancient religious revolutions and the modern God revolution is that where the former were instigated by single inspired individuals, the modern God revolution is a collective enterprise that involves numerous contributors working in many different fields of human knowledge. In addition, each contributor works with and has developed the thinking of those who went before. This means that the modern God revolution is not only collective, it is exploratory. So rather than seeking and arriving at definitive final assertions about God, modern God thinkers propose concepts that the rest os us are free to accept, reject, or adapt as we wish.

This exploratory process drives the modern era's thinking. During the eighteenth and nineteenth centuries much of the new thinking excited and engaged the wider public. Accordingly, publishers and newspapers gave much attention to new ideas of all kinds, including those concerning God. Edward Gibbon's *The History of the Decline and Fall of the Roman Empire* (1776–1788), Thomas Paine's *The Age of Reason* (1795), Ludwig Feuerbach's *The Essence of Christianity* (1841), Ernest Renan's *Life of Jesus* (1863), and James Frazer's *The Golden Bough: A Study in Magic and Religion* (1890) each questioned received wisdom, offered new ways of conceiving God, and in the process engendered considerable public debate regarding God.

This is not the situation today. While our public media continue to engage with significant discoveries made by those working in quantum physics, cosmology, biology, and technology, the revolution in thinking about God is no longer given such prominence. In fact, today's media coverage of thinking about God largely focuses on anti-God contentions made by outspoken atheists such as Richard Dawkins and pro-God responses offered by conservative religionists. The limitation of these debates is that they focus on pre-modern concepts of God and avoid contemporary ideas that are far more complex, more nuanced, and definitely more stimulating than backward-looking wrangling over the existence of the bearded God of yore allows.

Revolutionary modern ideas about God also deserve more public attention than they are given because they have been developed to accord with the scientific, philosophic, psychological, and social insights that underpin today's Western secular liberal outlook. They strive to make sense in the context of our modern worldview. Accordingly, there is a need for a survey of key thinkers of the modern era. *The God Revolution* has been written to fill this need.

Of course, a short work such as this cannot include all significant thinkers or explore all their ideas in depth. There are a number of important thinkers who could have been included but who are not. Brevity required that choices be made. Nonetheless, my aim throughout has been to provide an overview that introduces major trends in modern Western thinking about God to readers interested in the question of what God might, or might not, be.

By way of a final observation, I need to acknowledge that this book has developed out of my personal fascination with God. I was nominally raised a Presbyterian, but in my teens I found that perspective unsatisfying. I wanted to know more, to dig deeper. So I began exploring the origins of Christianity, the world's religions, mythologies, and mystical traditions, and Greek and Indian philosophy. I also engaged in spiritual practices.

As a result of my combined reading, experiences, and thinking I came to the conclusion that my conditioned childhood belief in God as a personal being living "up there" who is looking after each of us personally was insufficient to account for what happened in my life, and it certainly did not accord with the dramatic discoveries made by scientists during the past three hundred years. And in the process of exploration I discovered ideas that are far removed from the God of Sunday school.

What makes my personal journey significant is that all the revolutionary thinkers represented in these pages took the same journey.

The first phase of this journey, the initial questioning and eventual rejection of the personal God of Christian theism, is presented in Part One. These seven chapters explore why, from 1600 to 1900, theism came to be seen as unable to account for the existence of the world and what occurs in it. This inadequacy culminated in a widespread rejection of the metaphysically justified myths and dogmas that underpin all traditional religious beliefs.

Part Two examines ideas that were developed by twentieth century thinkers in response to this rejection. Some of their thinking is actually grounded in ideas first offered in the 1600s and 1700s, or earlier. Over the following centuries these ideas were refined into the intriguing concepts they are today. A selection of key thinkers, perspectives, and ideas are surveyed in the seven chapters of Part Two.

Part Three draws together the strands explored in Part Two, showing where thinking about God currently stands. No single concept is approved over any other. Instead, I offer a range of suggestions on possible future directions for thinking about God. This stance reflects the book's intent as a whole, which is to provide a survey of thinking about God that readers, if they feel inspired, may subsequently explore in greater detail for themselves.

PART 1

THE DEATH OF GOD

CHAPTER 1

An Impertinent Proposal

"God is dead." This famous statement has reverberated around the world ever since the nineteenth century European philosopher, Friedrich Nietzsche, first wrote it in 1882. By it he meant not that God had literally died, but rather that the Christian concept of God, as a supernatural being, that had long prevailed in Western culture was no longer valid.

In *Also Sprach Spach Zarathustra* (*Thus Spoke Zarathustra*, 1887) the work Nietzsche considered the greatest fruit of his genius (he was as certain of his own talent as he was of God's demise), Nietzsche made Zarathustra, the ancient Iranian founder of the Zoroastrian religion, the mouthpiece of his new philosophy: "Whither is God? he cried. I shall tell you. We have killed him – you and I. All of us are his murderers."[1]

While Nietzsche made one of the most radical statements about God in Western culture, he was not alone. By the time he wrote those words numerous men and women of his era had already thrown themselves into a complete re-evaluation of God, of the nature of reality, and of Christian beliefs as the long-held bases of Western culture. In fact, for over two hundred years before Nietzsche, scholars, scientists, field researchers, and thinkers had been carrying out wide-ranging investigations into biology, geology, mythology, cultural history, philosophy, and religion, making discoveries and developing ideas and theories that led to an extensive reassessment of humanity's knowledge of the world and the nature of reality as it stood at that time.

What made these discoveries and theories so influential was that they were not written up in specialized academic reviews for the learned few, but in book form that was easily accessible to the general public. That public responded by making many of these books best-sellers. The result was that their ideas produced immediate and long-lasting reverberations not just in the hallowed halls of academia, or in the lecture rooms of religious colleges, but in streets, cafes, and drawing rooms across the world. In order to taste the tenor of the time, and to place Nietzsche's cry of "God is dead!" in its historical context, we need a little scene setting.

The nineteenth century was when human beings first started to experience what today we accept as normal – the sensation that daily life is speeding up. By 1800 the Industrial Revolution was well under way in Great Britain, with the textile industries being mechanized and other industries, such as mining, metalworking, and farming, adding automation to their labor. James Watts' improvements to the steam engine, coupled with ready access to coal to fuel those engines, led to the establishment of factories. These in turn drew hundreds of thousands of workers off the land and into the cities. Gas lighting was introduced in 1812, allowing the burgeoning industries to work longer shifts and stimulating cities to develop a buzzing nightlife.

Buses providing public transport for workers were introduced to French cities in 1832 and to New York by 1836. The world's first department store was opened in Paris in 1838. The first photograph of a person was taken in 1839, postage stamps were introduced in Great Britain in 1840, and the world's first inner city subway opened in London in 1863. The Gatling gun was invented by Richard Gatling in 1862 to enable his fellow Americans to kill each other with modern efficiency during their Civil War, Alexander Graham Bell patented the telephone in 1876, and to complete the feeling of urban pressure, the modern world's first urban serial killer, Jack the Ripper, did his worst in the streets of London in 1888. Completing this teaser list of accomplishments, in 1895 France's Lumière brothers screened the first moving pictures, the modern Olympic Games was founded in 1896, and the British ensured the out-going century set the tone for the next by going to war with the South African Boers over gold, with the Nobel company (of Nobel prizes fame) providing the explosives. The Boers engaged in guerrilla tactics, hitting hard then vanishing into the countryside, to which the British responded with a scorched earth policy, incarcerating women and children in concentration camps, poisoning wells, and burning farms in order to starve out the Boer freedom fighters. So we can see that much of what we accept as the proper conduct of modern civilization was in fact set in motion during the 1800s.

Intellectually, the nineteenth century ushered in equally epoch transforming changes. In 1800 Western scholarly currents were dominated by Christian thought. All European countries shared a belief in one God, who was the God of Abraham, Moses, David, and Isaiah. They all agreed this God had caused a morally cleansing flood to purify the Earth, but had ensured the survival of animals and humanity via Noah's ark. They agreed that their God sent down his son to Earth as humanity's savior, and that the world was headed towards an eventual apocalypse, after which God's son would return and rule on Earth. As a result, all European nations – along with many of the countries they colonized – shared a common history that extended from God's creation of the world, through the present day, and into the apocalyptic future.

Europeans also shared the same divinely inspired Word of God, the Bible. This ensured everyone was grounded in the same religious stories: the creation of the world in seven days, the Fall and the subsequent expulsion of Adam and Eve from the Garden of Eden, Noah's task of building the ark, the descent of all the Earth's peoples from Noah's sons, the parting of the Red Sea when Moses led the tribes of Israel out of Egypt, the Ten Commandments delivered to Moses on top of Mount Sinai, the subsequent warnings of the long line of Jewish prophets, and the sacrifice of God's own Son in the form of Jesus Christ, sent to expunge humanity of its sins.

Of course this shared God, metaphysics, morality, history, and divinely inspired text didn't stop Europeans from disagreeing over how the texts should be interpreted, resulting in the formation of schisms, the instigation of the Protestant Reformation, the establishment of the Lutheran and Anglican Churches, and the creation of sects such as the Quakers, the Pietists, and the Methodists. Nor did sharing the same history, texts, morality, and metaphysics stop Europeans from bullying or killing each other when it suited their purposes. Nonetheless, throughout all their disagreements and battles, they continued to share a belief in the one God, the one creation, the one Bible, the one history, and the one human destiny.

This certainty regarding what they knew of themselves and the world was such that the Irish Anglican Archbishop of Armagh, James Ussher, drawing on Biblical chronology, confidently calculated that the Earth was created on the evening of Sunday October 23, 4004 BCE.

It was also accepted that humanity was progressing upwards, morally, intellectually, and technologically. Or, at least, it was in Europe. Thus European culture was not only the pinnacle of all that had gone before, but as European countries became colonial powers they considered themselves the deserved rulers of the world's "lesser" races. As the English historian, Thomas Henry Buckle, observed in 1857: "The great division between European and non-European civilization turns on the fact that in Europe man is stronger than nature, and that elsewhere nature is stronger than man, the consequence of which is that in Europe alone has man subdued nature to his service."[2]

Europeans were "stronger than nature" because they functioned according to reason, rationality being the leading characteristic of the civilized, while non-Europeans were ruled by their senses, which made them irrational and inferior. Therefore, according to European values, it was not only just, but in the best interests of the world's uncivilized and irrational "lesser" races, that they be ruled by the "greater" Europeans.

Then, in the 1800s, all this certainty received a series of shocks. Almost two thousand years of Christian culture, and several hundred years of European smugness, was suddenly challenged. A succession of ground-breaking discoveries, each presented in equally ground-breaking books, questioned Europeans' common understanding of humanity's place, role, and purpose in the world, their knowledge of God and of the world He created, and their view of humanity's moral and intellectual purpose. In just a handful of decades, the European world view was turned upside-down.

The books that embodied this challenge were predominantly scientific and scholarly in nature, presenting the public with the latest discoveries in the disciplines of biology, comparative religion, Biblical studies, psychology, archaeology, social sciences, philosophy, and philology. A historical survey is required in order to understand what was happening in these areas of study, and why these books should have had such an impact.

I'll begin by considering the immense impact scientific thinking has had on Western thought and culture.

CHAPTER 2

The Challenge Of Science

The provocation that was Charles Darwin's *The Origin of Species*, first published in 1859, still reverberates today. In his book Darwin published the results of decades of research, in which he advanced the radical idea that rather than being created in 4004 BCE, humanity had instead evolved over vast eons of time. Furthermore, this evolution had occurred not through God's intervention, but as a result of the biological process of natural selection, a process that functioned without recourse either to God or to any religious doctrine.

The scientific outlook that underpinned Darwin's book, and the methodologies he used to examine the natural world, had developed over the preceding three centuries. In order to understand not only why Darwin's theory had the impact it did, but also to place his thought in the context of the scientific discoveries of his era, we need to look briefly at how the sciences developed.

During the Middle Ages Europeans considered that religion and nature were one. There existed one Holy Catholic Church and it taught that God created the natural world in seven days, and that humanity, as the pinnacle of God's creation, had been created by God to rule the natural world and all creatures in it. This was known to be true because it was stated in the Bible.

In the thirteenth century Thomas Aquinas, the Catholic Church's greatest theologian, summed up all that was known about God at that time. He argued that the existence of God was self-evident, because God had implanted knowledge of Himself in human beings when He created them (that is why we can conceive of God in the first place), and because truth exists, and truth is God itself. Aquinas was himself powerfully influenced by the ideas of the ancient Greek philosopher Aristotle. Aristotle had theorized that God was the First Cause, the Unmoved Mover who animated the world and all in it. This led Aquinas to make three key assumptions regarding God.

First, the natural world that God, as first cause, had created was perfect. This was because God, as the perfect Being, could not create anything that was imperfect or flawed.

Second, Aquinas argued that God had given human beings reason so that we may "peer into" God's perfect world and use it discern God's perfect intention and thought as it is manifested in the world.

Third, and despite the power of human reason, revelation remained the ultimate guide as to God's intentions. And the Bible provided revelation. So no matter what human beings discovered via their reason, their thoughts were only correct if they agreed with the Bible.

These three assumptions – that the natural world was perfect, that human reason may understand the mind of God as it manifests in the natural world, and that statements about the world necessarily need to accord with the Bible – led directly to the tensions created by the discoveries of the sciences.

THE BIRTH OF THE SCIENCES

In the two centuries following Aquinas Europe changed radically. Politically and religiously, the Catholic Church's position as God's sole Earthly authority was challenged by the Reformation, which was triggered in 1517 when Martin Luther nailed his Ninety-Five Theses on a church door in Wittenberg. Luther's key contentions were that believers should reject all Catholic religious authority and traditions, and that the Bible, unmediated by Catholic dogma, should be believers' sole source of guidance. Thus, while Luther challenged the authority of the Catholic Church, he endorsed the Bible as the arbiter of truth.

Not long after Luther's declaration, in 1534 England's Henry the Eighth, irritated that the Pope wouldn't allow him to divorce an infertile wife, broke from Rome's domination by establishing the Church of England, with himself as its head. Other Reformist Protestant Christian sects and states followed, with the Netherlands and Germany also breaking from Rome's rule.

Suddenly, the Catholic Church's religious and political power was broken. Europe split into Catholic and Protestant camps, and they promptly went to war: the Eighty Years' War, fought by the Protestant Dutch and the Catholic Spanish from 1568 to 1648, and the Thirty Years' War, fought by France and Germany from 1618 to 1648.

Intellectually, Europe also underwent a radical change during this period, with the power of reason advocated by Aquinas being taken up and applied in ways Aquinas could never have anticipated. During the Italian Renaissance of the 1400s artists and thinkers looked back to Greece for inspiration and knowledge. In particular, Europeans hungry for new ways of thinking about the world embraced Aristotelian natural philosophy. Natural philosophy, coupled to reason, subsequently led to the development of scientific thought. Aristotle grounded his natural philosophy in observation. Francis Bacon (1561–1626) laid the foundations of the emerging scientific method when he similarly asserted in his *Novum Organum* (*New Instrument*, 1620) that the proper starting point for studying the world should be in observation:

> Man, being the servant and interpreter of Nature, can do and understand so much and so much only as he has observed in fact or in thought of the course of nature. Beyond this he neither knows anything nor can do anything.[1]

Bacon argued that what was required to progress human knowledge was a process of intellectual induction in which general principles and natural laws were derived from observed fact. Bacon also considered that previously accepted assumptions and ways of thinking had to be discarded, because they merely served to affirm what was already known; they did not lead to the discovery of what was not yet understood.

> Another form of induction must be devised than has hitherto been employed. ... For the induction which proceeds by simple enumeration is childish; its conclusions are precarious and exposed to peril from a contradictory instance; and it generally decides on too small a number of facts, and on those only which are at hand. But the induction, which is to be available for the discovery and demonstration of sciences and arts, must analyze nature by proper rejections and exclusions; and then, after a sufficient number of negatives, come to a conclusion on the affirmative instances.[2]

This process of reasoning was initially called the Baconian method. It was subsequently refined into the scientific method. Central to the scientific method was the idea that the natural world need not be examined only through the twin lenses of the Bible and Christian theology. Instead, the human eye, and the rational mind behind that eye, became the new lens through which to view the world. In this manner, Bacon took Aquinas' advocacy of rational thought to "peer into God's mind" further than Aquinas could ever have conceived.

However, this did not mean that Bacon and his fellow scientific thinkers rejected God. Far from it. Bacon himself considered that "the advancements of the sciences, are destined by fate, that is, by Divine Providence,"[3] and that the sciences revealed the power of God in the natural world, just as religion revealed God's will in the world. As such, Bacon considered that his new scientific methodology was the "handmaiden of religion."[4]

Bacon was not alone in believing in both God and the scientific method. The seventeenth century mathematician and philosopher, Rene Descartes, not only argued that knowledge of God is innate in us, but in *Principia Philosophiae* (*Principles of Philosophy*, 1644) he accepted that human reason is secondary to God's revelation:

> Regarding Him as the efficient cause of all things, we shall merely try to discover by the light of nature that He has placed in us, applied to those attributes of which He has been willing we should have some knowledge ... but we must keep in mind what has been said, that we must trust to this natural light only so long as nothing contrary to it is revealed by God Humself.[5]

The outlooks of Bacon and Descartes may not have been orthodox, and certainly they used reason rather than Biblical texts when seeking to discover the principles of mathematics and scientific inquiry. However, neither did they consider themselves to be stimulating doubt in Christian belief in God.

Nonetheless, the results of the new scientific thinking presented a direct challenge not only to the limits of the knowledge of the day, but to traditional Christian thought. Both Bacon and Descartes made that challenge in a way that brought them no censure – possibly because, in working in the areas of mathematics and philosophy, they were not directly confronting Church dogma. But another scientific genius of the same era was not to escape so easily. That genius was the Italian mathematician, astronomer, and physicist, Galileo.

THE BEGINNINGS OF SCIENCE

The immense contribution made by Galileo Galilei (1564–1642) to the beginnings of science resulted from his application of Bacon's methodology. He made observations, and then constructed mathematical formulae to connect what he observed. He established the idea that science should utilize measurable and repeatable experimentation, conducted experiments himself that laid the groundwork for the understanding of motion, established the foundations for astronomy, and presented mathematical descriptions of the laws of nature. His book *Il Saggiatore* (*The Assayer*, 1623), was the first to demonstrate how science should be practiced. In his spare time he also improved the design of the compass and refined the recently invented telescope, which enabled him to see mountains on the moon and the moons circling Jupiter. For all this he is revered today as the father of modern science, astronomy, and physics.

Of course, Galileo is best known because of the controversy he stirred when he claimed that the Earth travelled around the Sun. The Catholic Church regarded the Ptolemaic view, that the Sun, Moon and stars circled the Earth, as being the truth, on the grounds that it accorded with the Bible. *Psalms* 93, 96 and 104 each stated that the world and the Earth had been firmly set on their foundations by God, and could never be moved, while *Joshua* contains an account of how, with God's help, Joshua made the Sun stand still in the sky. In addition, Aristotle had also argued that the Earth was the centre of the universe. Indeed, Ptolemy had constructed his system under the influence of Aristotle's natural philosophy. With Aquinas in turn advocating for Aristotle's views, the Ptolemaic system became an official doctrine of the Catholic Church.

The first challenge to the Ptolemaic system actually occurred before Galileo was born, when *De Revolutionibus Orbium Coelestium* (*On the Revolutions of the Celestial Spheres*) by Nicolaus Copernicus (1473-1543) was published in 1543. Using intellectual reasoning and mathematics, Copernicus developed a heliocentric model of the solar system, in which he showed how the planets travel around the Sun, and how the turning of the Earth explains the apparent movement of the Sun and the revolutions of the stars. Copernicus' theory initially created much interest among Catholic and Protestant clergy who were fascinated by astronomy. Even Pope Clement VII was intrigued. After Copernicus' death two mathematicians, Tycho Brahe and Johannes Kepler, added further detail to Copernicus' model without creating any controversy.

This remained the case until Galileo's telescope enabled him to observe moons actually circling Jupiter, and to see that Venus had phases, just like the Earth's Moon, that resulted from it circling the Sun. Galileo also observed sunspots on the Sun. Suddenly, what for sixty years had been an interesting theory now had physical confirmation. Confirmation that Galileo promptly published. In *Sidereus Nuncius* (*The Starry Messenger*, 1610) Galileo presented the discoveries he had made via his telescope. His book attracted both support and ridicule from prominent clergymen. Those clergy who were supportive were as fascinated as Galileo was by his confirmation of the heliocentric theory. Those who couldn't accept the heliocentric model did so because it contradicted the Bible and contravened Christian Ptolemaic doctrine.

The problem was that both the Catholic and Protestant Churches considered that because, as Aquinas had argued, the natural world was perfect, the heavens must be fixed, unchanging, and perfect. Galileo's claim to have seen blemishes (sunspots) on the Sun meant the Sun was not perfect. And Galileo's claims the Earth was not fixed, and therefore not unchanging, implied that the entire universe was imperfect. Because Christian apologists could not concede that the perfect God could have created an imperfect world, they necessarily concluded that Galileo was wrong. He was accused of blasphemy and heresy. Consequently, the Inquisition was called to investigate.

After conferring with a committee of bishops, in 1616 the Inquisition decreed that there was insufficient evidence supporting Galileo's heliocentric claims. He was commanded to stop advocating heliocentrism. Galileo agreed to do as he was commanded.

However, the decision continued to rankle with Galileo. Eventually, he decided he wanted to defend his claims. So in 1630 he sought permission from the Inquisition and Pope Urban to write a book on his theory. This permission was granted, but with the proviso that he present both the geocentric and heliocentric views even-handedly. The result was *Dialogo Sopra i due Massimi Sistemi del Mondo* (*Dialogue Concerning the Two Chief World Systems*, 1632).

Unfortunately for Galileo, he was too polemical in his presentation. The Inquisition considered that he had neglected to present significant material in support of the geocentric position. An even bigger problem was that he had put the weakened geocentric position in the mouth of a character named Simplicio, and placed the Pope's own ideas in the mouth of the same character. The book's overall balance clearly tilted in favor of the Copernican position over that of Ptolemy and the Church. Scientifically, it was a ground-breaking work. But politically it was not a clever move, as it left the Pope, who considered he had tried to help Galileo, feeling insulted. Accordingly, the Inquisition was again brought in to investigate.

The judgement was clear-cut. Galileo was required to recant his views, the book was placed on the Inquisition's Forbidden Index of banned books (with Copernicus' *De Revolutionibus* now added for good measure), Galileo was kept under house arrest for the remainder of his life, and the publication of all his books, including those he was yet to write, was forbidden.

As history shows, none of this prevented the heliocentric view from becoming established over the next hundred years. Eventually, intellectual pressure and Galileo's continued renown pushed the Inquisition to allow the publication of a censored version of the *Dialogues* in 1741. Finally, in 1835, both Galileo's and Copernicus' books were taken off the Inquisition's Index of banned books. But by this time, two hundred years after Galileo's *Dialogo* was first published, a vast change in the European intellectual outlook had occurred.

THE DEVELOPMENT OF SCIENTIFIC THINKING

Isaac Newton (1643–1727), arguably the greatest scientist of all time, took to another level the experimental methodology of Bacon that Galileo had so brilliantly applied. Newton is best known as the scientist who discovered gravity when an apple fell on his head. While this story is folklore rather than fact, he was the first to describe, in mathematical terms, the force of gravity and how it influenced objects in the world. His theory of gravity extended to planetary bodies, adding significantly to Kepler's discoveries regarding planetary motion. Galileo thought planets orbited the Sun in circles, because the circle was the most perfect shape, but Kepler showed planetary courses actually followed ellipses. Newton improved the mathematical proof of this. In fact, Newton's mathematics was so accurate that his equations were used to calculate the trajectories of space flights to the moon in the 1960s. These, and other ideas dealing with mechanics, were presented in his masterwork *Philosophiae Naturalis Principia Mathematica* (*Mathematical Principles of Natural Philosophy* 1687), considered to be the most important scientific book ever written. Newton also developed the science of optics, showed how prisms split white light into colors, and developed a reflecting telescope that improved on Galileo's model.

Newton's discoveries, and especially the realization that the natural world functioned according to regular movements of material bodies that could be mathematically described, had a huge impact on his contemporaries. An impact that was both positive and negative. The scientific world was obviously profoundly impressed by Newton's achievements. But others were not enamoured at all. William Blake, reflecting the opinions of many, considered Newton and his physics were a blight, because the mechanistic view of the universe that resulted from Newton's laws was antithetical to human imagination and freedom. However, Blake wasn't impressed by religion either. He considered that religion propagated laws which bound humanity "more and more to Earth, closing and restraining, till a philosophy of Five Senses was complete. Urizen [the restrictive creator God] wept & gave it into the hands of Newton and Locke."[6] For Blake, Newtonian materialism completed the process of confining human imagination that religion had begun.

Newton's developments of mathematical laws by which the natural world functioned reflected the rise of reason as the principal means of understanding the world. As the above quote from Blake makes clear, the scientific outlook was based in the senses. The world of science was the world we see, feel, hear, taste, and smell. Human beings could "peer into" this material world by making observations of aspects of it, then use rational thought to discover the mathematical and measurable laws which governed what occurs in the world.

John Locke provided a philosophic rationale for the new materialist outlook. Considered the first British empiricist, Locke argued that the mind is a *tabula rasa* (blank slate) which obtains impressions from only two sources: sense experience, and rational reflection on sense experience. There was no room in Locke's thought for innate ideas or tendencies with which we are born, which also meant no place for the Christian concept of original sin – because human beings, being born blank slates, could not carry any moral stain into the world with them. Locke believed in God, and that human beings possessed a spiritual element. However, because both God and the spirit exist beyond either sense experience or rational reflection, he considered neither can be known.

Newton, despite Blake's view of him, also believed in God. Both humbler regarding what he had achieved, and somewhat more religious than how he was popularly portrayed, Newton observed: "Gravity explains the motions of the planets, but it cannot explain who set the planets in motion. God governs all things and knows all that is or can be done."[7]

However, despite the willingness of the early scientists and empiricists to accommodate God within their outlook, their materialist perspective marked a huge intellectual shift. The world as seen through the lens of Christian theology was fundamentally magical. It was a world in which God created the world in seven days, spoke to his prophets through whirlwinds, fire and visions, carried visionaries to heaven in chariots, sent His son into the world via the womb of a virgin, justified His ways through miracles, and resurrected lifeless bodies.

In contrast, the scientific outlook viewed the world through the lens of sense perceptions, and analyzed those perceptions using rational thought. Thus today's clash between religion and science, which has at its roots a clash between the miraculous and the rational, can be seen as beginning in the seventeenth century. This was when Copernicus and Galileo argued that, no matter what the Bible said, the Earth circled the Sun, and when Newton's experiments revealed that a rainbow was not God promising not to flood the Earth again, but resulted from white light splitting into its constituent colors. Furthermore, Copernicus, Galileo, and Newton each provided the mathematical formulae that showed how such events occurred.

"THE ORIGIN OF THE SPECIES"

By the time Charles Darwin was born in 1809, the scientific method had become common practice in geology, biology, botany, mechanics, and medicine. While Darwin was baptized in the Anglican Church, his father was a freethinker and his mother a Unitarian.

Freethinkers arose throughout Europe from the 1600s, hand-in-hand with the rise of scientific thought. They rejected the traditions and authority of the Church, along with miracles, the supernatural, and literal belief in the Bible. Instead they considered people should use reason and common sense to decide what is truthful and what is not. Their outlook is perhaps best summed up in the credo of British mathematician William Clifford who maintained that "It is wrong always, everywhere, and for anyone, to believe anything upon insufficient evidence."[8]

Unitarians rejected the Trinitarian concept that God consists of three persons, the Father, Son, and Holy Ghost. Instead they considered God was one being, and that Jesus was a great man and a prophet of God who provided a model for morality, but he wasn't God. Reason, intellectual inquiry, and the rejection of miracles and traditional Christian dogmas underpinned nineteenth century Unitarian belief.

In 1825 Darwin followed his doctor father's career course and attended university to study medicine. However, he didn't enjoy medicine's surgical aspect, and gradually became more interested in natural history, particularly beetles, plants, and marine animals. During this period two key ideas attracted him.

One was the argument for God's existence based on divine design in nature – an argument today known as intelligent design – presented by the Anglican theologian, William Paley. Seeking to explain his theological position in terms relevant to people living in the industrial revolution, Paley argued that if we found a watch lying on the ground, we would naturally conclude that the watch had a maker. Similarly, he argued, nature was like a watch in that we perceive:

> That its several parts are framed and put together for a purpose, e.g. that they are so formed and adjusted as to produce motion, and that motion so regulated as to point out the hour of the day; that, if the different parts had been differently shaped from what they are, if a different size from what they are, or placed after any other manner, or in any other order than that in which they are placed, either no motion at all would have been carried on in the machine, or none which would have answered the use that is now served by it.[9]

This concept of the world being exactly fitted together struck the young Darwin powerfully, planting a seed that eventually grew into his proposition of natural selection to account for how organic life fitted so well together.

The second key idea that stimulated Darwin's thinking was a theory proposed by the French naturalist, Jean-Baptiste Lamarck. He was the first to offer a theory of evolution, a theory he developed as a result of studying fossils and realizing that today's invertebrates were more complex than their ancient predecessors. Larmack first presented his theory in a public lecture in 1800 and subsequently developed it in a series of books published over the next twenty years.

Lamarck theorized that more complex creatures have evolved out of less complex creatures, and that the trigger for evolution was environmental, with changes in their environment causing creatures to adapt in order to survive. Adaptation involved the development of new organs that facilitated survival, and the withering away of those organs that did not. Larmarck argued that creatures evolved by a process of acquired characteristics, with off-spring inheriting characteristics developed by their parents – such as a giraffe stretching its neck to eat leaves higher in a tree, and passing on to its off-spring that propensity of a stretched neck. Darwin's own grandfather, Erasmus Darwin, was a well-known advocate of Lamarck's views.

At the same time as Lamarck another French naturalist, Georges Cuvier, was also collecting evidence that contributed to Darwin's concept of evolution. In 1776 Cuvier presented a paper on his studies of elephant and mammoth fossils which showed that the mammoth and mastodon had become extinct. That species become extinct was yet another highly controversial proposal, with Christian apologists arguing that extinction, like sunspots on the Sun, was a blemish on God's perfect creation and therefore was an impossibility. Accordingly, the extinction of species, as shown by Cuvier through his study of fossil records, made another puncture in the Christian world view.

In 1808 Cuvier discovered a reptile fossil, which he named mosasaurus. The following year he discovered the first fossil remains of the pterodactyl. Cuvier postulated that these creatures, which became known as dinosaurs, lived in an era before mammals, and that they once dominated the Earth. A cascade of similarly ancient fossil finds through the Americas and Europe in the next few decades confirmed Cuvier's thinking. Thus by the mid 1800s fossil finds had pushed back Ussher's creation date of 4004 BCE by millions of years.

Other ideas regarding evolution were also much discussed during Darwin's formative years. Some theoreticians observed that industrialized culture was more sophisticated and complex than primitive, unlettered non-European cultures. This gave rise to the idea that cultures evolved historically through four principal stages: hunting and gathering, pastoralism, agriculturalism, and industrialization. And the key idea for Darwin that different species should develop out of one common type became prevalent:

> There exists but one animal. The Creator used only one pattern for all organized beings. An animal is an entity taking its shape, or rather its different shapes, from the environment in which it develops. Zoological species are the result.[10]

This statement is not from a scientific treatise. It was in fact written by the French novelist Balzac, in the preface to *La Comédie Humaine* (*The Human Comedy*), published in 1842. What it indicates is that when Darwin left for a five year voyage on the Beagle, the period during which he gathered materials which led to his theory of evolution, he had concepts at hand to help him frame his observations, and a free-thinking state of mind that was prepared to follow those ideas wherever they might lead.

On his voyage Darwin took the first volume of the best-selling *Principles of Geology* by Charles Lyell. Published in four volumes between 1831 and 1834, Lyell's work provided extensive evidence that geological processes occur over eons of time. His evidence included studies of volcanoes and the wearing of landscapes by the natural processes of wind, rain, sea, and gravity. During his time in South America Darwin observed geological formations that confirmed Lyell's ideas. In later years Lyell was the first scientist to discover fossils dating back to the Jurassic and Triassic eras, thus extending Cuvier's pioneering work. In all this Darwin became convinced that gradual accretions of change, occurring over vast periods of time, could account for colossal changes not only in geological formations, but also in organisms. Furthermore, there was extensive data, in fossil records and derived from observations of the world's living species, which provided empirical evidence for the evolution of species.

Darwin's great innovation was to offer natural selection as the mechanism by which creatures evolve from simple to complex, from unfinished to perfected. He considered that as the fossil records show that vast numbers of species that once lived have become extinct, the species that survive today must be descended from those now extinct species. As he wrote at the end of his *The Origin of the Species*:

> It is interesting to contemplate an entangled bank, clothed with many plants of many kinds, with birds singing on the bushes, with various insects flitting about, and with worms crawling through the damp earth, and to reflect that these elaborately constructed forms, so different from each other, and dependent on each other in so complex a manner, have all been produced by laws acting around us. These laws, taken in the largest sense, being Growth with Reproduction; Inheritance which is almost implied by reproduction; Variability from the indirect and direct action of the external conditions of life, and from use and disuse; a Ratio of Increase so high as to lead to a Struggle for Life, and as a consequence to Natural Selection, entailing Divergence of Character and the Extinction of less-improved forms.[11]

Darwin himself didn't coin the phrase "survival of the fittest." But it is clear that he advocated in his book survival by adaptation to changing environmental conditions, and that adaptation occurs by way of a variety of mechanisms, none of which involved God.

Gaps remained in Darwin's theory that were only filled in later decades. For example, Darwin didn't know what biological mechanism enabled inherited characteristics to be passed from parent to progeny. This mechanism was provided by Gregor Mendel, whose 1868 experiments with snow-peas established that there was an "hereditary particle," which we today call genes, that carried the hereditary information. Interestingly, Mendel was a Catholic monk, who carried out his experiments in an Austrian monastery.

Thus dispassionate inquiry into the functioning of the natural world did not exclude a belief in God. Nor did adopting a scientific outlook automatically require the abandonment of a religious viewpoint. And yet ...

THE METAPHYSICAL IMPLICATIONS

Neither Darwin, nor any of the other thinkers I have briefly surveyed, set out to eliminate God with their scientific theories. As noted above, most British nineteenth scientists happily believed in God, although Darwin's belief in the theistic God of Christianity faded in his later years as more and more consequences of his theory struck him. Then, as today, people adopted a range of responses to the materialistic, sense-based worldview that came with the scientific outlook. Many had no problem separating the physical from the metaphysical in their minds. However, others did seek to reconcile their physics and metaphysics. One such attempt was Deism.

A problem for a number of thinkers was that the discoveries of science showed that the world functioned according to natural laws – such as gravity, the laws of motion, optics – which didn't require God's constant intervention. Science hadn't revealed how these scientific laws came to be, but it did clearly show that once those laws were in operation the world could continue very happily without God's care. The result was the Deist idea that in the beginning God had created the world, including the laws that keep the world functioning, but since then had adopted a "hands off" approach. To extend Paley's clock metaphor, God had created a world that was, effectively, a clockwork mechanism. Having wound it up, God could now stand back and let it function according to its design.

By adopting this view of God as a kind of absentee landlord, Deists could reconcile the Christian idea of God as creator with the fact that the laws governing the natural world enabled it to function without God's intervention.

In taking such a metaphysical position, Deists were a function of the European Enlightenment, in which reason was considered to be the proper basis for human understanding and observing natural phenomena, and the best way to extend human knowledge. Deism also became popular among seventeenth and eighteenth century thinkers because it allowed for a rational belief in God, but without the paraphernalia of traditional Christian belief. God existed as an Aristotelian First Cause or Prime Mover, but He didn't intervene in human history in the ways described in the Jewish *Torah*, the Islamic *Qu'ran*, and Christian *Bible*. Accordingly, Deists questioned or rejected the holy scriptures of all religions on the grounds that they were human inventions, and rejected miracles on the grounds that they contravened natural laws. With the Unitarians, Deists believed in the freedom of the individual to exercise conscience with respect to religious belief, and that religious beliefs should be consistent with the natural laws discovered by Galileo, Kepler, Copernicus, and Newton.

The Deist perspective prevailed for a period of about fifty years, into the 1830s. As a philosophic outlook it fell away because the benign Newtonian view of a an orderly world, running like clockwork, started by a God who was happy to allow humanity, the pinnacle of all created creatures, to get on with improving itself, was on the decline. In its place was a darker view of life.

In the final chapter of his *Origin*, Darwin concluded that the battle for survival that constituted living was a positive: "Thus, from the war of nature, from famine and death, the most exalted object which we are capable of conceiving, namely, the production of the higher animals, directly follows. There is grandeur in this view of life … from so simple a beginning endless forms most beautiful and most wonderful have been, and are being, evolved."[12]

Others were less convinced. After all, there was that ominous phrase, "the war of nature, from famine and death." And there was the also subtitle Darwin had given his book: *The preservation of favoured races in the struggle for life*. The idea that nature was at war with itself was already widely accepted. As the geologist, Charles Lyell, observed:

> All the plants of a given country … are at war with one another. The first which establish themselves by chance in a particular spot, tend, by the mere occupancy of space, to exclude other species – the greater choke the smaller, the longest livers replace those who last for a shorter period, the more prolific gradually make themselves master of the ground.[13]

The phrase "survival of the fittest," is popularly used to express this concept. However, this was not Darwin's phrase, being coined by British philosopher and political theorist, Herbert Spencer, when writing about the free market. However, he had just read *Origin of the Species*, and immediately applied Darwin's ideas of adaptation and evolution to economics. Darwin acknowledged the appropriateness of the phrase when he adopted it himself in the 1869 fifth edition of *Origin*, equating "survival of the fittest" with natural selection.

Thus, underpinning Darwin's evolutionary theory was a harsh realization: nature was ruthless regarding the survival of species, and completely indifferent to the survival of individuals. The natural order was one of struggle and war. When one species became extinct nature had another take its place. Whether this or that individual creature survived, or even existed at all, might have been of great significance to the individual creatures involved, but to nature all that mattered was that improvements in the species were passed on to the next generation. This was a very new way of looking at the world.

For almost two thousand years Christianity had assumed that a beneficent personal God existed who cared for individuals. After all, the whole idea of a personal God is that the individual believer is able to have a personal relationship with his or her God. Of course there was also evil in the world. So the loving God intervened occasionally in the world's affairs to help humanity overcome evil and move towards Him. The way God intervened was via supernatural means, by speaking via prophets, and by sending down His own Son for humanity's salvation. In addition, individuals also occasionally received supernatural interventions in their own lives as a mark of God's loving attention.

In contrast, the Newtonian-Deist position was that a beneficent personal God created the world, and in the process set in train a raft of natural laws. The Deist God then stood back and let those laws govern the world. For the Deists, once the world was set in motion God didn't intervene any further, maintaining instead a benign but impersonal and detached stance, and remaining absent from proceedings. However, the imprint of the beneficent and benign God was still visible in the world by individuals who used rational thought to discern God's intelligence and design in the operations of the world.

In contrast, the Darwinist evolutionary position was that God may or may not have created the world and set its laws in motion – Darwin himself moved from believer, to doubtful, to a borderline non-believer through the course of his lifetime. The evolutionary position agreed with the Deist view that natural laws governed the world. But God was not benign, and neither was the world regular, orderly, or revealing of a beneficent design. Rather the natural world was a violent place, in which a raging mass of creatures fought to survive and developed traits that gave them an edge over their competitors for food and territory, traits that would also enable them to survive change in the environment with greater facility. The beneficent, benign God was nowhere to be found in all this violent activity.

As scientific enquirers looked deeper and deeper into the natural world and the way it functioned, the more doubtful they grew regarding the nature of God. If, indeed, God existed at all. This was because the more natural laws they came to understand, the less need they saw for a supernatural God to explain how the world came to be as it was. Natural laws increasingly appeared sufficient to explain the world by themselves, without the need to appeal to God. This gave rise to two positions: agnosticism and scientific atheism.

Agnostic is a term invented by Thomas Huxley in the 1860s. A self-taught biologist, Huxley invented the term because he was dissatisfied with both the theistic and atheistic metaphysical positions. His view was that empirical evidence was required in order for anyone to either accept or reject belief in God. But scientific inquiry failed to show any certain evidence either for or against God's existence. Huxley's agnosticism embodied a position of doubt that he shared with many during the Victorian era.

However, others didn't let doubt stop them, arguing that scientific materialism necessarily led to an atheism. As the French scientist, Baron D'Holbach, argued in his *Systéme de la Nature* (*System of Nature*, 1770):

> An atheist is someone who destroys human chimeras in order to call people back to nature, experience and reason. He is a thinker who, having meditated on matter, its properties and ways of behaving, has no reason to imagine ideal forces, imaginary intelligences or rational beings in order to explain the phenomena of the universe or the operations of nature.[14]

D'Holbach was one of a number of leading thinkers, a group which included the empiricist Locke and the sceptic Hume, who argued for a purely materialist conception of reality on the basis that nothing exists but matter and motion, and that when we look at the universe we see no more than "an immense, uninterrupted succession of cause and effect."[15]

The logical end result of scientific materialism, that the notion of God is unnecessary and should be rejected, was popular among French political and philosophic thinkers of the 1800s. But it was not a position that became widely accepted among the rest of Europe's intellectuals.

Many still sought answers to metaphysical questions either in natural phenomena or in the Bible. Unfortunately, at this time the sacred scriptures of Judaism and Christianity were also coming under the same intense scrutiny that the sciences were directing at natural phenomena. The result was that during the 1800s the seed of faith found, in the fecund fields of sacred literature, a much less nutritious ground in which to root itself than was previously the case.

CHAPTER 3

The Bible, Critically Examined

Just four years after the publication of Charles Darwin's *Origins of the Species*, another book caused an uproar of excitement across Europe. This was Ernest Renan's *Vie de Jésus* (*Life of Jesus*), published in 1863. The uproar resulted from the way it dissected the New Testament narratives in order to find a picture of Jesus that was historically accurate. Renan argued that much of what had been assumed to be history in the Gospels was really just mythologizing that embellished the historical facts, and the fact was that much in the Gospels had no basis in historical reality at all. Such as the resurrection.

> For the historian, the life of Jesus finishes with his last sigh. But such was the impression he had left in the hearts of his disciples and of a few devoted women that during some weeks more it was as if he were living and consoling them. Had his body been taken away, or did enthusiasm, always credulous, create afterwards the group of narratives by which it was sought to establish faith in the resurrection?[1]

For Renan, Jesus was only resurrected in the minds of his grieving followers, and he only became the Son of God when Christian theologians three centuries later declared him to be so. Even more sensational was the way that Renan showed Jesus as a man of his time – with the emphasis on *human*. Renan's portrait revealed Jesus not as God born on Earth, but as the best of men who taught many great spiritual truths and provided a role model for all humanity. And he was certainly not born of a virgin, nor was he resurrected after his death, whatever might be the wishes of his followers.

For Christians, Renan's was a shocking position. From pulpits across Europe accusations of blasphemy were flung at the author. On the other hand, numerous Free-thinkers and Unitarians had no problem with Renan's view. And the public, always ready to be shocked, made Renan's book an instant best-seller.

But it also became a best-seller because none of these ideas were entirely new. Over the preceding hundred years numerous books had cast doubt over various aspects of the Bible's stories. Thus, as with Darwin's theory of evolution, Renan's *Life of Jesus* did not arrive out of a vacuum.

INVESTIGATING THE PENTATEUCH

For nineteenth century Europeans the Bible provided the Word of God. For millennia it had been accepted as divinely inspired, and that it was unquestionable as a witness to Israel's history (into which God had directly intervened), and that it was unimpeachable as a presentation of God's plans for humanity. As such the Bible was spiritually, historically, and literally the Truth.

This certainty worked well when no one thought to question the text of Bible. But the downside of claiming that the entire Bible was literally true was that if *just one little doubt* regarding *just one small part* of the Bible was shown not to be literally true, then the edifice of certainty regarding the entire Bible threatened to fall. This is why the battle over the Word of God became, for many, a battle over the very spiritual foundations of humanity. The problem was that as the Age of Reason rolled on, and the objectivity of the scientific method spread, people started looking very hard at the Bible indeed.

The first chinks in the assumption of the Bible's infallibility occurred when scholars examined the first five books of the Bible, known as the *Pentateuch*. Both the Jewish and Christian traditions considered these books to have been written by Moses. However, the English political philosopher Thomas Hobbes noticed that in *Deuteronomy* 34:5-6 it is written, "There in the land of Moab, Moses the servant of Yahweh died as Yahweh decreed: he buried him in the valley, in the land of Moab, opposite Beth-peor; but to this day no one has ever found his grave. Moses was a hundred and twenty when he died, his eyes undimmed, his vigor unimpaired."

In *Leviathan*, published in 1651, Hobbes observed that Moses cannot have written about his own death, and that the statement that "to this day" no one knew where Moses' grave was situated suggests that a later editor must have added an epilogue. Thus the *Pentateuch*, contrary to tradition, could not have *all* been written by Moses. Naturally, there was widespread reaction to Hobbes' observations, particularly as Hobbes' political views had become unpalatable to the ruling classes. Consequently, he was not only labelled an atheist, he was also forbidden under parliamentary decree from publishing any more books in England. Around the same time the Dutch philosopher Baruch Spinoza went even further than Hobbes by suggesting that Moses wasn't the author of the *Pentateuch* at all, offering instead the prophet Ezra, who lived centuries after Moses, as the most likely candidate.

In the mid-1700s Jean Astric, a French philosopher, developed on these initial investigations of the *Pentateuch*. It is with Astric that the scholarly tradition of Biblical criticism officially began. Astrics' initial motive was to examine the *Pentateuch* in order to refute Hobbes' and Spinoza's conclusions. Using the same methods of literary analysis that scholars of his day were applying to classical Greek and Roman literary texts, he soon realized that two parallel texts were present in *Genesis*, because the first and second chapters both described the creation, but one used the name of Elohim for God, and the other Yahweh. Astric further saw that there were doubled stories, such as the creation itself which is told in two different versions, and the account of Sarah in chapters 12 and 20. Putting all the doubled stories into columns, he concluded that Moses had four different lines of stories before him when he wrote *Genesis*.

Astric's conclusions stimulated widespread and intense study of the Bible, with German Protestant theological scholars leading the way. These scholars rapidly developed a number of new disciplines with which to examine the Bible, including source criticism, form criticism, redaction criticism, textural criticism, and the higher criticism. Each examined the texts of the Bible from different angles. Together they presented an entirely new perspective on the Bible, its historical context, and who wrote it.

Source criticism involved examining texts to see which sources were used in the writing and compiling of them. For example, whether a text's sources included histories, genealogy lists, legendary material, letters, diaries, or oral traditions. Form criticism focused on a text's literary conventions, such as whether it included histories, court records, proverbs, parables, poetry, etc, then placed those conventions within their sociological context. Redaction criticism assumed that a text was a compilation drawn from different sources and genres, all of which were stitched together by an editor, who in turn had his own theological perspective which was influenced by the conventions of his era. Textural criticism, also known as the lower criticism, looked at the variant texts available (ancient texts were copied by hand, resulting in multiple versions of texts), then edited the variant texts together in order to establish a primary text that was, in the scholar's view, as close to the original as possible. The higher criticism drew on all these disciplines, seeking to place a text in the historical era in which it was written, to compare it to other documents written in the same era, and to discern the doctrinal, political, and social perspectives that influenced the text's writers and editors.

An example of the higher criticism was a theory proposed by German biblical scholar, Julius Wellhausen, in 1883. By that time it was agreed by German scholars that the five Mosaic books of *Genesis, Exodus, Leviticus, Numbers,* and *Deuteronomy* not only had multiple sources, but they were edited together over several centuries. Wellhausen's theory, known as the documentary hypothesis, suggested that there were four sources. These were identified as J, the Jahwist (Yahweh) source, written around 950 BCE in southern Judah; E, the Elohim source, written in northern Israel around 850 BCE; D, the Deuteronomist source, written around 620 BCE, possibly in Jerusalem; and P, the Priestly source, written around 450 BCE. A redactor, R, edited together the version of the *Pentateuch* we have today. Wellhausen further suggested that text was compiled progressively, with the J and E sources edited together around 750 BCE. D was subsequently added to them, and the redactor edited final form around 400 BCE. Wellhausen agreed with Spinoza that this redactor could very well have been the prophet and priest Ezra.

TESTING THE NEW TESTAMENT

With the Old Testament being thoroughly investigated it was only a matter of time before the same critical attention was focused on the New Testament. Another German scholar, F.C. Bauer, revolutionized New Testament studies through his contention, first published in 1831, that early Christianity was characterized by conflict between the apostle Simon Peter and Paul of Tarsus.

Bauer argued that Paul's was a universalized view of Christianity, which was shaped for and embraced Gentiles, while the Jerusalem-based Christians led by Simon Peter and James, called the "brother of Jesus", wanted the Church to adhere strictly to orthodox Jewish law and ritual. In Bauer's view the Jewish Christians considered Jesus to be the Jewish Messiah for Jews, while Paul broke with the Jewish Temple and Law by presenting Jesus as the resurrected Christ who was for all peoples.

Bauer saw reflections of this conflict in Paul's letters, of which, incidentally, he considered Paul actually wrote only four out of thirteen letters ascribed to him. Bauer also argued that *Matthew* was written by the Jewish-Christians, because of the way it repeatedly situates Jesus as the fulfilment of Jewish longing for a Messiah, while *Luke* was written by someone from the Pauline-Christian camp, given it generalizes Jesus' teaching and is much less aligned to a Jewish theological position.

Today's scholars don't agree with all of Bauer's conclusions. However, the way he attempted to look "behind" what was presented in the New Testament, and especially his use of literary tools to analyze its texts, played a key role in establishing today's New Testament scholarship.

Another German scholar went much further than Bauer in his analysis of the gospels. This was David Friedrich Strauss, whose work was instrumental in initiating what in later decades came to be known as "the search for the historical Jesus." He also unquestionably influenced Renan when he was developing his own view of the historical Jesus.

Strauss entered the seminary at the age of twelve to begin his theological training, where he was taught by Bauer. (As with Renan, many of the greatest nineteenth century German theological scholars started out training to be priests.) Bauer encouraged his students to treat Christian scriptures as literary texts rather than as sacred writings, and to apply the same principles of textural criticism to them as they would to any classical work. Strauss took to this approach with a devastating single-mindedness.

The result was that 1835 saw the publication, when Strauss was twenty-seven, of his ground-breaking *Das Leben Jesu Kritisch Bearbeitet* (*The Life of Jesus Critically Examined*). Strauss saw his task as being to draw together the random criticisms of the Bible that had been made over the last one hundred years, and to bring this criticism onto a higher, more consistent level of scholarship.

Strauss' central thesis was that the miraculous elements in the Christ narrative were all mythological in nature. Before Strauss there had been two principal schools of thought regarding Christ's miracles: the supernaturalist school, and the rationalist (Strauss called it the naturalist) school. The supernaturalist school argued that the miracle stories in the Gospels were, simply, accounts of miracles. In contrast, the rationalist school sought to reconcile the Gospels to scientific thought, and particularly to find naturalistic explanations for Christ's miracles, such as how Jesus was able to walk on water, and how exactly water was transformed into wine. Strauss put an end to all such quibbling. His view was that there were no historical miracles, there were just mythical stories the early Christians made up to enhance the status of their beloved Jesus. This was the same position Renan later adopted when he came to write his book.

Strauss' *Das Leben Jesu* created a sensation on its publication in Germany, and then again in 1844 when it was published in English. The reason was that it fulfilled the hopes of free thinkers, and the fears of defenders of Christian theology, by articulating in a scholarly manner what many people already felt – that much of the story-telling in the Gospels was not historical.

For example, study of historical documents from Jesus' period showed that King Herod died in 4 BCE, and that there was no record of him – or anyone else – having ordered the killing of young boys. The conclusion was that the Massacre of the Innocents did not occur. Where, then, did the story come from? As this story is only told in the *Gospel According to Matthew*, Strauss suggested that the story's purpose was an example of the Gospel writer's intent to show how Jesus' birth and childhood fulfilled various Old Testament prophecies, the writer's underlying motive being to make a case for Jesus as the Jewish Messiah.

Today much of Strauss' book reads as polemic rather than the presentation of scholarly evidence. Furthermore, Strauss' glee at debunking traditional beliefs is almost palpable in his writing:

> There is little of which we can say for certain that it took place, and of all to which the faith of the Church especially attaches itself, the miraculous and supernatural matter in the facts and destinies of Jesus, it is far more certain that it did not take place.[2]

Nonetheless, after both Bauer and Strauss no one could read the Gospels without being conscious that mythologizing contributed to the construction of the Passion narrative.

Another highly significant realization regarding the Gospels that was made at this time was that the *Gospels According to Mathew, Mark* and *Luke* shared a great deal of material. Each recounted the story of Jesus and his Passion in more or less the same order, and in places even contained very similar or the same wording. This observation led to these three being called the synoptic gospels (from the Greek *synoptis*, which means "seeing together"). It also led to the critical formation of the "synoptic problem," which addressed the question of how the three gospels came to be so similar.

This wasn't a new observation. As far back as the fifth century Augustine of Hippo had noticed the similarities between the three gospels. He drew up columns to compare the texts, and from his reading of the texts argued that *Mathew* was the oldest, with the *Mark* editing down *Mathew* to a more streamlined version, and *Luke* drawing on both. This remained the accepted view until the 1700s, when other orders were suggested. Then in 1863 a German Protestant scholar, Heinrich Julius Holtzman, proposed another way of accounting for the link between the three gospels. His theory became known as the two-source hypothesis.

Holtzman began by proposing that the *Gospel According to Mark*, being the shortest and having the simplest narrative, was the first written. *Mark* begins with Jesus' baptism by John the Baptist and the entering into him of the Holy Spirit. *Mark* then recounts various miracles Jesus performed, presents his teaching on Jewish law, has him speak in parables, and culminates with his crucifixion and the discovery of the empty tomb by Mary of Magdala, Mary the mother of James, and Salome. (The post-resurrection appearances of Jesus to his disciples are not in the oldest manuscripts of *Mark*. Indeed, strictly speaking, there is no resurrection, only an empty tomb – which is why Renan ended his *Life* with Jesus' death and accounted for the story of his resurrection as essentially wishful thinking by his grieving, loving followers.)

The two-source hypothesis is that the writers of *Mathew* and *Luke* both used *Mark* as a narrative backbone to their own gospels, to which each subsequently added separate material. For example, each adds a genealogy through Joseph, but lists different ancestors. *Mathew* traces Jesus back to David and Abraham while *Luke* goes all the way back to Adam. Each also presents differing infancy incidents, with *Mathew* telling the story of the Massacre of the Innocents and Joseph having to take his family to Egypt, and Luke the story of the Roman census requiring Mary to return to Bethlehem and the visitation by the three magi. What both share are sayings of Jesus that are not in *Mark*, such as the Sermon on the Mount in *Mathew*. Due to the number of Jesus' sayings that are in *Mathew* and *Luke* but not in *Mark*, Holtzman postulated that the writers of *Mathew* and *Luke* must have had access to a second manuscript, which consisted of sayings of Jesus. This second document became known as Q (from German *quelle*, meaning source).

Holtzman's theory remains the most widely accepted today. Other scholars have suggested variations on the theory, or other orders of precedence for the Gospels, but his methodology and conclusions remain fundamental to contemporary New Testament scholarship.

RENAN'S "LIFE OF JESUS"

Holtzman's book was published in the same year as Renan's. And Renan's book has not worn so well. Renan, like Strauss, received a seminary education from an early age. In his teens he prepared himself to enter the priesthood, so his education included Catholic theology, philosophy, mathematics, and philology, the last of which led to his study of Hebrew. This study included a critical appraisal of the Old Testament texts, which eventually led to a catastrophic falling out with traditional Christian belief.

The reason was that while pursuing his philological studies, Renan discovered that *Isaiah* consisted of two parts written in different styles and at different historical eras – the first thirty-two chapters being written prior to the exile of the Jews in to Babylon, and the remainder after the return to Jerusalem. (Scholars today accept that the text of *Isaiah* is actually the work of three distinct writers separated by hundreds of years). Renan affirmed for himself through a close study of the language of the *Pentateuch* that its texts must have been written hundreds of years after Moses, and also discovered that the book of *Daniel* was written centuries after the time in which it was set.

Similarly, Renan sought to understand the Christ narrative from a historical perspective. This led him to conclude that parts of the narrative were impossible. For example, his search of historical records indicated to him that the census of Quirnus, if it did take place, occurred ten years after Jesus' supposed birth. This meant that there could have been no real motive for Mary and Joseph to travel to Bethlehem for the birth. Further, Renan considered that the Gospel writer Mathew required Jesus to be born in Bethlehem because he wanted to fulfil an Old Testament prophecy that the Messiah would be a descendent of David. As a result of this line of thought, Renan concluded that Jesus could not have been descended from David. Therefore, Renan argued, this part of the birth narrative could have no basis in historical fact.

Understandably, on discovering all this Renan experienced a falling off of his Christian faith. In 1845 he left the seminary, gave up all his aspirations for a religious life, and instead became a schoolteacher. He went on not just to write his *Life of Jesus*, but numerous works on Christian history and French culture, including the eight-volume *Origins of Christianity* (1866–1881) and a five-volume *History of Israel* (1887–1893).

The studies of Bauer, Strauss, and Holtzman showed that Biblical texts were not the direct word of God, but were rather produced by human beings who lived in identifiable historical eras, used the language and ideas of their time, and wrote texts that reflected the cultural assumptions of the era in which they lived. Renan presented these discoveries in digestible form the public.

However, at the same time as the Bible was being dissected, an entirely different way of viewing Christianity and the Bible came into usage. This was the discipline that became comparative religion.

CHAPTER 4

Let's Compare Gods

At the same time as scientists and scholars were extending the boundaries of European intellectual perspectives, explorers were extending the physical horizons of knowledge of the world. The most famed of the early explorers was the Venetian Marco Polo.

Marco Polo's father and uncle were merchants who travelled into Central Asia to trade with the Mongols. They ended up in the court of the Mongol emperor, Kublai Khan. Several years after their return Pope Gregory X asked the brothers to travel back to the Mongol court, carrying Papal greetings and gifts and also taking with them two monks to spread the Gospel. Marco was eighteen when, in 1271, he left Venice with his father and uncle on their second journey. However, when the travellers encountered warring factions in Syria the monks turned back. But the Polos carried on, reaching the court of Kublai Khan two years later. The Polos were away from Venice for twenty-four years, with their travels including Japan, India, Sri Lanka, and Africa.

The book Marco Polo wrote of their travels, *Il Milione* (*The Million*, better known as *The Travels of Marco Polo*) was first circulated in 1298. It entranced generations of Europeans. Readers of Marco Polo's account learned of the complexity of Mongol customs and religions, including that they believed in reincarnation, and that rather than worshipping images of God the Mongols worshipped a tablet on which were written the words *tien* (heaven), *koang-tien* (supreme heaven) and *shang-ti* (sovereign lord). The world had suddenly extended thousands of miles – and years of travel – towards the mysterious East.

Over the following centuries maritime explorers further extended European knowledge of the world as they sought precious gems, metals, exotic goods, and foods. One of the most famed of these seafarers was Christopher Columbus, who "discovered" the Caribbean islands in 1492 while seeking an ocean passage from Europe to the East Indies. He reached the Central American coast in a subsequent voyage in 1498. Columbus' navigation was off, but he found gold, which he needed to pay his backers. As an unexpected bonus his men carried back syphilis, a sexual disease previously unknown in Europe. It spread rapidly, causing perhaps five million deaths over the following decade. But it was a reciprocal exchange: the smallpox the Spaniards carried with them into Central America caused the deaths of millions of Indians.

Spanish adventurers followed Columbus into the Americas, where they discovered cultural and religious practices very different from Christian beliefs. They found pyramids as mysterious as those of Egypt; witnessed strange rituals, including human sacrifice; and learnt of exotic gods, including Huitzilopochtli, the sun god who required human sacrifice in order to keep shining, and Quetzalcoatl, the plumed serpent. Quetzalcoatl had brought books, the calendar and maize to humanity, and as the patron of priests opposed human sacrifice. Meso-American myths maintained that he created the current cycle of human beings, and that he was born of a virgin.

The numbers of European seafarers rapidly increased. In 1497 Vasco de Gama lead a fleet of four ships round the South African Cape of Good Hope and reached Goa, establishing the first direct sea link between Europe and India. Another Portuguese sailor, Ferdinand Magellan, set out from Spain in 1570, hoping to discover the Spice Islands of Indonesia. He died during the voyage, but the remaining members of his crew became the first to circumnavigate the globe.

Commercial imperatives drove most of this exploration. From the early 1600s the British, Dutch, French, Spanish, and Portuguese all established East Indian Companies in order to discover, transport, and deliver exotic spices from the Far East to European tables. Collectively, these companies opened up the travel routes that made possible extensive European colonialization of Africa, India, China, and the Far Eastern islands. To protect their interests, soldiers followed the sailors, accompanied by importers, linguists, and accountants. With them all went scholars. And it was what the scholars discovered that contributed most to the widening of European cultural perspectives.

WHEN STONES SPOKE

In 1798 Napoleon's army invaded Egypt. Over 150 French scholars disembarked from the ships with the soldiers. Two years later the British sent an army to conquer the French and to take Egypt themselves. Egypt was significant for three reasons. Economically, the Suez region provided a trade route shortcut between Europe and the East Indies. But Egypt was also a puzzle. It was the oldest of the Mediterranean civilizations, and the pyramids and the Sphinx were the ancient world's oldest and greatest wonders. In addition, Egypt played a significant role in the Old Testament and in the early life of Jesus, which meant that investigating Egypt archaeological sites promised to reveal historical information that would confirm the veracity of Biblical history. The only problem was that no one could read the hieroglyphs in which the ancient Egyptian texts were written.

This situation altered with the discovery of the Rosetta Stone. Initially found by the French military, it was forcibly taken from them by the British military, and today is housed in the British Museum. The Rosetta Stone caused huge excitement because engraved on it was the same text written in three different scripts: Egyptian hieroglyphs, Greek, and demotic Egyptian (Egyptian written in Greek letters). It was clear that the other two scripts would provide the key to translating the hieroglyphics. However for twenty years, despite the efforts of both British and French scholars, the hieroglyphics eluded interpretation. This frustrating situation only ended when the French philologist, Jean-François Champollion, succeeded in deciphering the Rosetta Stone in 1822. His success caused an international furore among scholars and the public alike. Finally, it was hoped, the secrets of the past would be revealed, and the truths of the Bible would be confirmed.

Suddenly it was "hot" to be a philologist and to study ancient languages, their development, and their relationship to other languages. The race was now on to decipher the numerous other ancient stone markings that had been discovered throughout the Middle East, Anatolia (Turkey), Persia (Iraq and Iran), and the vast unexplored regions of Central Asia. By the middle of the 1800s a wave of researchers were translating long dead languages such as Old Persian, Elamite, Akkadian, Avestan, and Hittite.

However, the knowledge that was uncovered was not what was anticipated. Rather than confirming the historical truth of the Bible, very different conclusions were soon reached. Researchers saw that European languages shared many common words with ancient languages. For example, God is *deus* in Latin, *dio* in Italian, and *dieu* in French, and Zeus was the principal Greek god; while the sky god in Sanskrit is *dyeus*, and the word *deva* is a name for god in Sanskrit and a demon in the ancient Iranian Avestan language. Philological studies revealed that modern European and Indian languages shared not just specific words, but also cultural assumptions – for example, the ideas of kingship, thunder gods (i.e. Zeus, Thor, Varuna), armed fortresses, and the tripartite division of society into priests/aristocrats, warriors and workers. Studies of these common words soon led scholars to conclude that European, Iranian, and Indian languages were all part of one extensive linguistic group, which they called Indo-European.

This discovery was revolutionary because it challenged the history presented in the Bible. According to *Genesis*, the Semitic races of the Arabs and Jews, and the Hamite races of the Egyptians and Cushites, were fathered by Noah's two sons, Shem and Ham, respectively. Because Noah had only one other son, Japhet, he was assumed to have fathered the rest of the human race. Accordingly, scholars had long categorized the early peoples of Europe, including their languages and culture, as Japhetic. But philology demonstrated that this was not the way that modern Europeans came to speak, think, and live as they did. Scholars immediately stopped referring to European languages as Japhetic. They also dropped the *Genesis* account of human history, adopting in its place an Indo-European dispersion model to explain the connections between Indian, Middle Eastern, and European cultural developments.

Thus, within a period of just fifty years a vast array of ancient engravings and manuscripts, long thought to be impenetrable, were opened up by European scholars, and philologists were able to use the study of language to peer back into the past and "see" how cultures had lived thousands of years previously. Biblical history, far from being wholly confirmed by philology and archaeology, was shown to recount the stories of just one small group of people. The resulting divergence of scholarly knowledge and Bible-derived history was soon given far more public exposure by a new discipline that followed on from the discoveries of philology, comparative mythology.

THE IMPACT OF OTHER CULTURES

By the 1800s European East Indian Companies had set up offices throughout the East. While trade and the exploitation of natural resources was their primary object, the opened-up territories also provided opportunities for the amateur biologist, geologist, and explorer. Universities had not yet established schools in these disciplines, so these men – and they were men predominantly – were amateurs in the highest sense of the word. Most spoke at least half a dozen languages and were learned in several branches of the new sciences.

Richard Burton was one such man. When young he was a soldier in the Indian army of the East India Company. He fought in the Crimean War, and subsequently explored Africa on the commission of the Royal Geographical Society, accompanying John Speke when he discovered the source of the Nile in 1858. In subsequent years Burton was a diplomat, writer, ethnologist, and orientalist. He reputedly spoke twenty-nine European, African, and Asian languages, was the first European to enter Mecca, and became a Sufi in order to explore mystical Islam. And wherever he went, he strove to learn as much as he could about the local culture's social and sexual behavior.

Burton's cultural interests culminated in his translation of the Indian erotic classic, *The Kama Sutra*, published in 1883. He also translated *The Arabian Nights* and an Arab erotic work, *The Perfumed Garden*. Because of their sexual content the publication of these books created public outrage among conservative Victorians, to the extent that after his death Burton's wife burned many of his papers, including a revised translation of *The Perfumed Garden*, on the grounds that she needed to protect his reputation. However, Burton proved to be prescient of cultural change. His *Kama Sutra* has never been out of print since its first publication, and one hundred years later was adopted as one of the textbooks of the 1970's sexual revolution.

Burton's interest in the social and religious beliefs of other cultures was widely shared. The 1800s became a golden era of translations. Edward Fitzgerald's free version of *The Rubaiyat of Omar Khayyam* became a huge hit when published in 1859. Edwin Arnold's *The Light of Asia* had a similar impact. Published in 1879, and subsequently translated into many other European languages, Arnold's book presented in verse form the life and philosophy of the Buddha. Among other religious texts, parts of the Zoroastrian *Zend Avesta* were first translated into French in 1771, with English translations following in the 1820s; the key work of Indian spirituality, the *Bhagavad Gita*, was first translated into English in 1785, with Edwin Arnold publishing his famed version in 1900; the Chinese *Tao Te Ching* was first translated into English in 1868; and the Buddhist *Dhammapada* was translated in 1869.

With this access to non-European religious writings and thought writers started critically evaluating what religion was and how it had developed. One was Thomas Bulfinch, whose *The Age of Fables, or Beauties of Mythology*, first published in 1881, was a huge popular success. A compendiast rather than a scholar, Bulfinch gathered classical myths from Virgil and Ovid and put them together with mythological and legendary material from Europe and the East. He then rewrote all these myths in order to present easily digested versions to American readers for their edification and enjoyment.

The classical myths Bulfinch selected included the creation myths of ancient Greece and Rome, stories told of the Greek and Roman gods, and accounts of giants and monsters that folk traditions described as sharing the world with early humanity. Among non-Classical materials were Northern European myths which told of Thor and Valhalla (the underworld); legends regarding the Celtic priests known as the Druids; Egyptian myths of Osiris, Isis and Horus and other Egyptian gods; and stories selected from the mythologies of the Hindu, Zoroastrian, Buddhist, and Tibetan folk and religious traditions.

Bulfinch ensured his versions were suitable for the family drawing room by removing offending elements, particularly the sex and violence which loom large in many of the world's folk tales. Despite his censorship, Bulfinch's work was ground-breaking in that he not only presented a wide selection of Western and Eastern myths, but he offered them seriously and without judgement.

MYTHS OF THE WORLD

The word "myth" was first used in the Greco-Roman era to refer to fabulous stories of heroes or gods that were considered to be fictions, or even lies. Christian writers adopted this same usage, particularly in relation to the myths of other religions, in order to characterize them as false beliefs.

But from the 1840s Europeans started examining myths from a non-judgemental perspective, and rather than explaining them away on the grounds that they were primitive and ignorant began treating them as being as worthy of study as fossils or any other ancient geological, biological, or philological materials. The word "mythology" came into common usage in the 1840s, being used to refer to creation myths, stories of gods, legends of heroes, retellings of important events, eschatological narratives, and folk tales. This new attitude of openness led to *The Golden Bough: A Study in Magic and Religion* (1890) by the Scottish anthropologist, James George Frazer (1854–1941).

Anthropology, the study of human cultures, was yet another scholarly discipline that began in the nineteenth century. The word "anthropology" was first used in 1807 by the French naturalist, Francois Peron, when he published his findings regarding the Australian Aborigines. The idea of studying cultures as social phenomena quickly caught on. But it went both ways, with a number of scholars also casting their eye onto European culture and interpreting it as a social phenomena.

Frazer contributed to the development of anthropology by examining the origins of European religious beliefs. This was a highly contentious activity, and on publication *The Golden Bough* instantly generated an outcry, not just because it treated Christianity as another religion among many, but because he placed the sacrifice of Jesus Christ in the context of cultural anthropology. That is, he argued that because human sacrifice was common in the ancient world, Christ's sacrifice should be viewed in the context of all cultural phenomenon rather than as a unique historical event.

Frazer's book began when he became curious about an incident described by Virgil in his *Aeneid*, in which, Aeneas, a hero from the Trojan War who was accompanied by a prophetess, sought entrance to Hades (the underworld) by offering the gatekeeper a golden bough. Curious about the history behind this offering, Frazer delved into ancient mythology and religion in search of other versions of the story. His studies led him to explore the beliefs and practices of ancient fertility cults, among which were vegetation myths and rituals common to all the ancient world's agricultural societies. One ritual was the sacred marriage, in which a sanctified woman, either literally or symbolically a queen and representing the Earth goddess, married a specially selected male, an honorary king, who represented the Sun god. Frazer contended that in some cultures this male was ritually sacrificed at mid-winter solstice in order to help the Earth goddess, who had "died" with the onset of autumn, to be reborn in spring.

Underpinning this ritual was the concept of sympathetic magic, performed in the belief that a symbolic ritual act can affect natural processes, and can also bring about a connection to the divine. In some cultures this belief led to the flesh of a sacrificed symbolic king being eaten so the tribe might maintain a connection with their God. Frazer concluded:

> It is now easy to understand why a savage should desire to partake of the flesh of an animal or man whom he regards as divine. By eating the body of the god he shares in the god's attributes and powers. And when the god is

a corn-god, the corn is his proper body; when he is a vine-god, the juice of the grape is his blood; and so by eating the bread and drinking the wine the worshipper partakes of the real body and blood of his god. Thus the drinking of wine in the rites of a vine-god like Dionysus is not an act of revelry, it is a solemn sacrament. Yet a time comes when reasonable men find it hard to understand how any one in his senses can suppose that by eating bread or drinking wine he consumes the body or blood of a deity. "When we call corn Ceres and wine Bacchus," says Cicero, "we use a common figure of speech; but do you imagine that anybody is so insane as to believe that the thing he feeds upon is a god?"[1]

This line of thinking led Frazer to contend that the Last Supper, in which Jesus symbolically offered his blood and flesh to his followers in the form of wine and bread, was nothing more than a carry-over of ancient agricultural rituals. His viewpoint created outrage. As did his conclusion that Christianity was far from special, and that its rituals were merely a development of more primitive vegetation beliefs and myths. For Frazer the ultimate conclusion was that Christian beliefs, reliant as they were on myths regarding Jesus' divine birth, teaching, and resurrection, was ultimately as primitive as the beliefs it replaced. This was the real challenge presented by *The Golden Bough*.

The Golden Bough is not highly regarded by anthropologists today. Frazer's methodology is not sufficiently rigorous to meet modern standards. But as a foundation text for comparative religion and mythology it had immense impact. And it provided the thinking reader with a provocative explanation regarding how Western worshippers came to think of God in the way they had.

Other concepts that became familiar to those comparing religious rituals and mythologies during the 1800s included the nature of taboos, in which places or people were considered to be clean or unclean; totems that contained sacred power, including animals and fetishes; rites and narratives regarding rebirth; agricultural explanations for the development of sacred families such as the Egyptian Osiris, Isis, and Horus, or the Greek Zeus, Persephone, and Dionysus; worship of the dead and the use of ancestors to commune with the "beyond;" dancing and drug-taking to induce ecstatic communion with the God; the communal partaking of sacred meals; astronomy; the uses of symbolic languages; and the saviour gods and rites of redemption associated with the Mediterranean mysteries.

The Mediterranean mysteries in particular caused nineteenth century thinkers to look at Jesus Christ in a new light. It became accepted that the savior gods Osirus, Attis, and Dionysus were worshipped before Christ. Dionysus attracted special interest. Originally a vegetation god, like Jesus he had a sacred meal of wine and bread. Zeus, king of the gods, was Dionysus' father, his mother being Persephone, the seed-maiden. While still a child Dionysus was torn apart by the Titans, was subsequently resurrected, and in his resurrected form continued to help humanity.

A fundamental point about Dionysus was that he was a savior god. Like the Christian God the Father, Zeus was depicted as possessing human characteristics but he existed in a region inaccessible to human beings. He was wholly "other." In contrast, Dionysus lived among humanity and was depicted in four forms: as a baby, as a youth, as a mature man, and as a resurrected god. Worshippers called on him and he entered them via wine and ecstatic frenzy, filling them with himself.

In all this there was a clear connection between Dionysus and Christ. As observed by Joseph Campbell, the great twentieth century mythologist, the maiden goddess Persephone was in a cave weaving when she was approached by Zeus in the form of a giant snake, who impregnated her. "And the virgin conceived the ever-dying, ever-living god of bread and wine, Dionysus, who was born and nurtured in that cave, torn to death as a babe, and resurrected. Comparably, in the Christian legend, derived from the same archaic background, God the Holy Ghost in the form of a dove approached the Virgin Mary and she – through the ear – conceived God the Son, who was born in a cave, died and was resurrected, and is present hypostatically in the bread and wine of the Mass."[2]

What this revealed is that the symbols and metaphors we human beings have created over the centuries to depict God both shape, and are shaped by, the world in which we live. Thus the disciplines of comparative religion and of comparative mythologies provided nineteenth century scholars with a means for understanding how symbolic languages developed over the eons.

MAX MÜLLER
FOUNDER OF COMPARATIVE RELIGION

Throughout the 1800s scholars explored the myriad ways humanity conceived of God and how belief in God, or gods, was expressed in religious terms. The world's array of cults, religions, and philosophies were examined, and numerous theories and explanations were tested. Some, such as phallic explanations of religion or the idea of the dying vegetative god, became popular for a period then fell out of favor. But collectively this theorizing led to the development of a range of conceptual tools that enabled scholars to understand how religions had developed over the eons.

The scholar who laid the foundations for comparative religion was the German philologist Max Müller. Born in 1823, he studied philosophy at university in Germany but showed a natural facility for languages, learning Greek, Latin, Arabic, Persian, and Sanskrit. In 1844 Müller started studying Sanskrit, which soon led him to begin translating into German the Upanishads, the texts that embody Indian spiritual philosophy. He subsequently moved to England, as the British East India Company had the largest collection of Sanskrit manuscripts in Europe. He remained in England for the rest of his life.

Using a position he was offered at Oxford University, Müller initiated a twenty-one year project under the collective title of *Sacred Books of the East*. The series eventually comprised fifty volumes, which were published between 1879 and 1910. Drawing on the skills of over a dozen philologists and Oriental scholars, Müller presented English translations of the sacred texts of Buddhism, Hinduism, Islam, Taosim, Confucianism, Zoroastrianism, and Jainism. Müller himself translated numerous Hindu texts for the series, and his critical edition of the *Rig Veda* still remains one of the greatest works on Indian religion.

Based on his study of the *Rig Veda*, Müller theorized that the oldest form of religious beliefs consisted of nature worship, with the earliest divinities representing natural forces such as the wind, fire, stars, dawn, and water. These forces were then personified and given names, with Ap being the *Rig Veda's* god of water, Prithvi the Earth goddess, Dyaus Pita the sky god, and the Maruts who were the forty-nine wind gods. Intricate myths were subsequently woven around these deities. Thus Vajra, Indra's thunderbolt, was considered to be the bones of the ancient sage Dadhichi, who immolated himself to save the world. In this way humanity invented the innumerable gods that fill the mythologies of all cultures. The highest form of concepts regarding God involved a return to abstract thinking about the deity, as embodied in Indian philosophic texts such as the Upanishads. From his studies of Indian religion Müller also concluded that religious concepts may degenerate over time, and that rather than always leading from lower to higher understanding, religions may fall from the heights of spirituality into the depths of ignorant ideas and blindly practiced ritual.

Müller gave the foundational Gifford Lectures between 1888 and 1893. In them he developed the idea that God is not a personal being but should rather be conceived of as the Infinite. He further argued that a perception of the Infinite was common to all religions. This led him to conclude that there was a common truth in all religions, derived from a revelation that was not confined to one religion, and that was not miraculous in the traditional sense of the word. Human beings could have access to this natural religion because we intuitively grasp the idea of the Infinite, which is also called the Beyond and the Divine, because we participate in it. Müller suggested that the Infinite reveals itself in the natural world, and that we can learn something of the Infinite using reason to examine the natural world.

All this was at odds with Christian theology on three grounds. The first was that Müller's outlook sounded to many like pantheism (the belief that God is identical with the natural world), even though this wasn't what Müller meant, as he considered God, which he called the Infinite, transcended the natural world. Second, Christianity believed that God had revealed Himself through His Son, not in nature as maintained by Müller. And third, Müller's Infinite was an impersonal force or power rather than the personal God of Christianity.

Despite Müller being a practicing Lutheran all his life, he was accused of blasphemy, and even of atheism – this latter accusation being commonly used during the Victorian era to stigmatize those who argued for any concept of God that differed from the orthodox Christian theistic concept of God.

CONCLUSIONS

All this shows how powerfully exposure to world religions impacted on the European outlook. Seven points in particular emphasize the shift that occurred regarding the way people thought of God during the nineteenth century.

There were multiple ways of conceiving of God. The world was not just European and Christian, but consisted of a wide range of cultures. These cultures had their own stories and ideas about God. Some religious activities, such as crop rituals and human sacrifice, clearly reflected primitive ways of seeing the world. However others, such as the moral outlook of Confucianism and the metaphysics of Vedanta, could less easily be dismissed as "primitive."

Lifestyle influenced how human beings conceive of God. The sacred was an animal spirit for hunter-gatherers, a goddess among agricultural societies, a thunder god for early Indo-European warriors, the King of kings for those living in Bronze Age city-states, and a saviour god in Mediterranean cultures among populations who felt oppressed and exploited. The way people live influences their aspirations which in turn shape the frameworks used to conceive of God.

The Bible was not unique. Many cultures had their own sacred scriptures. And as with the various non-European concepts of God, while much was clearly "primitive," some texts showed a religiosity at least as sophisticated as Christianity's. With translations of many of the world's sacred texts now available, suddenly the doctrines of Christianity didn't stand alone; they could be compared and contrasted with those of other cultures.

Christian monotheism was not unique. Europeans knew that Islam and Judaism had monotheistic concepts of God, just like Christianity, because all three worshipped the God of Abraham. But now they discovered that Zoroastrians had a single God, Ahura Mazda; Indian spirituality had Brahman as the transcendent sacred power beyond the physical world; Taoism presented the Tao as the energy or force underlying all earthly activities; and even the ancient Egyptians had a sophisticated view of God as an single originating power that split into various powers and identities as it manifested the world.

Christian morality was not unique. Europeans had long considered that Christian morality was superior to the morals of all the world's other religions. Yet Socrates' ethical philosophy, coupled to the way he died, impressed many as being as inspirational as Christ's death. And all religious traditions had their own moral injunctions, dating from the ancient Egyptians and Mesopotamians of 3,500 BCE, that embodied the same notions as Christianity. Indeed, the Christian moral concept of being good in thought, word, and deed was actually taken from the Zoroastrian religion. Further, even secular social outlooks, such as that provided by Confucianism, showed that other cultures strove to live according to the highest moral standards.

The Christian personal God was not the only way to conceive of God. Christianity assumed that God existed in the form of a personal being who presided over the world that He created. Now Europeans learned of abstract conceptions of God, which possessed neither form, image, nor body, called Ahura Mazda (Lord Wisdom) by the Zoroastrians, Wakan Tanka (Great Spirit) by the North American Indians, and Brahman (the Absolute) by Vedic meditators.

Any enquiring Westerner seeking to understand God now had options. Christianity could no longer be assumed to be the only religion in the world that offered valid spiritual truths. The texts of all the world's other major religious and spiritual traditions were now available to anyone who wished to explore them.

What all this meant was that the intellectual bases of European culture were rapidly changing. But it wasn't just the new discoveries of science, the revelations of Biblical studies, and the ideas thrown up by comparative religion that were challenging and altering Western intellectual perspectives. Social forces were also radically re-shaping the European worldview.

CHAPTER 5

Signs Of The Times

A massive earthquake devastated Lisbon in 1755. It sank innumerable ships moored in the harbour and killed up to 100,000 people. F.M.A. Voltaire, among the most celebrated writers of the age, responded to this disaster by writing *Poem on the Lisbon Disaster*, which was published in 1756 to widespread acclaim. It began:

> Unhappy mortals! Dark and mourning earth!
> Affrighted gathering of human kind! ...
> Behold these shreds and cinders of your race,
> This child and mother heaped in common wreck,
> These scattered limbs beneath the marble shafts –
> A hundred thousand whom the earth devours,
> Who, torn and bloody, palpitating yet,
> Entombed beneath their hospitable roofs,
> In racking torment end their stricken lives.[1]

More than the deaths and suffering it caused, Lisbon's earthquake set in motion a tidal wave of religious doubt. The disaster occurred on a religious holiday, to a Catholic population, and it destroyed the most important churches in Lisbon. As news of the disaster washed across Europe numerous believers started questioning what it was exactly that their God did in the world, given that so many good Christians had died. If God was all-loving and all-knowing, how could He have allowed this evil event to have occurred to His own? Voltaire's poem struck home because he didn't just sum up the earthquake's emotional impact, he also gave voice to the religious doubts – doubts he personally had harbored for a long time – of his shattered fellow Europeans.

Voltaire is best known today as an Enlightenment philosopher and satirist. A significant part of his appeal is that, despite being an intellectual, he expressed himself plainly and unequivocally. In his day Voltaire had a reputation for dealing mercilessly to foolishness, humbug, and ignorance – and he considered Christian beliefs embodied all three.

A key view held by Christian apologists of Voltaire's day was that evil happens to people because they had been bad and deserved it. (God, being all-good, all-knowing, and all-powerful, couldn't allow bad to happen to undeserving people). Therefore, they argued, and despite appearances to the contrary, the people of Lisbon must really have been bad, for which God had duly punished them. Voltaire responded by asking if the people of Lisbon really were so much worse than those left dancing in London, Paris, or Madrid? In his poem Christian apologists offer pride as the sin God had punished: pride was a heinous sin, and God always responded to sin with His ironclad laws of retribution, which required death. Voltaire responded to these apologists:

> Say you, over that yet quivering mass of flesh:
> "God is avenged: the wage of sin is death"?
> What crime, what sin, had those young hearts conceived
> That lie, bleeding and torn, on mother's breast?[2]

This question of how innocent children could be deemed sinful by a good God has troubled many over the centuries. Voltaire also repeated widely held positions when he argued that a supposedly just God had acted unjustly; when he accused God, the enemy of evil, of having just done evil Himself (to which He further seemed indifferent); and when he had God's defenders say, "This misery is for others' good," to which he replied on behalf of Lisbon's suffering, "Fine consolation this in my distress!"[3]

Voltaire's aim in all this was to use polemics to bring into the light of reason religious concepts that he saw as contradictory, as defying common sense, or as inhumane. Thus the real thrust of his Lisbon poem can be seen as representing profound dissatisfaction with the way that the Christian God was failing humanity and not improving "this world, this theatre of pride and wrong."[4]

> A God came down to lift our stricken race:
> He visited the earth, and changed it not![5]

Ultimately, Voltaire's questioning of the Christian world view was far from an intellectual's play. His questions reflected the doubts increasing numbers of Europeans were having regarding the answers Christianity supplied to questions about how the world functioned and what kind of God ruled it.

DOUBTING THE AUTHORITY OF THE CHURCH

At the same time that Voltaire was stirring controversy in France, an English historian similarly sowed doubts that were to flower in the 1800s. The historian was Edward Gibbon, and his book was *The History of the Decline and Fall of the Roman Empire*, published in six volumes between 1776 and 1788. The first volume, which took Gibbon seven years to research and write, was applauded by critics and by the public, whose enthusiasm ensured it sold out three editions in less than a year.

Gibbon remains one of the English language's great stylists. It was as much for his glittering style and his ironic tone as for the content of his history that his huge work created its impact, his droll humor doing as much to undermine the sanctity of Christ's representatives on Earth as his recounting of their escapades. As he wrote: "The theologian may indulge the pleasing task of describing Religion as she descended from Heaven, arrayed in her native purity. A more melancholy duty is imposed on the historian. He must discover the inevitable mixture of error and corruption which she contracted in long residence upon earth, among a weak and degenerate race of beings."[6]

What Gibbon discovered, and laconically presented, was a Christianity full of violence: Christian on Christian, priest on populace, aristocrat on everyone. He showed how Christianity propagated superstition, became a vehicle for oppressing others, shrugged its shoulders at the misery it created, and dispensed the teachings of Christ in a less than Christian manner. After discussing the martyrdoms inflicted on the early Christians in Rome, Gibbon wrote:

> We shall conclude this chapter with a melancholy truth which obtrudes itself on the reluctant mind; that, even admitting, without hesitation or inquiry, all that history has recorded, or devotion has feigned, on the subject of martyrdoms, it must still be acknowledged that the Christians, in the course of their intestine dissensions, have inflicted far greater severities on each other than they had experienced from the zeal of infidels. ... The church of

Rome defended by violence the empire which she had acquired by fraud; a system of peace and benevolence was soon disgraced by the proscriptions, wars, massacres, and the institution of the holy office. And as the reformers were animated by the love of civil as well as of religious freedom, the Catholic princes connected their own interest with that of the clergy, and enforced by fire and the sword the terrors of spiritual censures. In the Netherlands alone more than one hundred thousand of the subjects of Charles V are said to have suffered by the hand of the executioner. ... It must be allowed that the number of Protestants who were executed in a single province and a single reign, far exceeded that of the primitive martyrs in the space of three centuries, and of the Roman empire.[7]

Of course this view was controversial. But what gave Gibbon's comments an even sharper sting was that there was no alternative history of Christianity available in English. Anyone wishing to read the history of the early years of the Christianity had no choice but to read Gibbon's version.

At the same time as Gibbon was desiccating the institutions of Christianity with his urbane wit, the French were adopting a much darker, more violent attitude towards the institutions that governed them.

DISMANTLING CHRISTIANITY

In the 1780s, France was in deep trouble. Politically, France was a feudal state, ruled by a king who was supported by an aristocracy closely intertwined with the Catholic clergy. The third party in this political structure was the middle classes, who contributed most of France's economic activity. However, the aristocracy and clergy together formed the *ancien régime*, a traditional power structure which financially exploited, and politically oppressed, the middle classes, the growing numbers of urban workers, and the peasants.

Economically, the previous king, Louis 15th, had created a huge national deficit due to warring, so when his son Louis 16th took the throne there was an urgent need to bolster the nation's coffers. This was done by taking money from the only people who were generating it in sufficient quantities: the hardworking middle classes. Meanwhile, the serfs were being taxed exorbitantly by the Catholic Church, which had a traditionally granted right to do so. Naturally, the middle and working classes developed an extreme resentment towards those ruling (and taking from) them. This resentment was exacerbated by the conspicuous consumption of the nobility and clergy, led by the extravagant Queen Marie Antoinette, sister to the Austrian king.

When harvests failed in 1787 economic and political turmoil followed. The masses of citizens were already chafing under their exploitation. So when a shortage of state funds forced the king to convene the ruling classes to address the crisis, the wider population saw this as an opportunity to force the political rulers to confront the social and economic inequality that was destroying France. However, the *ancien régime* preferred to protect its interests rather than to feed the starving, give work to the unemployed, or reform the economy. So when the King decided the answer to the country's economic woes was to go to war with his wife's brother, the King of Austria, with the aim of stimulating the economy and raising his own declining popularity (on the premise that there's nothing like a good war to glossy up a ruler's tarnished reputation), the middle and working classes went to war themselves by storming the Bastille in 1789. The French Revolution soon followed.

Initially, the Revolution was seen as an opportunity to get rid of the *ancien régime* and to create a new state built on egalitarian principles. The *Declaration of the Rights of Man and of the Citizen* (inspired by the American *Declaration of Rights* of 1776), recognized that all men were born free and had equal rights. The rights of the individual, the separation of the powers of executive, parliament, and judiciary, and a social contract between citizens and the state, were all established. The clergy was also disbanded, with the Catholic Church forced to sell many of its lands, the resulting income going towards paying off the national debt. Powers taken from the Catholic Church were vested in the state.

In the years leading up to the French Revolution, Denis Diderot, writer and philosopher, famously proclaimed that France would never be free until the last king had been strangled with the entrails of the last priest. He got his wish – and more. Revolution was followed by the Reign of Terror, in which between 18,000 and 40,000 perished by the guillotine or were killed by marauding mobs. The Terror was followed first by General Napoleon's dictatorship, then by the Napoleonic wars that engulfed much of Europe. France suffered a century of instability. Only in 1870 was the stable Third Republic born.

With respect to religion, and in reaction to the historical abuses of the Catholic Church, those behind the Revolution initially sought to de-Christianize French society. Jacques Hébert, a journalist and newspaper publisher who rose to prominence during the power struggles, advocated the rule of reason. This included declaring a young woman the Goddess of Reason and organizing public ceremonies in Paris in which churches were defaced. Alternative to Hébert, Maximilien Robespierre sought to establish a state religion that acknowledged a Supreme Being who watched over France, but without drawing on Christian beliefs. It could be argued that both Hébert and Robespierre were cynical in proposing a Goddess of Reason or a Supreme Being, because they really wanted a secular state but realized that so many citizens believed in God that a divine replacement needed to be conjured up to satisfy their desire to worship something. In an emphatic resolution to the argument between Hébert and Robespierre over what form this should take both men died under the guillotine. In due course, Catholic worship was reinstated.

The violence of the Revolution shook Europe and the Americas. Initially the French revolution had been seen as a unique opportunity for the old order to be overturned, for social injustices to be righted, and for a new social and cultural order to be instituted. So there was wide dismay when the Revolution guillotined itself into excess. Yet the anti-religious ideas the French Revolution politicized, which rose from a genuine desire to promote humane ideals of social freedom, to end the exploitation of one class by another, and to create a more equitable society, had a profound social and intellectual impact on Christianity. This was because humanist ideals were now being offered as alternatives to Christian morality. And, in the case of France, the Catholic Church had been forced to relinquish much of the power by which it had politically and economically controlled France.

The idea that Christianity was part of an old order that controlled, exploited, and oppressed the wider populace, and therefore that it had to go, resonated with numerous other thinkers. Among these was Thomas Paine.

"MY OWN MIND IS MY OWN CHURCH"

The French Revolution simultaneously manifested and caused many to question the critique of religious beliefs that gathered momentum during the 1800s. It particularly led to a polarization of perspectives. For the first time in Western culture the word "atheist" began to be widely thrown about.

Gibbon was branded an atheist for the way he portrayed the Church in his *Decline and Fall*. The Scottish philosopher, David Hume, who brought amiable dollops of common sense to his thinking, wondered in a series of essays and books how Jesus' miracles could physically have taken place, what might be the scientific processes by which he could have walked on water, and what chemical processes occurred to transform water into wine. He also showed that the proofs of God's existence offered by theologians such as Anselm and Thomas Aquinas, proofs long accepted by Christian thinkers of all sects, were logically flawed. In other words, Hume showed that miracles could be dismissed on scientific grounds, and that God's existence could not be logically proven. For his efforts, Hume was also labelled an atheist.

In reality, charges of atheism were made on emotional rather than on intellectual grounds. Few even among the most sceptical European and American thinkers considered themselves to be complete unbelievers. Instead, like other intellectuals of that time, Gibbon and Hume were Deists.

One of the fullest presentations of the outlook of leading thinkers was made by Thomas Paine (1737-1809) in his best-selling book, *The Age of Reason*, published in three parts between 1795 and 1807. Thomas Paine is best known as one of the Fathers of the American Revolution. In his booklet *Common Sense* (1776) he argued for not just the independence of the American colonies from Great Britain, but also proposed the basis for a Constitution. His book created a huge foment when it first appeared, selling in the tens of thousands. Among his many contributions, Paine came up with the name, the "United States of America," proposed advanced social concepts such as a basic wage for all and a pension for the elderly, and presciently saw that the USA could become the world's greatest advocate for freedom.

Paine was born in England. He had a Quaker father and Church of England mother. The Quaker independence of outlook, taking its cue from founder George Fox's free-thinking and dissenter attitude, stayed with Paine throughout his life. Essentially a humanist, possessing a natural affinity with the poor, and always opposed to the exploitation of the masses by the wealthy, in his twenties Paine became involved in labour disputes, advocating for the workers. But by his late thirties Paine's career advocating for workers had dried up and, at the instigation of Benjamin Franklin, in 1774 he moved to the American colonies where he started his life all over again as a journalist.

Paine's articles and pamphlets immediately created a stir, especially when he argued for the abolition of slavery, sought social justice for women, advocated for an end to cruelty towards animals, and, most significantly, asserted that the

American colonies needed independence from Britain in order to grow. Paine's articulation of these issues not only made a fundamental contribution to what subsequently developed into the American Revolution, but also inspired those who initiated the French Revolution.

This inspiration was so great that Paine was offered French citizenship and a seat in the French Convention of 1792. Recognizing the momentousness of what the French sought to achieve, Paine took up both offers. But his French sojourn did not play out as he expected. After voting for the establishment of the French Republic, Paine found himself caught up in the subsequent Terror. He was imprisoned, and was nearly guillotined at Robespierre's command, only avoiding death because his cell door was incorrectly marked. Paine was freed several days later, after Robespierre himself was executed.

It was during the brief period between hearing he would be arrested and actually being taken to prison that Paine wrote Part One of *The Age of Reason*. He had intended to write the book in his final years, but because of the carnage occurring in France he felt compelled to start the book immediately – while he was still alive. Ironically for a religious sceptic, one of Paine's central concerns was that with the abolition of the Catholic Church by the new French government there was a danger that, "in the general wreck of superstition, of false systems of government, and false theology, we lose sight of morality, of humanity, and of the theology that is true."[8]

What Paine considered to be true he articulated in the Profession of Faith that opens his book:

> I believe in one God, and no more; and I hope for happiness beyond this life. I believe in the equality of man, and I believe that religious duties consist in doing justice, loving mercy, and endeavoring to make our fellow-creatures happy. But, lest it should be supposed that I believe many other things in addition to these, I shall, in the progress of this work, declare the things I do not believe, and my reasons for not believing them.
>
> I do not believe in the creed professed by the Jewish church, by the Roman church, by the Greek church, by the Turkish church, by the Protestant church, nor by any church that I know of. My own mind is my own church. All national institutions of churches, whether Jewish, Christian, or Turkish, appear to me no other than human inventions set up to terrify and enslave mankind, and monopolize power and profit.

> I do not mean by this declaration to condemn those who believe otherwise; they have the same right to their belief as I have to mine. But it is necessary to the happiness of man, that he be mentally faithful to himself. Infidelity does not consist in believing, or in disbelieving; it consists in professing to believe what he does not believe.[9]

As would be expected, the usual accusations of atheism were thrown at Paine when *The Age of Reason* was published. The religious authorities and the politically powerful continued to work together by adding his book to the list of Paine's pamphlets and books that were already banned by the British Government on the grounds of sedition and blasphemy.

Yet it is clear from Paine's Declaration of Faith that he was not an atheist. On the contrary, he held a very strong belief in God. It was just that, along with other rationalists and Deists like Voltaire and Gibbon, he wasn't satisfied with the traditional Christian formulation of belief in God, which he dismissed as superstitious and absurd. As Paine wrote of Christ: "He was a virtuous and an amiable man. The morality that he preached and practiced was of the most benevolent kind; and though similar systems of morality had been preached by Confucius, and by some of the Greek philosophers, many years before, by the Quakers since, and by many good men in all ages, it has not been exceeded by any."[10]

Paine's position was not that belief in God was wrong and to be avoided, but that irrational assertions that went hand-in-hand with religious beliefs should be avoided, leaving each person to form a belief in God according to their own powers of reasoning.

But the changing times, and the rejection of institutional Christianity by commonsense thinkers such as Thomas Paine, were far from the only challenge to traditional beliefs regarding God. There was also the gauntlet thrown down by philosophers and their radical new thinking about reality and the world.

CHAPTER 6

Doubts Of The Philosophers

By the early 1800s increasing numbers of philosophers, all trained in the German universities, were offering their speculations on many issues, including God. Naturally, these new speculations involved casting aside the old, long-accepted certainties. But in doing so these philosophers were largely reflecting the mood for change that was sweeping through the Western world, as each decade brought new scientific, religious, and social ideas. So it was inevitable that philosophic thinkers would make their contributions.

From the 1600s the notion of doubt was central to European philosophic thinking. Doubt regarding what had been believed. Doubt regarding what was known. Doubt regarding how we know at all. For hundreds of years Europeans had all thought more or less the same things about the world, had shared the same certainties, and had assumed the same truths. But suddenly those long cherished certainties were challenged. New ideas piled on top of last month's. There was no refuge, with even the nature of thinking itself being questioned. Of all these ideas, I'll briefly examine the key concepts of four philosophers.

DESCARTES: I DOUBT, THEREFORE I AM

Modern doubt began, in a philosophic sense, with René Descartes (1596–1650). In his *Meditations of First Philosophy* (1641), Descartes sought to ascertain what could definitely be known. In order to achieve the certainty he considered essential, he began by doubting everything:

> It is now some years since I detected how many were the false beliefs that I had from earliest youth admitted as true, and how doubtful was everything I had since constructed on this basis; and from that time I was convinced that

> I must once for all seriously undertake to rid myself of all the opinions which I had formerly accepted, and commence to build anew from the foundation, if I wanted to establish any firm and permanent structures in the sciences.[1]

Doubting everything he had formerly accepted involved doubting even religious testimony regarding God. Descartes didn't doubt the existence of God Himself. Rather, what he sought was certain proof of God's existence, and certain knowledge of the world God had created. Thus in his *Meditations*, the full title of which is, *Meditations on the First Philosophy in which the Existence of God and the Distinction between Mind and Body are Demonstrated*, he began from a position of doubting everything. This doubt had four stages.

In the first stage, Descartes realized that the senses were unreliable. This meant the certainty of knowledge regarding the external world should be doubted. Yet against this argument Descartes proposed that he knew he had a body. So he could certainly accept that the material world existed.

In the second stage Descartes considered how waking and sleeping states were easily confused. Therefore he might be actually be dreaming that he had a body, which meant even his experience of having a body might be a delusion. Yet against this there was certainty in the way that extension, quantity, place, and time all existed in the world, with mathematics and measurement proving their continued, regular existence.

In the third stage Descartes wondered, what if all this was really a delusion? Then even these mathematical certainties regarding the world would be in doubt. However, against this was the realization that God was good, and therefore would not allow human beings to live in such delusion.

In the fourth stage Descartes asked, what if instead of God there was actually a deceiving spirit? Then even this certainty would be a delusion. However, in the midst of all this doubt, Descartes suddenly realized that even if he was being deceived, in the act of being deceived there is a certainty. This certainty was that in being deceived, he existed:

> Let him [the deceiving spirit] deceive me as much as he will, he can never cause me to be nothing so long as I think that I am something. So that after having reflected well and carefully examined all things, we must come to the definite conclusion that this proposition: I am, I exist, is necessarily true each time that I pronounce it, or that I mentally conceive it. But I do

not yet know clearly enough what I am. ... I am, I exist, that is certain. But how often? Just when I think. ... I am a real thing and really exist; but what thing? I have answered: a thing which thinks.[2]

Descartes' dictum, "I think, therefore I am," is proverbial today. There was a spiritual dimension to his thinking in that he identified the mind with the soul. Thus in his view the soul was a rational entity, the fundamental activity of which was thought. The implication arising from this viewpoint, however, was that the world consisted of a duality, because the mind was separate from matter. Three questions rose from this duality.

The first was if mind and matter were separate substances, how were they connected? Descartes answered this question by arguing that the mind was situated in the pineal gland, which became a bridge between the realm of mind and the realm of matter.

Second, how could the mind know God? Descartes' answer was that God was a perfect and infallible Being. In contrast, human beings were imperfect and fallible, which meant they couldn't have conceived of a perfect and infallible Being by themselves. God must have placed the idea of Himself in the human mind.

Third, how can we know anything, given that a deceiver might be causing thoughts to enter the mind? Descartes' response was that what we conceive as God cannot be a deceiver, because this would contradict the reality of God, which was one of perfection, and a deceiver God would not be perfect. Thus God not only existed, God was perfectly truthful and good. And this God had created a truthful and good material world. Hence human beings can examine the world of matter, safe in the knowledge that the senses and reason can be trusted, and that certainty and true knowledge can be derived from them.

Science assumed that the natural world experienced by the senses could be examined by the rational mind without reference to God. Descartes provided a philosophic justification that reinforced this scientific view. And for Descartes and his fellow scientists and philosophers, the way to understand the natural world was via the laws revealed by mathematics. These mathematically understood laws didn't need God's involvement: they could be understood in their own right.

But in arguing all this Descartes was separating God and the natural world, mind and matter, body and soul. As noted earlier, for medieval Europeans God was experienced in the natural world via prayer, Church rituals, and seasonal religious festivals. For them God and nature, mind and matter, body and soul were closely entwined. In contrast, Cartesian duality split off the sensorily experienced material world from God and maintained that reason was sufficient to understand the world.

Descartes himself didn't see his separation of mind and matter as such a decisive split. His view was that God created the world and the mathematical laws by which it functioned. God also created the rational mind used to understand those laws. For him mind and matter were two aspects of the one world. But the breach between mind and matter initiated by Descartes continued to widen over the following centuries.

KANT: GOD AS RATIONAL HYPOTHESIS

Immanuel Kant (1724-1804) injected yet another level of doubt into European thought. Kant was born in Lutheran Germany and was raised on a strict diet of prayer and Bible readings. The young Kant attended university from the age of sixteen, where he was attracted by both philosophy and the sciences. He was especially impressed by Newton's groundbreaking advances, Newton being revered then in much the same way that Albert Einstein was last century.

Kant lived during the Age of Enlightenment, the era when Europeans first adopted the view that reason, rather than religious faith, should be the criteria by which to comprehend reality. Kant considered the dictum of the Enlightenment to be *sapere aude* (dare to know).

> Enlightenment is man's emergence from his self-incurred immaturity. Immaturity is the inability to use one's own understanding without the guidance of another. ... The motto of enlightenment is therefore: *Sapere aude*! Have courage to use your own understanding! ... Dogmas and formulas, those mechanical instruments for rational use (or rather misuse) of his natural endowments, are the ball and chain of his permanent immaturity. ... For enlightenment of this kind, all that is needed is freedom. And the freedom in question is the most innocuous form of all – freedom to make public use of one's reason in all matters. But I hear on all sides the cry: Don't argue! The officer says: Don't argue, get on parade! The tax-official: Don't argue, pay! The clergyman: Don't argue, believe! ... All this means restrictions on free-

dom everywhere. But which sort of restriction prevents enlightenment, and which, instead of hindering it, can actually promote it? I reply: The public use of man's reason must always be free, and it alone can bring about enlightenment among men.[3]

From his early twenties, Kant wrote a number of popular treatises on science, philosophy, metaphysics, and morality. He speculated that both our Solar System and the Milky Way Galaxy had formed out of condensing clouds of spinning gases. However, after becoming a highly regarded and successful philosopher, university professor, and author, in 1668, at the age of forty-six, Kant stopped publishing and spent the next eleven years solving the philosophic problems that had developed out of his early work. The result was the *Critique of Pure Reason*. Plato and Aristotle provided the foundations for Western philosophy until the 1700s. Kant's *Critique* became the first work of modern Western philosophy.

In his thought Kant developed Descartes' ideas regarding the distinction between mind and matter. Kant decided that there was a much more complex relationship between the two than Descartes had allowed. For Kant human beings were rational beings (Aristotle had said rational animals). Reason provided humanity with the means for understanding the natural world. In adopting this perspective Kant was in agreement with his age. But he argued for this from an interesting perspective.

One of the key distinctions in Kantian thought is between noumenon and phenomenon. A noumenon exists "out there," in the natural world, as a thing-in-itself. But Kant considered that we don't experience the thing-in-itself. Instead, what we experience is our *perception* of the thing-in-itself. This perception Kant called the phenomenon. What this means is that our phenomenal experience stands between us and the thing-in-itself in the world.

From a common sense perspective, we can readily agree with Kant's distinction today. It is clear that we don't experience a hot fire directly; what we experience is the phenomenon of heat on our skin, and the phenomenon of red-orange-yellow colors on our retina. Our bodily senses mediate our experience of the world, giving us our knowledge of things "out there." However, this is not all that Kant meant by phenomenon.

Kant agreed with the materialist and scientific view that all our knowledge must necessarily derive from sense experience. But to sense experience he added reason, on the grounds that we can only understand what we experience through concepts that we comprehend via rational thought. Thus we perceive via our senses. And we develop our understanding of sense information through concepts. "By means of sense, objects are given to us, and sense alone provides us with perceptions; by means of the understanding objects are thought and from it there arise concepts."[4]

Kant spent hundreds of pages of intricate philosophic reasoning analyzing the concepts we use to understand the world. I'll draw out just a few conclusions that are significant in relation to this study. First, there is Kant's philosophic position with respect to God.

Metaphysical problems didn't exist for Kant. He argued that all the questions people had regarding God's existence or non-existence, or regarding what God's qualities might be, were based on a false assumption. The assumption is that we can ask such questions about God. Kant's view was that we cannot.

Kant's reason for claiming this is that God is not a Being we can perceive via our senses. And because our senses can never provide material evidence as to God's existence or non-existence, we have no basis for speculating on what qualities God might possess. However, Kant still believed in God. How so?

One of Kant's most famous statements was that he acknowledged, "the starry heavens above me, and the moral law within me." By "the starry heavens above" he meant the Newtonian and scientific view that the cosmos functioned according to mathematically determined laws; by "the moral law within me" he meant that morality was the highest mode of human existence. Further, Kant considered that our moral sense was derived from God. Thus just as Descartes argued that God implanted ideas regarding perfection in us, so Kant argued that the fact we have moral concepts proves that God exists. However, Kant's God was a distant Being, who we can only ever know through the "echo" provided by moral reasoning and by acting morally. Accordingly, the God of Descartes, who was a transcendent Being separate from the natural world, with Kant became a Deistic God almost completely removed from it.

In addition, where Descartes argued for a duality in existence, Kantian philosophy has at its centre some interesting contradictions. For example, on the one hand Kant considered that our perception and knowledge can only be of things in the world that we experience via our senses, and that all our rational understanding must be of things in the world. To this extent he was an empiricist. On the other hand, Kant also considered that we only experience sense-based phenomena, rather than the thing-in-itself, and we understand what the thing-in-itself is through ideas. Ideas thus became the key to rational understanding. To this extent he was an idealist. But empiricism and idealism are usually considered opposite approaches to understanding the world.

Ultimately, to us today, Kant was an idealist. Scientists conduct experiments to learn how to control and manipulate bodies and forces in the world. Kant didn't do this. He sought to understand the world through the application of pure reason, and to affirm God's presence through concepts which underpin moral action. Thus where the scientist is engaged experimentally with the world, building empirically-derived data, Kant was engaged in rationally-derived concepts and interacting with the world through moral choices.

In Kant's day, the sciences were still developing and little data had been collected on which to base an fully empirical view of the world. Nonetheless, his distinction between *phenomenon* and *noumenon* inspired subsequent thinkers, and led to the development of new ways of viewing human experience. We'll consider further implications of all this later. Right now we need to consider some of the responses that Kant's ideas stirred up among other German philosophers. In particular, from Hegel and Feuerbach.

HEGEL: GOD AS ABSOLUTE

The contribution G.W.F. Hegel (1770-1831) made to European thought was one of certainty as opposed to doubt. Influenced by German mystics, as well as by European philosophic thought, he sought to transform Christian theology by providing it with a new conceptual framework.

Hegel also reflected prevailing social interests of his time, philosophizing ideas that were "in the air," particularly the idea of historical development, embodied in the assumption that European culture was the pinnacle of human achievement. In addition, Hegel also extended Kant's concept of phenomenon, establishing in his first book, *The Phenomenology of the Spirit* (1807), the foundations for twentieth century phenomenological studies, including existentialism and contemporary forms of spirituality.

Hegel considered that "philosophy is its own time raised to the level of thought."[5] Behind this statement is his view that human experience is grounded in what he called the "finite-infinite." By "finite" Hegel meant conditioned historical experience; in other words, what we experience day-to-day. By the "infinite" he meant the Absolute, which he also called Spirit, and that he identified with transcendent consciousness. Hegel situated God in the midst of the finite-infinite. Thus God was an ideal that existed at the heart of our day-to-day experience.

> The concept of the spirit has its reality in the spirit. Since the subjective individuality in its free development is essentially a process that begins with immediate life, the highest identity which being has ... contains the significance of the essence of nature and of the spirit. The significance of the ideal is the substantiality as the identical and concrete essence of nature and of the spirit, a concrete essence which is called God.[6]

Hegel deliberately set up his thought in opposition to Kant. A key difference in approach was that he considered we primarily understand through intuition, not reason. It is through intuition, experienced in the midst of everyday life, that we come to understand God existing in the "finite-infinite." As Hegel put it, the Absolute "is not to be grasped in conceptual form, but felt, intuited; it is not its conception, but the feeling of it and intuition of it that are to have the say and final expression."[7]

Hegel's Idealist thought caused huge excitement among those who sought a new way of thinking about God and religion. His philosophy was considered to be far more positive and affirming than the thinking of Kant and his fellow sceptical rationalists. They argued that if there was a God, the existence of that God couldn't be proved; and even if God did exist, He was so far removed from humanity's experience that we could never know anything about Him. For Hegel, God was here and now. However, Hegel's God wasn't here in the form of the personal God of Christianity. And neither did Hegel's God come wrapped in the chains of Christian theology and tradition. No special belief, ritual, or profession of faith was required to experience the truth about Hegel's God. It was available in the spirit's subjective experience of the world.

> The truth is inherently universal, essential and substantial; and, as such, it exists solely in thought and for thought. But that spiritual principle which we call God is none other than the truly substantial, inherently and essentially individual and subjective truth. ... We encounter it as such in world history.[8]

For Hegel, the way we experienced and thought about God also emerged out of the zeitgeist, the spirit of the age. What he meant was that each historical era develops its own concept of God that is meaningful for those living in that era. But as that era passed away, so their idea of God passed away with it. Thus God was experienced in popular Greek religion as Zeus and the other Olympian gods. But when Greek civilization ended, Zeus and his fellow Olympians died with it. However, their death still had a use.

For Hegel, history had a purpose: the realization of God in human history. He didn't mean this in the Christian sense that Jesus Christ actualized God in history through his birth, death, and resurrection. Rather, for Hegel, God became actualized in human history through the individual. "The peculiarity of Hegel's form of idealism ... lies in his idea that the mind of God becomes actual only via its particularization in the minds of 'his' finite creatures. Thus, in our consciousness of God, we somehow serve to realize His own self-consciousness, and, thereby, his own perfection."[9]

What this led to was Hegel's idea that the death of one set of gods was followed by the birth of others, each more advanced than the previous. Thus humanity was in the process of advancing into ever higher concepts of God as the Absolute. The process of historical becoming was accordingly of great significance to Hegel, with the highest form of existence being that of freedom of the spirit. And in order to achieve freedom of the spirit human beings had to progressively cast off all those things that prevented freedom – such as slavery, religious dogma, social oppression of the individual, and culture that alienated individuals from their highest purpose. Thus Hegel advocated that just as the Greek Olympian gods died in human consciousness, so Christianity had to be cast aside because it was superseded by a superior (Hegelian) understanding of the way the Absolute and spirit functioned in the world.

Hegel's analysis of history as a progress towards freedom, along with his dialectic logic and liberal social criticisms, inspired many other nineteenth century thinkers, notably Marx. In addition, Hegel's idea that the perfection of the Absolute could only be realized by a great, self-conscious, World-historical individual, stimulated both Nietzsche's idea of the Übermensch (the individual who is beyond ordinary morality), and Hitler's concept of an Arian master race who had the historical and spiritual right to rule over all others.

Hegel's belief in the progress of history also had an ironic impact. It turned out that his wasn't the culminating philosophy for all time. Instead, as the years passed, other thinkers refined his concepts, used them as a jumping-off point, or by-passed them altogether. New ideas, reflecting the new zeitgeist, struck Westerners as more reflective of how things were. So Hegel's concepts of the Spirit and Absolute lost their relevance and died away.

Nonetheless, the new direction of thinking about God offered by Hegel and the other German Idealist philosophers – including Fichte, Schelling, and Schleiermacher – meant that the subjective human aspect of experience was now considered to be more significant than sense-based data. Thus while God was still considered to be transcendent, the place to find God was no longer "out there," in the world of things. Rather, it was within, in the everyday experience of human consciousness. This was where the future of understanding God lay. And Ludwug Andreas Feuerbach saw himself as just the man to take Hegel's thought to the next level.

FEUERBACH: GOD AS PROJECTION

Ludwig Andreas Feuerbach (1804-1872) studied under Hegel at the University of Berlin. After Hegel's death in 1931, a group formed called the Young Hegelians. Largely consisting of young bucks who sought to make their marks in German intellectual life, they opposed the mainstream, academic interpretation of Hegel's thought, which considered that Prussian culture was the apogee of human history. Instead, the young Hegelians argued that Prussian culture still had much to change, including the social conditions in which many of the working classes were struggling to earn enough to feed their families, in which a conservative form of Lutherism held religious sway, and in which political dissent was repressed.

The Young Hegelians came to include not only Feuerbach, but also two Biblical scholars whose work we have already examined, Bruno Bauer and David Strauss. Bauer's support of the Young Hegelians cost him dearly, because in 1842 the Prussian government withdrew his university professorship. Strauss himself never obtained a university position, surviving financially by writing books on philosophy, Christian thought and history, and through going pen-to-pen with other German writers on a variety of controversies. It was an aggressive intellectual environment, in which thinkers were constantly challenged to defend their perspectives, which explains why German scholarship remained at the forefront of European thought during the 1800s.

As with Bauer and Strauss, Feuerbach survived outside the academic mainstream. A university position was never a possibility for him because in his first book, *Thoughts on Death and Immortality* (1830), he criticized Christian theology, especially the idea of the immortality of the soul. Feuerbach argued that the concept of heaven was an illusion that distracted people from addressing the reality of life. He also defended the ideas of the highly controversial Dutch philosopher, Baruch Spinoza. This wasn't a good idea, since Spinoza had long been considered to be an atheist and not at all the type of person one should defend in "polite society." Fortunately, when Feuerbach married in 1837, his new wife's family owned a porcelain factory in a Bavarian town, which generated sufficient income for him to spend his time thinking and writing without having to seek employment with those who despised his thinking.

The book that made Feuerbach's reputation was *Das Wessen Des Christianity* (*The Essence of Christianity* 1841). In it he presented the proposition that humanity had invented religion, that religion was nothing more than an entrancing dream, and that what humanity needed was wake up and face reality.

> Religion is the dream of the human mind. But even in dreams we do not find ourselves in emptiness or in heaven, but on earth, in the realm of reality; we only see real things in the entrancing splendor of imagination and caprice, instead of in the simple daylight of reality and necessity. Hence I do nothing more to religion – and to speculative philosophy and theology also – than to open its eyes, or rather to turn its gaze from the internal towards the external, i.e. change the object as it is in the imagination into the object as it is in reality. But certainly for the present age, which prefers the sign to the thing signified, the copy to the original, fancy to reality, the appearance to the essence, this change, inasmuch as it does away with illusion, is an absolute annihilation, or at least a reckless profanation; for in these days illusion only is sacred, truth profane.[10]

These were times when an aggressive polemic was necessary to generate lively conversation in cafes and drawing rooms. So while Feuerbach extended Hegel's position, the way he framed his argument was deliberately provocative. In this mood, he was happy to take on both Kant and his old master Hegel.

Against Kant, Feuerbach argued that the grandfather of German idealism missed the essence of experience when he argued that we can't know the thing-in-itself, that all we ever experience is the sensual phenomenon of the thing. For Feuerbach this meant that we can never know the truth or reality of anything in our experience. Extending this criticism to the concept of God, Feuerbach argued that even if we experience God in the moral sphere, we can never know God in reality. So whatever we think about God is generated by us.

> God exists, but he is for us a tabula rasa, an empty being, a mere thought. God, as we imagine and think of him ... is only an appearance of us and for us, and not God in himself.[11]

Further criticizing Hegel's view, Feuerbach argued that self-consciousness boiled down to ego, and that Hegel had made the ego itself divine.

> The Hegelian philosophy ... objectified the ego as substance, as God. But in so doing, it expressed – indirectly and in a reverse order – the divinity of the ego ... meaning that man's consciousness of God is God's own self-consciousness. That means that the being belongs to God and knowing to man. But the being of God, according to Hegel, is actually nothing other than the being of thought, or thought abstracted from the ego, that is, the thinker. The Hegelian philosophy has turned thought, that is, the subjective being ... into the Divine and Absolute Being.[12]

So for Feuerbach, Kant presents a distant God we can never experience, while Hegel presents a God who is grandly called Absolute Spirit, but is really just an extension of our own self-conscious ego. Both were unsatisfactory to Feuerbach because they failed sufficiently to account for the materialist reality of life. They also kept people locked in the dream of religion.

In *The Essence of Christianity* Feuerbach argued that the abstract vagueness of both Kant and Hegel should be replaced by the one thing that truly is real – man himself. Man worships God and practices religion, valuing in them the highest qualities of human existence, whether these be love, knowledge, truth, or reality. But these qualities are really part of humanity's highest essence. Therefore religion and God consist of those concepts and qualities that are essential to man's highest self. Thus religion and God do not exist outside us, but inside us, as our highest essential aspects. "The absolute to man is his own nature."[13]

Feuerbach's next step was to ask, in that case, where did God come from? The answer he offered was, God came from us. We desired immortality, love, truth, knowledge. And out of our desire for these qualities we idealized a God, which was really just the objectification of our own highest desires. He added a caveat, however, for if the qualities we desired are negative feelings, then our God would be negative: "If in the heart there is fear and terror, in God there is anger; if in the heart there is joy, hope, confidence, in God there is love."[14] Whichever qualities we embraced as essential to our self-consciousness we then projected as God onto reality.

Did God, then, have a reality? Feuerbach answered yes. And no. The highest human ideals gave God reality. But it was a reality that existed according to the circumstances of the world in which we lived.

> The divine being is nothing else than the human being, or, rather the human nature purified, freed from the limits of the individual man. ... Therefore God is an existent, real being, on the very same ground that he is a particular, definite being; for the qualities of God are nothing else than the essential qualities of man himself, and a particular man is what he is, has his existence, his reality, only in his particular conditions.[15]

For Feuerbach, because human beings exist in their conditioned, historical reality, so God can only be defined in terms of that conditioned historical reality, having no existence apart from that reality.

CONCLUSION

During the period of two hundred years, from Descartes, through Kant, to Hegel and then Feuerbach, we can see a definite progression respecting the concept of God.

For Descartes, reality consisted of mind and matter, and God was "out there" somewhere, as a divine being who created matter, while at the same time transcending it. For Kant, God was still "out there," but the limitations built into human perceptions meant that we could never prove God's existence nor definitely ascertain God's qualities. We could only infer God via innate rational concepts, while through living morally, and by being a good person, we could feel an echo of God's existence within us.

Then, in Hegel's thought, a big shift occurred. Now the subjective aspect of our experience came to the fore, with God being considered to exist as an Absolute Spirit within the phenomenologically experienced historical moments of our daily existence. God was no longer "out there." Hegel thought of God as being perpetually present to us as the highest aspect of our own existence.

Finally, with Feuerbach, the Absolute is withdrawn completely into the human. There is no longer a God even in the historical moment. There is just the highest human qualities that we project onto the world around us. According to Feuerbach, we invented God, who now depended on us for His existence.

CHAPTER 7

The Fork In The Road

We now have a context in which to place Nietzsche's assertion, "God is dead." As we have seen, many European thinkers had long been making the same claim, in a variety of scientific, scholarly, and intellectual disciplines. So Nietzsche's 1882 declaration was far from novel.

It is clear that what Nietzsche was referring to was not the literal death of God, but rather the death of the concept of the theistic, personal God held by traditional Christianity. However, Nietzsche also had a greater goal. This goal was to transform European culture from a belief in what he considered to be a superstitious creed to a more rationally-based world view centred on human achievement. In this goal we can see that Nietzsche reflected his times, merely adopting to a more extreme degree the same stance that he shared with many other intellectuals and free-thinking believers in the late 1800s.

To recapitulate: Three hundred years earlier, in 1582, Europeans had believed in one God, one sacred book, one creation story, and one saviour. But by 1882 the one God had been shown to have interesting and sophisticated rivals, the one sacred book was known to have been written and edited by human hands, the one creation story was viewed as no more than a marvellous poetic myth among numerous other equally marvellous myths, and the one savior was thought of as a human being who after his death had been raised by his followers into a divinity in exactly the same way that Buddha and Krishna had been divinized by their followers.

The view of reality that Aquinas' theology justified had fallen. The world was no longer assumed to be the perfect creation of a perfect God. And while reason was unquestionably accepted as humanity's most powerful tool for understanding the workings of the natural world, divine revelation was no longer needed to guide reason. Reason could do very nicely by itself.

Among those who grappled with the implications of the ideas explored in the preceding chapters there was a growing realization that religious explanations regarding how and why the world was the way it was had lost their relevance. Mythological religious stories about the world had been superseded by scientific and rational explanations.

This was the cultural change that Neitzsche had sought. He contributed to that change. But, in fact, change came out of the collective efforts of thousands of scientists, mathematicians, philosophers, researchers, and scholars, efforts that were accepted by thinking people who took their discoveries to heart. Thus by 1882, when Neitzsche proclaimed God's demise, humanity's view of reality had changed and God could no longer be thought of as previously.

Yet, despite the traditional theistic idea of God having been cast down from its pedestal, many people still wished to believe in God. This wish led to a question that intrigued, vexed, amused, and infuriated many, then and today: Where did God fit into this new view of reality?

There were three basic ways of responding to this question: attempting to maintain Christian beliefs, rejecting all beliefs, and developing new beliefs.

THE RELIGIOUS ESTABLISHMENT'S RESPONSE

Conservatism is the tendency to maintain existing forms of doing, feeling, and thinking. Conservatives fight change out of a desire to keep things as they have been. And institutions, because they have so much invested intellectually, emotionally, socially, and economically in keeping things as they have been, are naturally the most conservative and fight longest and hardest against any momentum towards change.

This is why Christianity's many churches responded so defensively to the changes that occurred throughout the 1800s. The conservative authorities controlling the Christian churches adopted a head-in-the-sand attitude, predicated on the hope that if defenders of faith ignored the scientific, intellectual, social, and cultural advances that were happening around them, those advances would eventually run out of energy and evaporate.

The Catholic Church applied this strategy to an extreme degree when it called the First Vatican Council in 1869 to address the rise of rationalism, free-thinking, and doubt regarding the Bible and traditional doctrine. As is stated in the official records of the Council:

> Everybody knows that those heresies, condemned by the Fathers of Trent, which rejected the divine magisterium of the Church and allowed religious questions to be a matter for the judgment of each individual, have gradually collapsed into a multiplicity of sects, either at variance or in agreement with one another; and by this means a good many people have had all faith in Christ destroyed. Indeed even the holy Bible itself, which they at one time claimed to be the sole source and judge of the Christian faith, is no longer held to be divine, but they begin to assimilate it to the inventions of myth. Thereupon there came into being and spread far and wide throughout the world that doctrine of rationalism or naturalism – utterly opposed to the Christian religion. ... The abandonment and rejection of the Christian religion, and the denial of God and his Christ, has plunged the minds of many into the abyss of pantheism, materialism and atheism ... [threatening] to overthrow the very foundations of human society.[1]

The Catholic Church shared this fight for hearts and minds with the Anglican, Lutheran, and other Protestant churches. However, the Catholic Church had long ago taken the fight into the intellectual lives of its members by establishing an *Index of Forbidden Books*. These were books Catholics were not allowed to read for fear their beliefs and morals would be subverted. By the end of the 1800s the *Index* included a large percentage of the works of authors discussed here. The writings of Francis Bacon, René Descartes, Copernicus, Galileo, Edward Gibbon, John Calvin, Erasmus Darwin (Charles' grandfather), David Hume, Immanuel Kant, Martin Luther, Ernest Renan, Baruch de Spinoza, and Voltaire were all on the *Index*.

The solution the Catholic Church offered to this rash of free-thinking was to introduce the doctrine of Papal Infallibility. This gave the Pope the final word on all doctrinal and teaching issues within the Church. If a Catholic had any doubts about Church doctrine regarding the nature of reality due to being "tainted' by scientific or scholarly ideas, all they had to do was listen to what the Pope declared about the issue and doubt no more. This doctrine of Papal Infallibility created considerable unease among many in the Catholic clergy due to the impression of intolerance they feared it would engender. Accordingly, numerous bishops chose to leave Rome rather than vote on the measure. With those who disapproved not voting, the proposal duly passed, and continues in place today, although the *Index* was officially abandoned in 1996.

With Catholics forbidden from engaging in the intellectual advancements of the era, and with many Anglicans and Lutherans also being pressured to conform to traditional doctrine, it became increasingly difficult for thinking believers to reconcile their religious beliefs with the cultural, scientific, and social advances of the era. Indeed, it could be suggested that the head-in-the-sand attitude adopted by many mainstream churches led directly to two attitudes that remain prevalent today: the alienation of intellectuals from and within Christian churches, and the rise of fundamentalism.

ALIENATION AND FUNDAMENTALISM

Western cultural and intellectual advances created huge conflicts of conscience for many who wished to maintain institutional religious belief, but who did not want to ascribe to the "package" of myths, moral rules, ritual practices, and metaphysical concepts that went with belief. Yet the response of the mainstream churches largely required their laity to ignore the new discoveries – which were in their own way revelatory – and instead conform to traditional Christian teachings justified by readings of the Bible. The result was that, forced to make a choice, great masses of believers choose to leave the churches.

An interesting example of this exit is offered by Marian Evans (1819-1880), best known today as George Eliot, the author of *Middlemarch*. Raised in a devout Church of England family, Evans attended evangelical Christian services between the ages of fifteen and twenty-two. But she also had a prodigious intellect, reading voraciously in five languages, and devouring philosophical, political, and theological writings. This reading inevitably exposed her to critical interpretations of traditional beliefs.

All Evan's questioning of her own beliefs came to a head in 1842, when she read *An Enquiry Concerning the Origins of Christianity* (1838) by Charles Hennell. Hennell argued that a true account of the life of Jesus Christ could not deviate from the laws of nature (i.e. there were no miracles), that just because Jesus' tomb was empty when the women arrived did not mean he had been resurrected, and, in agreement with Renan, that it was the feelings and desires of Jesus' followers, influenced by attitudes customary in the era in which they lived, that they elevated their teacher to the status of divinity.

Hennell still considered himself a Christian. He just didn't want to be burdened by the beliefs that an intelligent, civilized, intellectually sophisticated, nineteenth century European no longer accepted as true. But that did not mean he considered Jesus' teaching was of no value. "Christianity thus regarded as a system of elevated thought and feeling, will not be injured by being freed from those fables, and those views of local or temporal interest, which hung around its origin."[2]

By 1842, at the age of twenty-four, Marian Evans had reached the same conclusion. She also decided that in good conscience she had to stop attending church. On the day she decided this, she wrote her father a letter justifying her position, saying of the Jewish and Christian scriptures:

> I regard these writings as histories consisting of mingled truth and fiction, and while I admire and cherish much of what I believe to have been the moral teaching of Jesus himself, I consider the system of doctrines built upon the facts of his life and drawn as to its materials from Jewish notions to be most dishonorable to God and most pernicious on individual and social happiness.[3]

Four years later, in 1846, living the life of an emancipated woman in London, Evans showed how far she had traveled intellectually by translating David Strauss' *Das Leben Jesu* into English. Seven years later she translated Feuerbach's *Das Wessen Des Christianity*. Her choice of rejecting traditional beliefs was also taken by many others brought up in Christian churches, to the extent that the Victorian age became known as the age of atheism.

The alternative course, adopted by many conservative believers, was to vociferously defend their religious beliefs. This path was followed by the scholar Edward Pusey. In 1821, while studying at Oxford, Pusey traveled to Germany to find out for himself what intellectual challenges German scholarship presented to the traditional Christian world view. A conservative Anglican, he was confronted by frightening statements made in the German lecture halls: that religion was not a God-given fact, but was rather something human beings made up; that religious history consisted of stories people tell each other about the creation of the world, about God, about how things came to be as they are; and that the Bible itself was a wholly human construct. Pusey was challenged further by the idea, first suggested by Hegel, that human perception shifted and altered over time, because it was shaped by tribal and national yearnings, by social conditions, and by prevailing modes of thought. Religion, as a part of human culture and perception, was not an intractable fact of reality, but rather similarly altered and shifted over time.

On his return to England Pusey confronted the new German perspective in a book, *An Historical Enquiry into the Probable Causes of the Rationalist Character Lately Predominant in the Theology of Germany* (1827). However, because he discussed the German scholars' issues seriously, other Christian apologists branded him a sympathizer of the radical German thought. Pusey, seeking to show he was a good traditionalist, eventually decided that the German scholars' positions were too strong to refute. He decided that what was needed to defend both the authenticity of the Bible, and the religious status quo, was "an absolute intolerance, amounting to fanaticism, of anything that threatened the entrenched position of Christianity as a revealed Religion."[4] He was not alone in adopting this strategy. Another apologist of the time stated:

> The Church must renounce rebellion as of all evils the greatest. ... I do not shrink from uttering my firm conviction that it would be a gain to the country were it vastly more superstitious, more bigoted, more gloomy, more fierce in its religion than at present it shows itself to be. ... Rationalism is the great evil of the day.[5]

Thus does conservativism, when faced by its own intellectual inadequacies, descend into fundamentalism. But all this occurred because the nineteenth century was a fluid era, full of social, political, economic, and intellectual change. It was during this period that the practical application of liberal democracy and free markets were worked out, and the newly educated middle classes were politically and economically empowered. Further, with more people able to read than at any time previously in history, and more books being published than at any other time in history, increasing numbers of people were in a position to question for themselves what over the centuries had been automatically accepted because people were unaware of any alternative perspectives.

So those who wished to grapple with the nature of God now had three main options. First was the conservative option of defending traditional beliefs, no matter how much out of step with the times they became. Second was the sceptical option, arising out of alienation, of choosing to withdraw from conservative mainstream religious organizations and beliefs. And the third option was to change the conceptual context by adopting non-traditional forms of belief.

THE SEARCH FOR NEW FORMS OF BELIEF

One Sunday morning in September 1893, Mrs George W. Hale looked out the front window of her house and saw an unshaven and somewhat dishevelled Indian man sitting on the pavement outside. What made this sight so incongruous was that she lived in one of the mansions that lined Lake Shore Drive, among Chicago's wealthier areas, and that the Indian was wearing the orange robes and turban of a Hindu monk. The man was Narendranath Dutta, better known as Swami Vivekananda (1863–1902).

Vivekananda was in the United States to attend the World Parliament of Religions, which had been organized to run in conjunction with the great Exposition being held in Chicago. However, the Parliament had been postponed by several weeks, and the delay had caused him to run out of funds. Luckily, the hungry and exhausted Vivekananda had come to a rest under the right window because Mrs Hale was a personal friend of Dr Burrows, the President of the Parliament's organizing committee. She took Vivekananda in and, with others, gave him food and housing for the duration of the Parliament.

This inauspicious event, involving an Indian monk and a Western society lady, may be seen as emblematic of a new approach in Western spirituality that also occurred during this age of scepticism and doubt. With the leading authorities of mainstream Christianity not wishing to engage with the rapid changes that were occurring in the world, the field was open to alternative possibilities, and the translations scholars were making of the texts of all the world's religions and spiritual traditions provided those new possibilities.

The impact made by translations of the world's major spiritual, ethical, and philosophic texts on eighteenth and nineteenth century readers cannot be underestimated. Today we expect to go into any quality bookstore and find translations of the *Bhagavad Gita*, the *Analects of Confucius*, the *Dhamapada*, and the Egptian *Book of the Dead*. In the eighteenth and nineteenth centuries these were still new texts, brim full of exciting new concepts, offering new ways of seeing the world and God in relation to it. Voltaire had been attracted to Chinese thought and culture, among the German thinkers Hegel, Goethe, Schopenhauer, and Nietzsche each found much to enthuse over in Buddhism, and Max Müller was far from alone in being impressed by the Indian *Upanishads*, their ideas equally inspiring the poet Samuel Coleridge and the Transcendentalists Henry David Thoreau and Ralph Emerson.

Indeed, such was the general enthusiasm for non-Western spirituality that by the 1870s Western culture had become a great mixing bowl in which various currents of religious, mythological, spiritual, scientific, literary, and philosophical thoughts were swirling. This was the period which saw the founding of Christian Science in 1866 by Mary Baker Eddy, while in 1875 Madam Blavatsky drew together a range of Eastern and Western beliefs to establish the Theosophical Society. This was also when spiritualism and mediumship became popular, along with an appreciation of the spiritual implications of diet, health, psychology, and environment. Collectively, these all laid the foundations of what we today call New Age practices and beliefs.

Accordingly, when Vivekananda, a real Indian swami dressed in authentic robes, appeared at the World Parliament of Religions, he had a primed audience. This was an ideal opportunity for a charlatan to take the eager and open Parliament attendees for a ride. However, Vivekananda had genuine depth. He possessed a commanding presence, a sharp intellect, a Western-style education, and a profound understanding of Indian spirituality and philosophy, and he proved to be the ideal person to introduce the practical aspects of Indian spirituality to Westerners.

Naren, as Vivekananda was called by his family and friends, was born and raised in Kolkata (Calcutta). As a child he was naturally drawn towards spirituality, even meditating with his friends after school. However, at school he was introduced to Western science and philosophy, including the philosophy of Hegel. As a result he developed not just a sceptical attitude towards the existence of God, but also towards the excesses of Indian religion. For a time he even became an atheist, as he could find no rational basis for maintaining a belief in God. However, because he felt that the only way of knowing something is to experience it, the teenage Naren then developed an intense desire to find someone who had perceived God and so settle for him the question of God's existence and nature once and for all. Over the years he visited a variety of professors, teachers, and holy men, but none could affirm that they had seen God. Then, in 1881, he met Ramakrishna Paramahamsa. To Naren's question of whether he had seen God, Ramakrishna replied, "Yes, I have seen God. I see Him as I see you here, only more clearly."[6]

Ramakrishna was considered to be one of India's greatest holy men. He was engaged in the task of reviving an understanding of India's ancient spiritual traditions at a time when the impact of Western science and social attitudes were causing many of India's educated to discard their country's spiritual and philosophic traditions. Ramakrishna's impact on Naren was profound. He not only answered Naren's questions regarding God, but took him into deep meditative states, and taught him the deepest aspects of Indian spirituality, particularly the non-dualist principles of Advaita Vedanta. After Ramakrishna's death in 1887 Naren became the leader of a group of young monks. It was in this role that it was suggested he travel to Chicago and attend the World's Parliament of Religions. The Rajah of Khetri gave him the funds to do so, and also gave him the name of Vivekananda.

Vivekananda became the sensation of the Parliament. While representatives from most of the world's major religions were present, from his first appearance it was Vivekananda who attracted all eyes. Newspaper reports focused on him due to his singular and authoritative appearance, and Chicago buzzed with anticipation as to what he would say, an anticipation that was intensified when he declined his first opportunities to speak due to extreme nervousness.

Finally, Vivekananda approached the rostrum. He began his speech with the words, "Sisters and brothers of America." While the other speakers had used the much more formal, "Ladies and gentlemen," Vivekananda's opening words were typical of his relaxed outlook. The response was electric. Most of the seven thousand attendees immediately stood, their applause lasting a full two minutes.

Vivekananda's message to the Parliament was a simple one of tolerance and acceptance. He spoke of how Indian spirituality assumed that all religions and all creeds were variations on each other, and how there were no missionaries in India because Indians considered that all religions worshipped the same God – this at a time when large numbers of Christian missionaries were arriving in India to convert the "heathen" Hindus to the "one true" religion of Christianity. Vivekananda also called for an end to fanaticism and intolerance, and for their replacement with the universal acceptance of all creeds:

> If the Parliament of Religions has shown anything to the world, it is this: It has proved that holiness, purity, and charity are not the exclusive possessions of any church in the world, and that every system has produced men and women of the most exalted character. In the face of this evidence, if anyone dreams of the exclusive survival of his own religion and the destruction of others, I pity him from the bottom of my heart and point out to him that

upon the banner of every religion will soon be written, in spite of resistance: "Help and not Fight," "Assimilation and not Destruction," "Harmony and Peace and not Dissension."[7]

After the Parliament was over Vivekananda travelled the country giving lectures on Indian religion, philosophy, and spirituality. He ended up staying for four years, establishing the Vedanta Society there in 1894.

In many ways Vivekananda's arrival in the United States can be seen as the real beginning of the impact of Eastern spirituality in the West. Previously, Westerners had translations of the ancient texts of the Vedas and Upanishads. Vivekananda brought a personal understanding of what those texts meant and how Westerners could use them in their own personal search for God.

OUR GOD DILEMMA

This is where we find ourselves today. Traditional religions and their mythologically-based outlooks continue to have a say in our cultures, but religion is no longer at the centre of Western life. Furthermore, day by day what traditional religions assert is losing its relevance.

The ways we think today about the world, about ourselves, and about the nature and processes of reality, have been progressively and ever more radically altered since 1620, when Frances Bacon's *Novum Organum* laid the foundations for the scientific method. Radical change sped up throughout the 1800s, when so many ground-breaking discoveries about the world were first made, and when the bases of knowledge, technologies, culture, and social practices that we today take as axiomatic were first proposed.

By 1900 the world had changed irrevocably. And it wasn't just the lives of millions that had been altered. The way those millions perceived reality had also been transformed. The old social and intellectual orders had collapsed, and in their place stood a new world full of possibilities. Liberal freedoms, along with education and economic opportunity, offered the world's millions the chance to create a brave new world for themselves, materially, emotionally, intellectually, and spiritually.

In the world's cities anyone could now read books, attend public lectures, join groups of like-minded people, and become involved in whatever they felt was most significant to them. Travel had also become much easier for everyone, with colonialization, the increased wealth of the middle classes, and developing trade suddenly making the whole globe available for physical and intellectual exploration. And for those who sought a brave new concept of God to match the brave new world in which they now lived, profound and wide-ranging critiques of Western thought, religion, and life were being introduced by a new generation of thinkers, including Marx, Freud, Jung, Adler, and William James. Every year, old proposals were being questioned and overturned, and new theories about the world and humanity's function in it proposed.

However, this openness of possibilities also created doubt. Because everything was possible, nothing was certain. And this situation applied particularly to God. With the old certainties gone:

- Increasingly people no longer believed that every single event in the world was initiated and overseen by a supernatural being called God.
- People no longer automatically accepted that the myths recounted about this supernatural being in sacred books such as the Bible were historically and literally true.
- Religious revelation was no longer considered to offer the highest and truest form of knowledge about how the world worked.
- Humanity knew it did not live in a magical world in which God could willfully set aside the laws of nature.

What the collapse of the old certainties added up to was a removal of the support structures for traditional theism. The concept of a personal supernatural God was, at best, in deep trouble and, at worst, no longer tenable. Of course, individual thinkers had questioned the nature of God long before this time. But this was the first period in human history that a significant proportion of *an entire generation* was able to so seriously question long-established truths.

For some this was a terrible situation, as it meant the old certainties were gone, yet there was nothing to replace them. It was as if a void had opened up beneath them. But for others it was an excellent situation to be in, because they now had the opportunity, an opportunity not afforded to their great-great-grandparents' generation, to make up their own minds. To reiterate what Thomas Paine observed in *The Age of Reason*:

> I do not believe in the creed professed by the Jewish church, by the Roman church, by the Greek church, by the Turkish church, by the Protestant

church, nor by any church that I know of. My own mind is my own church ... [and] it is necessary to the happiness of man, that he be mentally faithful to himself.⁸

One of the principal glories of the twentieth century was that it continued the momentum of the previous three centuries by generating a host of new ideas regarding the nature of the world. But this also required rethinking God.

On the one hand God was seen as irrelevant. On the other God was seen as just as necessary as ever, but was to be approached in an entirely new way, one freed of the social, institutional, and conceptual restraints of the past. On the one hand enquirers had the freedom and opportunity to follow Paine's dictum and find their own accommodation with God. And on the other was the fear that freedom generated, the fear we naturally experience when we commit ourselves to exploring the unknown and undefined.

Part Two examines how this tension played out.

PART 2

GOD'S RESURRECTION

CHAPTER 8

World War And Its Discontents

The twentieth century did not ease up on the rate of change initiated by the preceding three centuries of scientific discoveries, technological advances, cultural advances, and social restructuring. On the contrary, everything was now up for grabs.

New literary movements, including Imagism, Dada, and Surrealism turned European writing on its head. Similarly, artistic movements developed by the newly emerged middle classes, beginning with Impression in the 1870s and continuing with Expressionism, Cubism, Futurism, Dada and Surrealism, first challenged then overthrew the power of the official art academies. By 1910 art-making had been transformed from illustrating scenes drawn from the Bible and classical mythology to capturing the vibrant, steaming, grimy, immediacy of modern life. The staid repetitions of the academies were replaced by the experimentalism of the avant-garde, which illuminated the streets of culture with the flashing neon of the New.

Socially, the twentieth century presented ever more radical challenges to ideas of how societies should be organized. World War One began as a battle between Europe's aristocrats, but proved their death-knell as shocking numbers of working class men were stirred into killing each other while choking on poisonous gases, drowning in mud, and dying in droves while attempting to capture hilltops in the middle of nowhere. This "war to end all wars" was followed two decades later by World War Two, a conflagration driven by middle class politicians, military elites, and industrialists who, between wars, had replaced Europe's bumbling aristocratic classes as rulers. They brought a business-like efficiency to war, killing more second time round than anyone anticipated.

And even when peace brought an end to the rain of bombs, the cultural demolition continued as the post-war era continued to overturn established ways of thinking and living. Progress became the new catch word for a generation eager to put the horrors of two world wars behind them as they immersed themselves in a wide-reaching remodelling of the world.

However, the horrors were not so easily buried. This was because where the Lisbon earthquake of 1775 that so troubled European believers had killed one hundred thousand by a single act of nature, the gas chambers of the Third Reich murdered over six million, an achievement that required sustained human ingenuity. Arguably, sheer stupid bloody-mindedness from the German and Russian leaders caused the deaths of twenty million on the battlefields of Russia. But ingenuity was again to the fore in the creation of the two nuclear bombs that the Americans dropped on the Japanese to end the Pacific war. In total, over nine million were killed during WW1, while a staggering seventy million died during WW2. And after all that destruction what did humanity get out of it? A Cold War driven by a brand new doomsday technology that had the potential to wipe every living creature from the face of the planet.

Finally, when it was all over, and the enormity of what had occurred struck home, the obvious questions began to be asked. Where was God when all this was going on? How could the all-loving, all-knowing, all-powerful God have stood back and allowed so many people of all nations and religions to suffer and die? If everything occurred in accordance with God's purpose, what was His purpose in creating so much misery and destruction? And given that God had directly intervened by holding back the waters of the Red Sea so Moses could lead the tribes of Israel out of Egypt, and given that He was so concerned about the spiritual state of humanity that He had descended from heaven to Earth in the form of His own Son to expiate our sins, why didn't He step in and prevent all this murder and insanity? Didn't He care any more? Wasn't He motivated to do something? Was He even paying attention?

Much in twentieth century intellectual culture was shaped by a negative response to these questions.

GOD IS BURIED

Where the nineteenth century had to deal with doubt, in the twentieth century the default intellectual mode became cynicism. Thus a natural response to the above questions was that, clearly, God was not in charge. Furthermore, according to thinkers such as Karl Marx and Sigmund Freud, God never had been.

Marx asserted that God was a mirage invented by human beings and religion an opiate used by those in power to pacify the working classes, whose hopes of reaching heaven in the afterlife, Marx argued, were cynically exploited by the ruling elite to stop them from rebelling over their misery in this one.

Taking up Feuerbach's contention that God is a projection onto reality of human aspirations, Freud argued that God was no more than the neurotically generated image of an exalted father, which humanity had created out of an infantile need to feel protected and cared for. Freud thought that belief in this God was no more than a childish phase. To him God was a psychologically created illusion which we grew out of as we matured into adults and came to grips with the true nature of reality. Thus the twentieth century rejection of God and religion was no more than a necessary emergence from illusion into reality. As Freud wrote in *The Future of an Illusion* (1927):

> Observe the difference between your attitude towards illusions and mine. You have to defend the religious illusion with all your might. If it becomes discredited – and indeed the threat to it is great enough – then your world collapses. There is nothing left for you but to despair of everything, of civilization and the future of mankind. From that bondage I am, we are, free. Since we are prepared to renounce a good part of our infantile wishes, we can bear it if a few of our expectations turn out to be illusions.[1]

Adopting with a vengeance the contention of the French scientist Baron D'Holbach that God was a hypothesis we no longer needed, post-war Western intellectual culture jettisoned the illusion of God and became atheistic. Marxism and, for a time, the psychoanalytic writings of Freud, provided the new sacred texts of what became a post-religious age.

During the pause between world wars philosopher A.J. Ayer offered an increasingly common perspective, arguing that nothing but physical reality, experienced via the senses, can sensibly be spoken of. But because assertions about God could not be empirically tested, and because they could not definitely be shown to be either true or false, they were invalid propositions. Which meant that God was also now an invalid hypothesis.

Existentialism, which placed the responsibility for human actions wholly on human beings, became influential in the aftermath of WW2. The French philosopher and atheist Jean-Paul Sartre, who became one of its leading flagbearers, considered that with the demise of the personal God of Christianity humanity now had a "God-shaped hole" in its psyche. This hole was a void into which surged a profound sense of the absurdity and meaninglessness of human existence – which, when we think about it, was actually a perfectly understandable response to the psychotic butchery of two world wars.

Further feeding this anti-metaphysical, anti-religious, and anti-God outlook were the ground-shaking discoveries of the sciences.

THE TWENTIETH CENTURY SCIENTIFIC REVOLUTION

In the early decades of the twentieth century the sciences not only provided some of the most exciting discoveries in human history, but they radically and profoundly altered our understanding of reality today.

As noted in Part One, Western theologians had long agreed that God, as the transcendent first cause of all that is, could never change. And neither could the world He had created. Aquinas articulated the rationale for this view when he proposed that God is perfect, infinite, immutable, simple (has no parts), and an indivisible unity. Because nothing God created could be less than perfect, and because perfection was necessarily complete, the world God had created was conceived as being a perfect fullness to which nothing could be added or subtracted. Furthermore, the world would maintain this state for all time.

This is why the discovery of fossils in the 1700s was such a shock – because fossils, being the remains of extinct species, contradicted the view that no part of God's creation could cease to be. This in turn also threatened the idea of God's perfection, for species that went out of existence appeared to be a clear blemish on God's good work. However, if fossils rocked the ark of traditional religious thinking about God and the world, scientific discoveries made in the early years of the twentieth century turned the ark upside-down.

The turning began with the publication of Albert Einstein's Special and General Theories of Relativity in 1905 and 1916 respectively. Einstein showed that there was no absolute time and space against which moving objects could be measured. Almost three hundred years earlier, when Newton formulated his laws regulating the movement of bodies through space, he had assumed that all movement should be measured against absolute time and space. As a Christian Newton accepted Aquinas' view that the world was complete and unchanging. Accordingly, he considered that his concept of absolute unchanging time and space provided a scientific justification for the metaphysical view that God is perfect. Einstein's dismantling of Newton's absolute time and space was therefore not just scientifically significant, it also overthrew a key concept by which scientists and theologians had found an accommodation with each other.

In 1919 Einstein's General Theory of Relativity became accepted as fact when English astrophysicist Arthur Eddington observed starlight being bent as it passed the Sun. The news was trumpeted in newspaper headlines around the world. The discovery also created huge excitement among physicists, mathematicians, and cosmologists, stimulating a flurry of revolutionary ideas.

In 1922 Russian mathematician Alexander Friedman, on the basis of equations derived from Einstein's Theory of Relativity, suggested that the universe was expanding. In 1925 American astrophysicist Edwin Hubble discovered that the Milky Way was not the entire universe, that actually the universe is full of vast numbers of galaxies. Hubble backed up his conclusion with equations and observations related to redshifted light emanated by galaxies as they moved away from our galaxy, thus confirming Friedman's proposal that the universe is expanding. And in 1927, Georges Lemaître, a Belgian physicist and a Catholic priest, proposed that the universe originally exploded out of what he called a "primeval atom." It was this originating cosmic explosion that provided the impetus for the expanding universe. Decades later Lemaître's proposition became better known as the "big bang."

All these discoveries actually took Einstein by surprise. He had previously realized that one of the consequences of his equations was that the universe could be contracting or expanding. But he had assumed with everyone else that the universe was static. Accordingly he inserted into his equations a formula that he called "the cosmological constant." This ensured that the equations derived from his theory described a static universe. When he later realized that Hubble was right, and that the universe indeed was expanding, he called this cosmological constant the biggest blunder of his life. Einstein's assumption shows just how firmly the idea of a static universe was entrenched at the start of the twentieth century, even for otherwise radical thinkers.

Nonetheless, and despite Einstein's initial doubts, the Theory of Relativity, backed up by empirical observation, showed that the universe was actually much more complex and interesting than anyone had imagined. It was full of strange features, including supernovas, pulsars, white dwarf stars, singularities, black holes, and all space was filled with microwave radiation left over from the big bang. Previously inconceivable ideas were introduced, such as event horizons, quantum gravity, galaxies that devoured other galaxies, and wormholes that offered a means of travelling through space-time. So not only was the universe not static, it was full of fascinating entities that were born, matured, and died over periods of billions of years. The idea of a perfect, unchanging universe was taking a pummelling. The knock-out was arguably made by quantum physics.

During the late 1910s and 1920s, Niels Bohr, Werrner Heisenberg, Max Planck and Einstein himself (along with a number of other contributing physicists) explored the implications of relativity at the sub-atomic level. The result was that a new description of sub-atomic reality was formulated, a description now known as quantum mechanics.

One of the key concepts of quantum mechanics is that sub-atomic particles such as electrons are best understood not as things but as packets of wave probabilities. This means that all the possible states in which a sub-atomic particle may exist do so in the form of wave functions. These wave functions exist simultaneously and anywhere in space. According to the Copenhagen interpretation of quantum mechanics, the wave functions that contain all the particle's possible states only collapse into one specific state at the actual moment of observation. But what complicates the situation is that observation can tell us *either* where the electron is *or* what its motion is, but not both at the same time. So we can make accurate predictions about a sub-atomic particle's location and momentum. But we can never definitely observe both. This feature became known as the Heisenberg uncertainty principle.

The implications of quantum mechanics radically challenged Newtonian physics. Newton had assumed that all bodies in the material world interact according to mathematically defined laws, and that if we understand the laws that connect two bodies then the effect of one body on another can be calculated and known with absolute certainty. In this sense Newton thought of reality as innately determined. One body's activity affected another, and we can determine to what degree. Heisenberg's uncertainty principle asserted that Newton was wrong.

According to quantum mechanics material reality is rooted not in determination but in probability. This means that we cannot precisely determine the effect of one particular body on another. Even worse for Newtonian determinacy, the probability wave functions that are inherent in reality mean that what happens in the world *can never be fully determined*. While deterministic Newtonian physics continue to be applicable on the level of everyday activity, Newton's laws fail when applied at the sub-atomic level, where probability rules.

Einstein personally remained uneasy with the philosophical implications of quantum physics. He responded to Heisenberg's uncertainty principle by claiming that "God does not play dice." (Which in turn stimulated Niels Bohr to reply, "Einstein, stop telling God what to do!") Yet by the time Einstein died in 1955 both relativity and quantum mechanics were had become the accepted descriptions of the universe on the cosmic and sub-atomic levels respectively.

Meanwhile, Darwin's theory of evolution had also been considerably advanced. Darwin never worked out the details of how natural selection works biologically. However, over the decades following Darwin's death the genetic details were progressively unveiled, culminating with the double helix model of DNA that Crick and Watson's proposed in 1953. The unravelling of the human genome, genetic engineering, and cloning subsequently followed.

As the biological processes by which natural selection occurs were clarified in ever greater detail, the concept of evolution became ubiquitous, entering numerous non-biological disciplines, including economics, social history, psychology, and literary analysis. The process of never-ending change that underpinned biological evolution also fitted with the idea that reality is cosmically relativistic and driven by quantum probability.

The result was that relativity, quantum mechanics, and evolution sank forever the idea of a static, unchanging universe.

THE TWENTIETH CENTURY INTELLECTUAL REVOLUTION

During the last decades of the twentieth century new ways of thinking came to the fore. Textual analysis, structuralism, constructionism, post-structuralism, and deconstruction became the accepted intellectual lenses though which to consider the nature of reality. These were all gathered under the general rubric of postmodernism, an outlook which questions prevailing norms, critiques the structure of identity, and challenges the validity of dominant cultural narratives, especially grand narratives such as the metaphysical story that the perfect and unchanging God created the perfect and static universe.

Driving the postmodern critique is an insight regarding the degree to which our view of reality is a construction. This applies both to the social aspects of our lives and to our individual identity.

On the social level, postmodernist thought emphasizes the degree to which all positions and perspectives are culturally and historically determined. Thus if we consider a Paleolithic hunter-gatherer who followed migrating herds of reindeer in what is now France around 20,000 BCE, a worker on the pyramids in Egypt near modern Cairo in 2,200 BCE, and an Argentinian accountant travelling to work on the subway in Buenos Aires in 2010 CE, for each their language, clothing, lifestyle, education, occupation, skills, world view, leisure activities, religion, and social identity are socially determined. They are *what* and *who* they are because of *where* and *when* they are. Our choices, tastes, lifestyle, work, outlook, thoughts, concerns, the way we talk, and our personal possibilities are each determined by our upbringing, our education, our social conditioning, our social and physical environments, our genetic make-up, and our psychophysical tendencies. Three conclusions may be drawn from this realization.

The first is that grand narratives fail because rather than being the eternal truths that they purport to be, they are really no more than stories that are told from perspectives that have been culturally, socially, and historically determined. So the grand narrative Europeans told themselves in the nineteenth century (that they were innately superior to the non-European cultures they were colonizing) was not a great truth for all time. Instead, it was just one story among many possible stories. And all stories are relative to the tellers and the cultural contexts in which they are told.

The second conclusion is that if we wish to understand the nature of the social and identity constructions in which we live, we have to deconstruct them. So if we look at the grand narrative of European colonialization we can see that claims that Europeans were superior to non-Europeans on intellectual, cultural, and religious grounds were really just justifications one group used to exploit, terrorize, and plunder others.

Third is the realization that embedded in grand narratives are assumptions that become mythologized, and that over time those myths become accepted as actual truths. So in order to develop new perceptions and constructions of reality we first have to deconstruct and demolish the old myths.

In this sense postmodernism can be seen as an outgrowth of the spirit of inquiry that fueled Enlightenment thinkers. The critique of the Bible carried out by German form critics was deconstructive. Similarly, geologist Charles Lyell deconstructed landscapes to discern underlying patterns of geological change, and botanist Charles Darwin deconstructed species, identifying patterns of inherited traits in order to discern species' evolutionary paths. Philology, archeology, anthropology, and comparative religious studies deconstructed the sequence, antiquity, and interactivity of cultures throughout history. Collectively, these disciplines engaged in a multi-disciplinary deconstruction of the grand religious narrative of Christianity derived from the Bible.

Accordingly, postmodern critiques may be seen as a reworking of the Enlightenment quest for knowledge and understanding. It is just being carried out in a different cultural context using different terminology and different conceptual frameworks.

The upshot of all these twentieth century cultural changes, along with scientific developments and intellectual scepticism, created huge problems for the concept of a personal interventionist God. Scientific discoveries replaced mythological descriptions of reality, and deconstructive thinking provided intellectual tools to question the assumptions of the past and past assumptions that had been carried into the present. Accordingly, the world in which we live today may be characterized as post-mythological, post-metaphysical, and post-religious. All of which suggests that by the late twentieth century God was well and truly dead and buried. And yet …

GOD REVIVES!

Interestingly, and despite a general dismissal of God by twentieth century intellectuals and academia, God never actually went away. It was only that one particular grouping, consisting of the Western scientific, academic, political, economic, literary, and cultural elite had removed God from their thinking.

However, for numerous others a desire to grapple with the notion of God remained. In the wider Western cultural context outside the academies God remained a significant presence in human activity. People continued to fill churches, synagogues, mosques, and temples each holy day; texts ascribed to God continued to be quoted in public moral and cultural debates; God continued to be used to justify actions performed; and priests continued to bless the soldiers of all nations as they went off to war, including to kill those who worshipped the same God. All this occurred no matter how vaguely God might be conceived, and no matter that for many God had now become an absence, a shadow that darkened and tormented human beings rather than illuminated humanity in its bleakest hours.

Yet, as life keeps reminding to us, our lives are an ebb and flow. And while the out-going tide of Victorian doubt reinforced by twentieth century scepticism revealed traditional ideas of a personal God to be a skeleton beached by history, with the rivets of religious justifications rusted and popped, and the central planks of belief buried in mud or having floated out to sea, an in-coming tide of reevaluation of God floated radical new ideas about God.

Accordingly, while many agreed with Freud that we have outgrown the personal God of theism, and with Sartre that growing up has left us with a God-shaped hole in our collective psyche, all thinkers did not then choose to feel their existence was meaningless or to wallow in despair. Instead, they saw the death of the theistic God as an opportunity to reconsider what God is. Freed from the intellectual and theological bric-a-brac of the past, they reveled in what an opportunity to redefine God in terms that are relevant to us today. Three concepts of God are currently the most widely advocated by those who continue to grapple with God.

The first is the personal God of traditional theism, which is obviously still held by many. This is God as a perfect super-being who transcends the universe, who is described in anthropomorphic and mythological terms, and who has the power to intervene in human existence, supernaturally and miraculously putting aside the laws of nature in order to do His will, which is always for the good. We have already seen that there are many problems with this concept of God. Further concerns will come to light in the following chapters.

The other two concepts of God most widely explored today are the immanent God of pantheism and the immanent-transcendent God of panentheism. Pantheism and panentheism both developed in parallel to the social, scientific, philosophic, and cultural developments outlined in Part One. Pantheism was conceived during the late 1600s to provide a concept of God that was consistent with the nature of reality being newly revealed by the sciences. Panentheism was proposed in the early 1800s as a way of reconciling traditional theism and pantheism, with which many remained uncomfortable. Panentheistic concepts of God were subsequently developed by a wide range of twentieth century thinkers.

Accordingly, the following chapters survey a range of twentieth and twenty-first century ways of thinking about God. However, before embarking on this exploration, we first have to consider the issue of what is involved in discussing God and God's nature.

CHAPTER 9

God-Talk Is A Human Invention

One cold winter in December 1273, Thomas Aquinas, the Catholic Church's greatest theologian, had an experience while saying the Mass that caused him to re-evaluate his life's work. He later wrote of this experience: "All that I have written seems to me like so much straw compared with what I have seen and with what has been revealed to me."[1]

As a result of this experience, which is thought to have involved a mystical vision of Jesus, Aquinas gave up his theological writing, leaving unfinished the third part of his magnus opus, *Summa Theologiae*. For anyone who has struggled with the dry doggedness of the *Summa*, the fact Aquinas did not finish his book is not necessarily a bad thing. However, at the heart of Aquinas' life work was the goal of *felicitas*, a direct perception of God. Aquinas' belief, which is also the mainstream Christian view, was that such a perception is only possible *after* the body's death. What Aquinas experienced was an intimation of *felicitas* while still in his body, *before* he died. In relation to this experience Aquinas saw that the theologizing to which he had dedicated his entire adult life, for which he still remains revered today, was "so much straw."

The word theology comes from the Greek: *theos* (god) and *logos* (word, rational speech). So theology literally means God-talk. It is talk in which we discuss, theorize, and speculate about God. As Aquinas' experience intimates, the reality of God is one thing, and our talk about God is something else.

For us living today in the twenty-first century the certainties that Aquinas sought to define, certainties that were stamped and certified by religious institutions, have gone. Where, for our forebears, God-talk had to use an agreed vocabulary and follow an established line of thinking in order to be acceptable, we live today in secular, democratic, pluralist societies. Within legal limits, we can say what we like about anything, including about God. In the past Jewish,

Christian and Islamic God-talkers had to take care regarding what they said, otherwise the arbiters of "legitimate speech" would step in and ostracize, imprison, or execute them. Today, we are happily free of this fear.

Of course, for those employed by religious organizations talking about God in ways that depart from the company line is an employment issue that may lead to being fired (as has happened to a number of controversial God-talking clergy in the twentieth century). But at least they no longer have their entrails torn out for saying it. And, naturally, those of us who are not aligned to any institution are completely free to formulate our own ideas about God. Yet despite this we also have to acknowledge that limits are inherent to all God-talk.

First there is the realization that, like all our talk, God-talk is unavoidably and inextricably bound up in our world view, our education, our culture, our established ways of thinking, and our language. Just as our lives are a social and historical construct, so whatever we say about God is similarly a construct.

Accordingly, while we may assume that God-talk strives to make definitive statements regarding God, in fact whatever we say necessarily reflects what we hold to be significant. And the concepts and words we use to express what we think and feel about God are unavoidably a product of our life and times.

Aquinas' God-talk reflected what was significant to him, in the context of his education, up-bringing, and life experiences. His God-talk was expressed in the language and conceptual framework of his times. We do exactly the same today. If social and economic freedom is important to us, then we speak of God in terms of freedom. If following rules and morality is significant to us, then we speak of God in terms of moral retribution and rewards and punishments. If we consider that personal feeling and social responsibility is important to us, then we talk about God in those terms. We can't avoid talking about God using ideas that are significant to us. And we can only express those ideas in the language we have grown up with, using ideas and vocabulary common to our times.

But, in doing so, are we really talking about God? Are we really making valid assertions about God's nature? Or is what we say inextricably bound up in our own talking? Of course, any talk about God has value, because it concerns what we consider to be most significant and ultimate in our lives. But in doing so how can we be sure we are actually saying something valid *about God*? How can we know we are not just talking *about ourselves*?

I will start considering this issue by examining the kinds of statements we make about God.

ABOUT TALKING ABOUT GOD

God-talk depends on words. But words are slippery. The ideas I associate with a word are not necessarily the ideas you associate with the same word. Education, authority, personal desires, fears and hopes, and our personal experiences each necessarily impact on the words we use and on the ideas we associate with those words. This is why doctrinal conventions have developed in all religions, out of an attempt to ensure that all believers are reading from the same page, and deriving the same meaning from that page.

Historically, the desire for clarity has led to the development of two broad ways of talking about God. One is making positive statements about God by asserting that God possesses this or that particular quality. The second is defining God negatively, by asserting that God does not possess this or that quality.

The ninth century Indian philosopher, Shankara, provided one of the classic statements of the negative approach when he wrote of Brahman (God conceived of as the transcendent Absolute):

> If the desire is to express the true nature of the Absolute, void of all external adjuncts and particularities, then it cannot be described by any positive means whatever. The only possible procedure then is to refer to it through a comprehensive denial of whatever positive characteristics have been attributed to it in previous teachings and to say "not thus, not thus."[2]

If God is thought of as being the ultimate transcendent existent, then our limited words can never adequately describe the full reality of what God is. So, the thinking goes, better not to say anything at all. In the Christian tradition, the fifth century Dionysius the Areopagite was the first to articulate this negative position. Calling God the One and the Good he maintained that God is beyond definition because God is beyond our ability to conceive or name. We can't even say that God exists, because God precedes existence itself.

> The One which is beyond thought surpasses the apprehension of thought, and the Good which is beyond utterance surpasses the reach of words. It is a Unity which is the unifying Source of all unity and a Super-Essential Essence, a Mind beyond the reach of mind, and a Word beyond utterance, eluding discourse, intuition, name and every kind of being. It is the Universal Cause

of existence while not existing Itself, for It is beyond all being and such that It alone could give, with proper understanding, a revelation of Itself.³

In agreement with Shankara, Dionysius denied that any attributes could be given to God. He saw God as a "light which surpasses Deity" and there is "no more fitting method to celebrate Its praises than to deny It every atttribute." Even deity was denied to God, because "Godness" itself is a positive attribute, and all positive attributes, including deity, were inadequate to express what God fullness.

The Jewish religion acknowledges the inadequacy of positive assertions about God by not allowing God's name to be spoken or written down, using instead the term *El Shem* (The Name) or conventions such as YHWH and G-d. In Islam it is forbidden to create an image of God, because God exists beyond all images. And Augustine proclaimed, "If you have understood, it is not God."

So where does that leave us when we attempt to make positive statements about God? Catholic theologian Elizabeth Johnson offers three ground rules for engaging in God-talk.

The first is that "the reality of the living God is an ineffable mystery beyond all telling."⁴ We can never uncover all that God is. The second is that because our God-talk cannot capture what God is, "No expression for God can be taken literally. None. Our language is like a finger pointing towards the moon. It is not the moon itself." And the third is that because no single word encompasses the mystery of God, many words are valid. As Johnson puts it, "If human beings were capable of expressing the fullness of God in one straight-as-an-arrow name, the proliferation of names, images, and concepts observable throughout the history of all religions would make no sense at all. But there is no such name."

Along the same lines, theologian Catherine Keller proposes that, "What we call 'God' is literally – *not*. The only proper name for God, from the perspective of negative theology, is the infinite: a purely negative term. Theology, however, ... is perpetually tempted to mistake the infinite for the finite names and images in which we clothe it. And this is idolatry. Idolatry of the most deceptive kind, the truth made lie: we might call it *theolatry*."⁵

So God-talk is tricky. God-talk can be thought of as a finger, a generator of metaphors, a lamp that we use to help us peer into reality. But if we focus too much on the talk itself, if we become so involved in the talking that we confuse what we are saying with what we are talking about, then we lose our way. Keller uses the term idolatory to indicate how replacing God with talk about God causes us to worship the signifier instead of the signified and to miss the mark.

In respect to this, Buddhist thinkers have traditionally considered there are three categories of statements we make about reality.

THREE CATEGORIES OF GOD-TALK

One of the key assumptions of Buddhism is that we live in mental constructs. These constructs are generated by conventions, which include what today we identify as social norms, customary practices, prevailing cultural attitudes, accepted traditions, lawfully-limited behaviour, and intellectual orthodoxy.

The aim of Buddhism is to deconstruct all mental constructs in order to perceive reality without using the lenses that mental constructs provide. However, Buddhism also recognizes that we have to function within our social environment. This means that in actuality we need to use the same concepts and language as everyone else in order to interact, communicate, and live. So the reality is that we can't avoid engaging with and using conventions. As a consequence, Buddhists divide our thinking into three categories, which they have named conditioned, illusory, and unconditioned.

Conditioned thinking is our everyday pragmatic thinking. It is what we use to make a shopping list, to do our work, and carry out the activities of our day. Religious doctrines and rituals are manifestations of our conditioned thinking. Indeed, Buddhists consider much in Buddhism itself is a reflection of conditioned thought, because it has to do with social and religious conventions. Ethically, conditioned thinking is neither right nor wrong. Rather, it is necessary to live with others. But it remains limited because it doesn't provide us with an unfettered and unconditioned insight into reality.

In contrast, illusory thinking creates conceptual prisons that have little to do with reality. Illusory thinking is present in the madness that fills our everyday world, whether as a result of personal desires or of socially generated delirium. Using notions of God or democracy to justify going to war and to harm and exploit others "for their own good" are examples of illusory thinking.

Unconditioned thinking has two aspects. Its initial aspect consists of thought that occurs when people seek to rise above their everyday mental constructs, above the known and the done. Its second aspect is thought that occurs in those who personally have risen above their everyday mental constructs, have experienced reality in that unconditioned state of heightened awareness, and who consequently seek to express what they experienced to others.

Buddhism uses the example of a rope to indicate the differences between these three ways of thinking. If we see the rope and view it as a snake, this is illusory thinking. If we see the rope and use it to tie a dog to its kennel, this is conditioned, conventional thinking. And if we see the rope and use it to remind ourselves how we are bound in conditioned reality and that we need to transcend our limitations, this is unconditioned thinking.

In the context of God-talk, conditioned thinking keeps us embedded in what we already know, illusory thinking drags us down into fantasy and madness, and unconditioned thinking helps us rise above what we already know and enter into what we do not know but wish to. (Note: This third position is a contentious statement, because the contemporary Western constructivist perspective is that we cannot rise above conditioned reality. This will be discussed further in Chapter Thirteen.)

In today's terms we could see these three categories as apologetic, justification, and discovery. We have God-talk that aims to clarify the circumstances of our everyday existence, we have God-talk that is used after a decision has been made to justify that decision in religious and cultural terms, and we have God-talk that we use to help us arrive at a new level of understanding.

Accordingly, God-talk is not just talk. It is not just words. Whether our God-talk is conditioned, illusory, or unconditioned makes a difference. Whether we strive to fit in with others, work out ways to dominate them, or wish to rise above the known to enter the unknown, necessarily has a fundamental impact on the orientation of our life.

Because this study is focused on investigating new perspectives with respect to God, I'll briefly explore the implications of God-talk as discovery.

GOD-TALK AS DISCOVERY

Thinking about how we think is important because the assumptions that underpin our thinking shape where our thinking starts from and therefore where it ends up. For example, if we think we can't afford to visit a particular place that is special to us, or if we believe that we don't deserve to go there, then we never will arrive.

Similarly, if we accept someone else's ideas about God, not only are we eliminating other approaches as possibilities, but we are ensuring we will never discover what else God might be for us. In God-talk, as in travelling, package deals are not necessarily the best way to visit distant lands, especially if we wish to find that special marvellous place that is discovered only when we travel off the beaten track. By our own thought we limit or free ourselves.

So God-talk as discovery involves a journey in which we try to minimize the number of assumptions we make, and to keep open for as long as we can the possibilities of where we might end up. As Catherine Keller puts this in relation to the tradition of Christian theology:

> Theology is one hulking body of truth-*claims*, including that made by the present sentence. Theology – not the truth it seeks – comprises a shifting set of propositions, frayed and porous at the edges. Some of its propositions will *propose* more attractive, more healing and more redeeming possibilities than others. To propose is not to impose – but to invite... Theology then is a truth-process, not a set of truths.[6]

All the ideas of the thinkers surveyed in the following chapters share this sense of God-talk as discovery, as consisting of propositions rather than impositions, and as an invitation to enter into an exploratory process.

Having clarified the nature of God-talk, let's now move on to address one of the foundational concepts of today's God-talk: the death of the God of traditional theism.

CHAPTER 10

Beyond The Mythological God

On the cusp of the twenty-first century, in a deliberate echo of Martin Luther's 1517 Reformation, American God-talker John Shelby Spong proposed a New Reformation of Christian beliefs. But where Luther had nailed his theses to a church door in Wittenburg, in keeping with the conventions of a very different age Spong posted his on the internet. His propositions for a New Reformation began:

> Theism, as a way of defining God, is dead. God can no longer be understood with credibility as a Being, supernatural in power, dwelling above the sky and prepared to invade human history periodically to enforce the divine will. So, most theological God-talk today is meaningless unless we find a new way to speak of God.[1]

For Christian theologians, acknowledging the death of the supernatural theistic God obviously presents a huge dilemma. If the old God is no more, what God should Christians now conceive of and worship?

In this chapter I will examine the ideas of three Christian thinkers who have faced up to the reality of living in secular Western culture and have sought to bring the Christian concept of a personal God "up-to-date." Each of these thinkers starts from the premise that the theistic God of Christianity has died and cannot be revived. But they arrive at different positions regarding what God is or should be considered to be.

Two shared ideas are central, however. The first is pluralism, which recognizes religions as social constructs, and therefore proposes that no one religion or belief system can validly claim that it alone holds the keys to truth. Furthermore, religious perspectives are never fixed for all time. Instead, believers are involved in an on-going process of adjusting their beliefs to fit in with the times. Hence just as the ancient Jewish prophets offered their communities new ways of approaching God, so these God-talkers are a new generation of prophets, walking in advance of mainstream believers, pointing out new directions for those grappling with God.

The second idea is that the stories human beings have created about God, the myths which our forebears told about God, are not literal stories or truths. Rather, they are cultural creations, devised to respond to specific issues. As a result they are historically determined ways of talking about God that made sense to those who originally spoke them. However, we live in different times to our forebears, our culture diverges markedly from theirs, and we have to face very different issues. We live in a world shaped by globalization, secularity, the sciences, ecological concerns, and by troubled forms of national and international engagement and discourse (this last, of course, is far from new in human history). In this context our forebears' mythological ways of viewing the world have understandably lost their relevance for us.

The bottom line is we live in a post-mythological age. And, to reflect this fact, our God-talk has to move beyond mythological concepts of God. One of the first twentieth century God-talkers to make this move was Paul Tillich.

PAUL TILLICH: GOD AS GROUND OF BEING

Born into a Lutheran family, Paul Tillich (1886–1965) was one of Germany's leading pre-WW2 theologians. Ordained a Lutheran minister in 1912, Tillich taught in many of Germany's most prominent universities. However, during the early 1930s he criticized the rising Nazi party, and when they were elected in 1933 they fired him from his lectureship at Frankfurt University. He then took up an offer to teach in the United States, where he lived for the rest of his life. It was there that he wrote the books for which he remains acknowledged today. His theological masterwork is *Systematic Theology* (1951–63), while his most influential and popular book is *The Courage To Be* (1952).

Tillich's contribution to twentieth century God-talk is significant because he strove to express his position in terms of the existential philosophy that was developed in response to the horrors of WW2. In the process he proposed a number of ideas that subsequently became key for many other spiritual thinkers, Christian and non-Christian.

In *The Courage To Be*, the book that popularized his ideas, Tillich started with an existential analysis of anxiety and fear. He began there because he considered they were the principal forms of non-being that threaten the existence of our individual being. For Tillich, anxiety and fear exist as three pairs: fate and death, emptiness and meaninglessness, and guilt and condemnation.

> Non-being threatens man's ontic self-affirmation [personal being], relatively in terms of fate, absolutely in terms of death. It threatens man's spiritual self-affirmation, relatively in terms of emptiness, absolutely in terms of meaninglessness. It threatens man's moral self-affirmation, relatively in terms of guilt, absolutely in terms of condemnation.[2]

Tillich saw anxiety and fear as existential in nature, in the sense that they impact on us at the most basic level of our existence in the world. Neither drugs nor therapy will "cure" us of them or make them go away. Rather, for Tillich, the key to overcoming existential anxiety and fear is by spiritually confronting our situation in the world. This confrontation requires us to have courage, specifically the courage to be. If we manage to do this then we have the possibility of becoming a new being.

For Tillich, as a Christian, this new being was most powerfully characterized by Jesus, a man who, when the Spirit that is God entered him, became the Christ. This human Jesus is our ideal model for new being, spiritually and morally. As such Jesus also symbolizes the Divine. Symbols were highly significant for Tillich, as he considered that they point beyond themselves. And the ultimate "beyond" to which all religious symbols point is God. So Jesus the Christ, as a symbol, points beyond himself to God.

Who or what is this God which filled Jesus and made him the Christ? For Tillich, God is not *a* being. And God is definitely not the supernatural personal being of theistic Christianity. Instead, he posited God as Being-Itself, the Ground of being, which gives all creatures their individual being. Thus Tillich differentiated Being-Itself from the personal God of theism.

This differentiation was highly significant because Tillich considered that the personal God of theism had contributed to and shaped the anxiety of modern life. This was because the personal God was a being who not only commanded, judged, and demanded, but who also had been appropriated to the cause of war and totalitarianism. Thus for Tillich this personal God of theism:

... deprives me of my subjectivity because he is all-powerful and all-knowing. God appears as the invincible tyrant, the being in contrast with whom all other things are without freedom and subjectivity. He is equated with the recent tyrants who, with the help of terror, try to transform everything into a mere object, a thing among things, a cog in the machine they control. He becomes the model of everything against which Existentialism revolted. This is the God Nietzsche said had to be killed because nobody can tolerate being made into a mere object of absolute knowledge and absolute control.[3]

So we must reject God and seek what Tillich called the "God above God." Furthermore it is only from this God above God, which is Being-Itself, that our courage to confront non-being derives: "The ultimate source of the courage to be is the God above God; this is the result of our demand to transcend theism."[4]

Tillich also suggested that the God above God may be thought of as an expression of ultimate concern. This has turned out to be a slippery term, but may be understood as an attempt to express why the idea of God remains important to us: because it is an expression of our ultimate concern with our existence.

So, for Tillich, humanity's spiritual quest involves us in rising above our anxiety, fear, and despair and seeking Being-Itself, the God above God. Jesus, who became the Christ, symbolizes the result of this quest.

Tillich's spirituality remains controversial for many because he denied not only Jesus as God incarnate on Earth, he also denied that God is an objectively existing entity at all. But other theologians have gone further.

LLOYD GEERING: RELIGION WITHOUT GOD

New Zealand Presbyterian minister and theologian, Lloyd Geering (b. 1918), is among the leading proponents of post-mythological theology. He offers a more radical take on Christianity's God than Tillich by arguing we no longer need God at all. Theologically, his position is termed non-realism.

Geering's non-realism includes maintaining, with Tillich, that God does not exist as a being, that the resurrection is not an historical event, and that there is no life after death. A charge of heresy was made against Geering in 1967 by conservative Presbyterians. He was found not guilty, but Geering's non-realism remains problematic for many traditional Christians.

Lloyd Geering summarizes his spiritual perspective in *Tomorrow's God* (1994). He begins from Neitzsche's position that the theistic God of Christianity is no longer valid. Orthodox religious doctrines have been overturned, and God has been overturned with them. God, which is no more than a symbolic idea human beings have created, has passed its use-by date, which means we are left having to face up to the reality of our lives.

Geering considers humanity's quest for meaning is fundamental to our existence. It is a manifestation of the creativity that is inherent in the universe. This creativity drives biological evolution that has created the huge diversity of life on Earth. It also manifests in the endless creativity of human self-consciousness. Because of this human beings are natural makers of meanings. And historically religion has been accepted as the peak of human meaning-making.

However, Geering argues that the meanings we generate about reality and our place in it are never constant. They change over time. This is seen in the way that the world's great religions, which all originated in the Axial Age, between 800 BCE and 200 CE, have gone through stages of growth and decline. Geering adopts the ideas of Robert Ellwood to identify five stages. The first stage begins with a religion's founding. Religions blossom during their second stage, when they are linked to an imperial power. For Christianity this occurred when Constantine made it the religion of the Roman Empire, for Buddhism when King Ashoka adopted it, and for Confucianism when it was adopted by the Han Dynasty. The third stage occurs when the imperial power fractures politically and the religion is forced to turn inward, as happened between 1000 CE and 1500 CE in Christianity, and from 1258 CE for Islam, with the fall of Baghdad and the Abbasid Caliphate. These were also periods when the classic mystical forms of Christianity and Islam attained their peaks. The fourth stage is reformation, when religious beliefs are adjusted to the changing times. Martin Luther's 1517 Protestant Reformation is an example. The final stage is when religions fall from their previous influence and are transformed into forms of private worship. This is the phase "in which the great religion is no longer overtly observed in the official organs of society, is no longer dominant in the intellectual leadership, and is no longer providing the chief motivation of the on-going culture."[5]

Geering identifies duality as one of the key concepts of the great religions in general, and of Christianity in particular. All the world's religions divided reality into two realms, Earth and Heaven, this-world and the other-world. This-world was filled with unhappiness, suffering, illusion, and death, while the other-world offered happiness, fulfillment, truth, and eternal life. Believers put up with the pain of living in this-world for the spiritual reward of being reborn, after death, in the eternal other-world.

The power of this duality was that the other-world gave this-world its meaning and purpose. However, that was also its weakness. Because with the rise of scientific materialism, the existence of other-world came to be questioned, then rejected. And with its rejection the source of humanity's religious meaning-making was lost. As a result the world became meaningless, and so we entered the phase of existential fear and angst identified by Paul Tillich.

Geering agrees with Tillich regarding the significance of symbols. He argues that we create symbols as bearers of meaning. This is why symbols are fundamental to religions, for which God is the culmination of human language making, with God being the greatest symbol, the greatest meaning, and the greatest word.

Who or what, then, is the God of Christianity? Geering sees the Christian conception of God the Father as resulting from a fusion of the unchanging, transcendent, other-worldly, philosophic God of Greek philosophy with Yahweh, the very human-like angry, vengeful, loving God of the Old Testament. Because it combines these two ideas, the Christian God is a human invention.

> At last we have reached the point where we can acknowledge that 'God' is a word, a very important word, a symbolic word. It has no external referent which is open to public confirmation. ... The word 'God' has a function, but no content or meaning except that which we supply. When we use this word we are affirming something about ourselves. It is a religious symbol which has the meaning we choose to give it.[6]

However God, as a symbolic word, still has meaning and value for us. Geering identifies two criteria as important to our continued use of the word God.

The first is that we need to remember that God is a symbol that we can use to express our deepest concerns. But we can't return to the old mythological mode of thinking about God as a real existing entity. We can't turn God into a idol and worship it.

The second is that we have to jettison the old concept of duality: that God is infinite and humanity finite, that God is good and humanity is sin-filled, that God is all knowing and humanity is ignorant, and that God is the authority and judge to whom human beings must submit and be judged. In particular, we must get rid of the idea of the other-world. And while we're at it should also jettison the idea of God as "Him," along with the subjection of women that the male pronoun involves. Duality and all its implications must go.

To replace duality Geering proposes that we adopt the scientific perspective of material monism, in which the universe is conceived of as infinite but made of one "stuff." In this vision of the world there is no supernatural realm nor any metaphysical spiritual domain.

Geering's summarizes his vision in six points. As a result of globalization, whether we wish it or not, we live *globally*. We obtain *knowledge* via the scientific method, which can never obtain all that is to be known, and so is in a never-ending quest for new knowledge. Nonetheless, we can obtain definite knowledge about our world. Our culture, values, and beliefs are *humanly based*, being generated by us. Our global world is also continually *changing*, as new knowledge comes to light and as we develop new values, new beliefs, and new expressions of culture. All this means that the closed societies of the past are steadily being replaced by *open societies*, in which we are each free to creatively develop our own views. And in order to sustain these differences we need tolerance and an acceptance of diversity. Finally, with the demise of the ancient religious systems of meaning, each of us is now left to *create meaning* for ourselves, in the context of our lives.

There is one down-side to all this, however. This is that with the emphasis now firmly on this-world we need to acknowledge that the Earth itself, and particularly the Earth's ecosphere, is central to humanity's biological survival. So issues of ecology, pollution, conservation of non-renewable resources, and of living harmoniously with our environment come to the fore. Accordingly, what we need today is a new set of values, new contexts of meanings, and new stories, that encapsulate the new relationship we have to forge with this-world, the Earth on which we live. In a sense, we need a new religion that embodies all these, even though it will be a religion that looks nothing like the religions of the past. And how does God fit into all this?

Geering argues that we are faced now with an opportunity. An opportunity to consciously create the values, aspirations, and goals we wish to associate with the symbolic word God – that is, if we wish to use the word at all. In this open sense God may be understood in three ways. First, we may use God in reference to the Earth in which we live. Second, we may consider that our inner quest for meaning is God within. And third, given that our own human being is an embodiment of the creative self consciousness that has emerged from the universe:

> God is rising to self-awareness in the (as yet) confused collective consciousness of the global human community. This is tomorrow's God, calling us from a world yet to be created. But, to create this world, this God has no hands but our hands, no voice but our voice, no mind but our mind, and no plan for the future but what we plan.[7]

JOHN SHELBY SPONG: GOD WITHOUT RELIGION

American Episcopalian minister John Shelby Spong (b. 1931) offers an interesting contrast to the views of Lloyd Geering. Where Geering argues that today we need a new set of religious values, meaning, and stories, which reflect the scientific interpretation of reality, and which we could use as the basis of a new religion in which God is an optional extra, Spong argues that he needs and wants a concept of God to help him make sense of reality, but for him religion is the optional extra.

As his starting point Spong agrees with Geering's analysis that the personal God of theism can no longer be maintained in today's world, a world he characterizes as post-Christian. Yet rather than saying, with Geering, that God is no more than a symbolic word, Spong considers that there is a spiritual reality to which the word God may still be attached. However, for Spong this spiritual reality does not involve the supernaturalism associated with the personal God of theism. Instead, he accepts Tillich's concept of God as Being-Itself, the Ground of being. And so spirituality becomes the activity of embracing and manifesting God as the Ground of being in our lives.

Spong, as a Christian, sees Jesus Christ as the ideal human being who historically most perfectly embodied Being-Itself. But Spong acknowledges that all religions and all spiritual traditions, and the greatest sages of those traditions, offer exactly the same "porthole" into Being-Itself as offered by Christ. Embracing spiritual pluralism, he asserts that no tradition is greater than any other, and that all equally offer ways of entering into Being-Itself.

In *A New Christianity For a New World* (2001) Spong describes his vision of what happened to the personal God of theism and what is required to replace it.

Following Tillich, Spong sees the key to humanity's uneasiness regarding being in the world as a function of self-conscious, and self-consciousness leads to existential fear and angst. To these Spong adds Freud's insight that humanity's key response to being self-conscious is hysteria. Spong suggests that a thermostat is required to control the heat of that hysteria, and that illusory personal gods projected onto reality by theistic religions have historically provided this.

> Theism was created by frightened self-aware humans to assist them in the task of banking the fires of hysteria brought on by the trauma of self-consciousness, the shock of non-being. God, understood theistically, is thus quite clearly a human construct. ... Theism was the means whereby that which was experienced by newly self-conscious human beings was personalized. ... [Theism] put a pious face on human fear and made the threat of non-being and the trauma of self-consciousness manageable.[8]

For all the reasons previously recounted, Spong agrees theism as dying. He further views today's religious fundamentalisms as manifestations of religious hysteria, hysteria which increases as naive believers struggle – and fail – to hold onto dying concepts mired in the past that are increasingly become out-of-sync with today's world. He agrees with Geering that we need to find a non-theistic concept of God in order to move into the future.

However, complicating this search for Spong is his view that language in general, and God-talk in particular, cannot fully encapsulate any new non-theistic concept of reality. "No human words, no human formulas, and no human religious systems will ever capture that reality."[9] Yet we need words of some kind in order to describe God and to comprehend the ways that Being-Itself impacts in the world. So Spong offers three definitions of the non-theistic God. These are:

1. God is the ultimate source of life. One worships this God by living fully, by sharing deeply.
2. God is the ultimate source of love. One worships this God by loving wastefully, by spreading love frivolously.
3. God is being – the reality underlying everything that is. We worship this God by having the courage to be all that we can be.[10]

Living fully, loving wastefully, and having the courage to become new spiritual beings are the qualities by which Spong considers we come to understand reality in non-theistic terms. And, consistent with his view that we can't discover the God above God through words and language, he considers any new understanding needs to be situated in experience. New experiences will enable us to understand Being-Itself as it manifests in the world. We can then use words to approximate what we have experientially discovered. What this adds up to is a philosophy of achieving knowledge through participation:

> We human beings cannot *know* God; we can only *experience* God. Thus there is no way that we can say God is anything. When we talk about God, we can say only that the experience of God is "as if _____." Adding whatever human words we can find to characterize our experience.[11]

Because God cannot be defined in ancient mythological terms and still remain relevant in today's world, Spong considers that Christianity will have to change radically in order to remain meaningful. His vision is that religious seekers will grow beyond the limitations of the traditional theistic God by dropping outmoded myths, rituals, and doctrines, and by becoming part of humanity's worldwide urge to seek God via the growth of personal being. Writing of this new ecclesia (church), Spong asserts:

> The new ecclesia will offer opportunities for people to grow into new being – a being not bounded by tribal claims, superiority claims, gender claims, or even religious claims. ... Those who once called themselves Catholic and Protestant, orthodox and heretic, liberal and evangelical, Jew and Muslim, Buddhist and Hindu, will all find a place in the ecclesia of the future. ... There we will all walk together into the meaning of God – the joy, the wonder, the mystery of God – a God not bounded by our formulas, our creeds, our doctrines, our liturgies, or even our Bible, but still real, infinitely real.[12]

This concept of God which exists beyond religion, which is experienced rather than defined via language, is what attracts Spong. This is the way we may best understand God today. This will enable us to discover what Tillich called the God above God.

Philosophically, the concept of God that both Spong and Tillich propose is called panentheism. In contrast, Geering's proposal that we should conceive of God in relation to the Earth on which we live is more naturally aligned to pantheism (although, because Geering prefers not to use the word God, his outlook is not pantheism).

Because pantheistic and panentheistic perspectives have been explored in depth during the modern era, in the next two chapters I will explore their key implications.

CHAPTER 11

Pantheism: Everything Is God

The assumption underlying pantheism is that reality consists of the natural world, the world we experience via our senses. Therefore, because this natural world is where we human beings "live, breathe, and have our being," pantheism considers God in this context.

Consequently, pantheism rejects the idea of a supernatural God who interjects Himself into the activities of the world and in doing so bypasses the natural laws that govern the world. In rejecting supernaturalism, pantheism brings us, literally, back down to Earth, seeking the sacred in the here and now.

Of course, there is no need to bring God into the picture at all. Many people besides scientific materialists consider that we can understand the world perfectly well without recourse to God. Pantheists broadly agree with the scientific view of the world, but add a sense of the sacred to the equations.

Pantheism offers two directions to explore: immanence within and transcendence beyond. Pantheistic immanence places God within the natural world, seeing God in the patterns discernible in matter and life and in the laws that govern all natural forms, processes, and activities. In contrast, pantheistic transcendence identifies God with the natural world in a holistic sense, in which the totality that is the natural universe may be conceived of as God.

In adding the concept of God to physical reality pantheism reflects a feeling that life is not just about bodies and equations and mindless molecules bumping into each other, but that it also involves subjectively experienced values and meaning, values and meaning that we associate with God.

Accordingly, we are being pantheistic when we feel awe looking at the stars in the night sky, or when we appreciate the incredible variety of forms, colors, and patterns in nature, or when we wonder that there is a world at all, and when we appreciate that we exist in it. Pantheist feelings of this kind are present in the work of writers such as Walt Whitman, Ralph Waldo Emerson, William Wordsworth, and D.H. Lawrence, who each reverenced the power of nature but without turning their feelings into religious ritual or dogma.

Before considering how pantheism manifests today, I'll briefly examine the development of modern pantheism.

JOHN TOLAND, PANTHEIST

The word pantheist was first coined by John Toland (1670-1722). An Irish-born philosopher and writer, Toland spent the majority of his adult life writing professionally in London. In harmony with the advanced thinking of his day Toland considered that liberty was the key to human progress, and that the oppressive hierarchies of the state and of the church should be dismantled in favor of rule by reason and tolerance.

In his mid-twenties, having completed his studies, and being filled with the exuberant sense of being right that makes the naivety of youth so endearing, Toland published a book called *Christianity Not Mysterious* (1696). He wrote it in response to a sermon given by the well-known cleric Robert South, titled *Christianity Mysterious, and the Wisdom of God Making It So* (1694), in which South claimed that religion is a mystery that reason cannot penetrate, and therefore that believers needed to give up thinking and accept the dogmas of religion with resigned faith. Toland rejected this view, arguing that there is no mystery and that the propositions of Christian faith could and should be justified entirely by reason. In arguing this he sought not just to take the supernatural claims made by Christianity out of the religious equation, but to assert that the claims of the clergy were, in fact, disingenuous:

> There is nothing that men make a greater noise about, in our time especially, than what they generally profess least of all to understand. It may be easily concluded, I mean *the mysteries of the Christian religion*. The Divines, whose peculiar province is to explain them to others, almost unanimously own their ignorance concerning them. They gravely tell us, *we must adore what we cannot comprehend*. And yet some of them press their dubious comments upon the rest of mankind with more assurance and heat than could be tolerably justified, though we should grant them be absolutely infallible. ... We hold that reason is the only foundation of all certitude;

and that nothing revealed, whether as to its manner or existence, is more exempted from its disquisitions than the ordinary phenomena of nature. Wherefore, we likewise maintain, according to the title of this discourse, that *there is nothing in the Gospel contrary to reason, nor above it, and that no Christian doctrine can be properly called a mystery*.[1]

We have already seen in Part One how the controversy between the naturalist and supernaturalist camps played out during the following centuries. In a sense Toland established the advanced guard of a position that is still being explored by today's post-mythological God-talkers.

Indeed, Toland was so far ahead of his time that his book was soon being investigated by the authorities. Toland responded by doing what many in his situation have done over the ages – he left town. But when he sought refuge in his home city of Dublin the authorities there soon heard of his arrival, had his book burnt by the public hangman, and ordered his arrest. The seriousness of Toland's situation is indicated by the fact that a student in Edinburgh was hanged for blasphemy in that same year.

Toland promptly returned to London where the controversy continued to simmer for several years in the form of answering essays, missives, and books. And it wasn't only the printers who had reason to thank Toland for the work that his controversial book stimulated. One who profited was Peter Browne, a fellow of Trinity College in Dublin, who wrote the most popular riposte to Toland, and partly on that basis was appointed Bishop of Cork and Ross in 1710.

Over the following years Toland kept his head down. But he remained under continued pressure to repudiate his views. He eventually genuflected to the authorities by joining the Church of England (he had been born a Catholic) and by publishing a book, *Vindus Liberius* (1702), in which he publicly admitted his errors. Thereafter, Toland limited his pronouncements on God and religion to the discussions of London's freethinkers who met in secret to explore these exciting – albeit dangerous – new ideas.

Over time Toland came to call these groups of thinkers pantheists. What they shared was a rejection of a supernatural God on the grounds that there is no supernatural realm, there is only the physical universe. Drawing on the ideas of the Renaissance philosopher Giordano Bruno, Toland proposed that the universe was infinite and that the stars were suns just like our sun, spread throughout infinite space. He also considered that the infinite universe was in continual flux, and that two fundamental principles underpinned this flux: action, which was manifested by matter in general and by each material object locally, and intellect, which human beings used to comprehend the universe. Action, in turn, resulted from the interactions of oppositions such as heat and cold, gravity and levity, hardness and fluidity, with the flow between these opposites creating the universal flux. However, all these oppositions and motions human reason could intellectually harmonize in God.

Accordingly, Toland considered God to be the meaning we derive when we intellectually discern what is occurring in the universe. Because Toland preferred to situate all his ideas in the practical world of day-to-day living, he avoided abstract descriptions of God. So he likened God to a political leader who, from the perspective of ignorant citizens, embraces all the contradictory aspects and forces of the nation he rules. This makes God an idea, a way of thinking about material reality, and not an existing entity of any kind.

In 1720 Toland published *Pantheisticon: or The Form of Celebrating the Socratic Society*, in which he sought to characterize the freethinking philosophic groups he was part of. It was in this work that Toland first used the word pantheist, although for him the word was synonymous with one who followed Baruch Spinoza's ideas. (Spinoza is examined shortly.) Toland was also careful not to upset the authorities. This time round his book was written in Latin, and it wasn't translated into English until 1751, well after Toland's death.

Toland was not a pantheist in the modern sense. However, his attempts to think about God in a new way was a reflection of the restlessness of the times, a restlessness that could perhaps be described as a form of commonsense materialism, with a pinch of idealism. He sought to understand God in the context of the physical reality he could perceive and comprehend, and he sought to do so without recourse to the religious myths, superstitions, supernaturalism, and thought-inhibiting prejudices that he considered were so prevalent in his day. In this he anticipated thinkers such as Lloyd Geering who similarly advocates viewing reality from a commonsense, non-supernatural, rational, materialistic perspective.

Toland, of course, was far from the first to argue for a view of reality based on the naturally perceivable world. The Daoist philosophy of Laotze has been identified as pantheistic, as has the outlook of a number of ancient Greek and Stoic philosophers, and parts of the Upanishads. In particular, Toland's ideas were influenced by a philosopher whose thinking has had a profound impact on subsequent Western ideas about reality and God. This philosopher was Baruch Spinoza.

THE GOD OF SPINOZA

Baruch Spinoza (1632-1677) has to be included in this study, if only because he had the unique distinction of being called both God-obsessed and an atheist. His thinking is significant because he laid the philosophic foundations for scientific materialism, pantheism, and religious naturalism.

Considered the first pantheist of the modern era, Spinoza didn't shy from the abstractions that the realist Toland preferred to avoid. He was not only an extremely rigorous thinker, but he sought to create a philosophic framework that included all the principal aspects of human thought known in his day, including metaphysics, ethics, politics, perception, knowledge, and theology. He succeeded so well that his ideas had a stimulating effect on numerous later thinkers. For example, Hegel considered Spinoza to be the greatest of all philosophers, to the extent that he argued that anyone who didn't appreciate Spinoza was not a philosopher. Spinoza's twentieth century admirers included Albert Einstein, who stated unequivocally that his God was Spinoza's God.

Spinoza was born in Amsterdam and was of Portuguese Jewish descent. A brilliant student, he was educated at the city's Jewish school, but had to leave at seventeen to work in the family business after his oldest brother died of tuberculosis. The next significant event in his life occurred at the age of twenty-three, when he was officially excommunicated by Amsterdam's Jewish community for proposing "monstrous heresies," and refusing to retract them. While the reasons for his excommunication were not made public, his later writings indicate it was likely for asserting such ideas as that the soul was not immortal, that God was not a benevolent being who comes to humanity's aid, and that the Jewish law was not given by God nor was it binding. As was noted in Chapter Four, Spinoza also made an important contribution to the embryonic discipline of Biblical criticism, arguing that Moses did not write the *Pentateuch* and suggesting instead Ezra as its editor, a view that is widely accepted today.

The order of excommunication meant that no one in the Jewish community, including his own family, was allowed to have any kind of communication with Spinoza, no one was allowed to employ him, and no one could read anything he wrote. Essentially, he was cut off from the Jewish community, not just in

Amsterdam, but throughout Europe. Consequently, Spinoza left Amsterdam and moved to a small town near the city of Leiden (where John Toland later attended university), where he worked as a lens grinder. He spent his final six years in The Hague. As his mother and older brother had, he died of tuberculosis, in his case at the age of forty-four.

Because Spinoza's ideas diverged so far from the prevailing religiously-dominated doctrines of the seventeenth century, only one of his books, a response to Descartes' philosophic principles, was published in his name during his lifetime. A second work, *Tractatus Theologico-Political*, published anonymously in 1670, created an enormous stir due to asserting that all revealed religions should be analyzed and explained by reason, that the Torah had passed its use-by date, and that God not only possessed no intrinsic purpose, but only acted within the laws embedded in His own nature. The public reaction to this work was violent, and word soon spread as to who had written this book that troubled Christians as much as it appalled Jews. Consequently, Spinoza became known throughout Christendom as "the atheist Jew," or even just as "that Jew."

The notoriety of the *Tracticus* was likely linked to an attempt on his life, when an unknown assailant tried to knife him as he came out of the theatre one evening. Fortunately, only Spinoza's cloak suffered. He kept the cloak as a reminder of the consequences of bucking prevailing views. The incident also reinforced for him the way that superstitious emotionalism so commonly ruled reason with respect to religious beliefs:

> Superstitious persons, who know better how to rail at ice than how to reach virtue, and who strive not to guide men by reason, but so to restrain them that they would rather escape evil than love virtue, have no other aim but to make others as wretched as themselves; wherefore it is nothing wonderful if they be generally troublesome and odious to their fellow men.[2]

Spinoza may have been notorious, but he survived because the Netherlands was actually far more tolerant than any other European country at that time. Living in meagre but contented circumstances, with financial support from friends, he never married. Instead, he worked, debated his ideas with friends, developed his philosophy, and wrote his books.

Spinoza attempted to publish his masterwork, *Ethics*, during his lifetime, but when word went out of his plans tongues across Europe immediately spawned such a brood of viperous statements about the book that concerned friends persuaded him not to do so. Those friends published his *Ethics* after his death.

The idea and reality of God permeates all Spinoza's thinking. Spinoza began his *Ethics* by proposing that the entire universe consists of one substance. Nothing exists that is not part of this substance. He called this substance God.

> God, or substance, consisting of infinite attributes, of which each expresses eternal and infinite essentiality, necessarily exists ... Besides God, no substance can be granted or conceived ... Whatsoever is, is in God, and without God nothing can be, or be conceived ... God is the indwelling and not the transient [ie. external] cause of all things.[3]

Spinoza envisaged God as the only existent. The consequence of this is that everything in existence is a modulation of God. In addition, he conceived of God as the *indwelling cause*. That is, God is not a being of some kind, personal or otherwise, standing outside the universe, causing what happens in it. Rather, because the universe is the substance that is God, God is embedded in the universe, so God necessarily causes what occurs from *within*.

It needs to be made clear that Spinoza's substance should not be understood in the modern sense of matter. Spinoza's concept of God-as-substance includes matter but is not limited to it. To explicate this Spinoza called God *Deus sive Natura*, that is, *God, otherwise known as Nature*. But just as substance is not identical with matter, this is not a simple identification of God with the natural world. Rather, Spinoza divided Nature into two aspects, *natura naturans* and *natura naturata*.

Natura naturata is the natural world we perceive via our senses, while *natura naturans* is that which organizes the natural world. To use theological language, *natura naturata* is the created world and *natura naturans* is what created that world. To use scientific language, *natura naturata* is the material world and *natura naturans* is the combined laws that orchestrate what happens in and to what exists in the material world. However (and this is key to Spinoza's philosophy), while *natura naturans* and *natura naturata* are the two basic aspects of God, they are equal aspects. Without the other, neither can be.

Spinoza developed this idea in response to his reading of Descartes. Descartes famously divided reality into two aspects, intellect and extension, a division more popularly known as mind and body. Moreover for Descartes, while the mind was rational and possessed free will, the body functioned like a machine according to mathematically-stateable formulae. The Cartesian split between mind and body has created huge controversy over the centuries. Even in Descartes' day people wondered how do mind and body, being so different, connect in a human being? Or was the mind, which Descartes identified with the soul, actually no more than a kind of ghost occupying a machine?

Spinoza eradicated this problem at one stroke by asserting that Descartes' intellect and extension were not two separate qualities at all. Rather, they were two aspects of the one substance which is God. Accordingly, we can think of *natura naturata* as the natural world as it extends into the material universe and through time and space. And our intellect, our rational mind, is what enables us to "peer into" *natura naturans* and discern the natural laws that underpin the material universe. So just as God consists of *natura naturans* and *natura naturata*, so we consist of body and intellect. Take away either, and the other cannot and does not exist.

> God is, and acts solely by the necessity of His own nature; He is the free cause of all things. All things are in God, and so depend on Him, and without Him they could neither exist nor be conceived; lastly, all things are predetermined by God, not through His free will or absolute wish, but from the very power of God or infinite power.[4]

It was in this idea of pre-determination that gave to Spinoza's philosophy its truly innovative element. What Spinoza proposed was a vision of the universe in which God as substance predetermines what happens in the world. But God doesn't do so actively, in the manner of the anthropomorphic God of the Old Testament who knows and controls everything. Rather, Spinoza considered that God determines what happens in the world in a passive sense, by virtue of His own nature.

Thus just as the laws of motion tell us what will happen when a speeding car hits a wall (how much inertial energy the car possesses and therefore how big a dent the car's chassis will incur), so the laws innately existing in *natura naturans* determine what will occur in any part of the natural universe.. Accordingly, it is not predetermined in an active, interfering sense. Instead the world is predetermined in a material sense. For example, it is predetermined that a kite that goes into the air will inevitably return to the ground, and it is predetermined that a body that is born will one day die. Both are predetermined in the sense that that is the way the universe is. And, for Spinoza, "the way the universe is" is God. It is due to this line of thinking that Spinoza's philosophy attracted the attention of scientific thinkers.

SCIENTIFIC SPINOZISM

Intellectual inquiry was held in the highest esteem by Spinoza. He considered that there are three kinds of knowledge. The first consists of opinions and imagination, the second, which he called reason, involves commonly understood notions about things, and the third is knowledge of God, which he termed intuitive knowledge.

> The highest endeavour of the mind, and the highest virtue, is to understand by the intuitive kind of knowledge. ... As all things are in God, and are conceived through God, we can from this knowledge infer many things which we may adequately know, and we may form [the intuitive kind of knowledge]. ... The more we understand particular things, the more we understand God. ... The laws of His Nature are so vast as to suffice for the production of everything conceivable by an infinite intelligence.[5]

For Spinoza, God as intellect and extension, that is, God as idea and particular thing, are one and the same. So when we come to know a particular thing, for example, a drawn circle, we can make use of intuitive knowledge to move from that particular drawn circle to a knowledge of all circles. And that idea of the perfect intellectual circle exists eternally in God. So knowledge of things in the world provides us with knowledge of the substance that is God.

One caveat is that Spinoza considered that human reason is finite and limited in comparison to God's infinite Intellect. Therefore human thought can never encompass the vastness that is God. Nonetheless, the endeavour of seeking to know God brings us closer to comprehending the nature of reality. And all this accords with the scientific aim of understanding the laws that govern the universe.

Of course, a major point of difference between Spinoza's thinking and scientific thought is that Spinoza's is a metaphysical system, in which everything is related to God, whereas the sciences deal with reality as a physical system.

However, the fact that Spinoza identified God not with consciousness or being, which science finds problematic, and instead identifies God with substance, with which science does not have a problem, offers a key point of commonality. In addition, two aspects of Spinoza's thinking make a resonance between his philosophy and contemporary science possible.

The first is that Spinoza sees the universe as self-contained, with all that is required to understand the universe already existing within it. So the universe is explicable in its own terms, without recourse to any additional factors existing outside or beyond the universe. The second is that everything in the universe is produced by natural laws, and we can understand these laws through the use of reason. So we possess the means to understand what makes the universe tick, even if we will never be able to comprehend it in its entirety.

Stephen Hawking, the physicist, reflects this Spinozian outlook when, in his book *A Brief History of Time,* he discusses the quest to formulate a single unified theory that would describe the universe as a whole. Einstein spent his final decades seeking a unified theory, without success. Other scientists continue that quest today. But, writes Hawking, if scientists ever are able to formulate a unified theory, "it would be the ultimate triumph of human reason – for then we would know the mind of God."[6]

Einstein himself was deeply moved by Spinoza's vision of a universe that is unified in God, but that may be understood intellectually. He stated:

> If something is in me which can be called religious then it is the unbounded admiration for the structure of the world so far as our science is concerned. ... I am a deeply religious non-believer. This is a somewhat new kind of believer. ... I have never imputed to Nature a purpose or a goal, or anything that could be understood as anthropomorphic. What I see in nature is a magnificent structure that we can comprehend only very imperfectly, and that must fill a thinking person with a feeling of humility. This is a genuinely religious feeling that has nothing to do with mysticism.[7]

Einstein didn't believe in the personal God of Christianity or Judaism. What he did believe in were the laws that govern the universe, laws that he spent his working life so passionately – in his own words, religiously – striving to understand. It is in relation to these laws that Einstein situated his concept of God.

The scientific project of investigating the nature of reality is a quest that has at its heart, in Hawking's terms, a desire to know the mind of God. In this sense the scientific quest may be thought of as a religious quest, albeit in the Spinozian sense of knowledge of the universe being humanity's highest spiritual goal.

In contrast to this intellectual approach, others have adopted a more emotion-centred perspective in relation to their scientific quest.

RELIGIOUS NATURALISM

Physics is the most abstract of the sciences, and physicists are naturally attracted to a concept of God that is consistent with geometry and mathematical formulae. One consequence of this view is that it tends to reduce the material universe to mindless particles. Thus what we experience as the teeming diversity of life is reduced to chance encounters in the atomic dark – dark because it lacks consciousness or intelligence. This means that our view of life itself is drained of purpose, meaning, and values. Physicist Steven Weinberg famously summed up this view when he stated, "The more the universe seems comprehensible, the more it seems pointless."[8]

The problem many have with this view of reality is that if we agree that life has no purpose or point, what are we left with? The empty purposelessness of particles mindlessly bumping into each other?

Biologist Ursula Goodenough (b. 1943) confronted this question in her early twenties. Goodenough was raised a Methodist, but was unable to believe in a theistic God. Instead, she found her vocation in the biological sciences. However, when faced with the reductive materialism of the sciences during her early twenties, and particularly with the stark coldness and potential nihilism of Weinberg's assertion that the universe is pointless, she decided: "I can deflect the apparent pointlessness of it all by realizing that I don't have to seek a point. In any of it. Instead, I can see it as the locus of a Mystery."[9] This appreciation of life as a mystery, but a natural mystery, not a supernatural one, gave Goodenough a sense of wonder and awe at the fact that life is at all, and that we exist within it. In her later years Goodenough re-evaluated her upbringing and felt a pull towards traditional religions. This led her to articulate what she believed in the form of what she calls religious naturalism. She offers five key points.

Taking on ultimacy. We human beings like to ask ultimate questions, such as why is there something rather than nothing, we wonder where the laws of physics came from, and we contemplate the universe's apparent strangeness.

Goodenough argues that our existence is a mystery, in which such questions are unanswerable. In fact, any answer we provide can be no more than an unverifiable belief. But the asking of ultimate questions continues to be central to human experience of living in the midst of a mystery.

Gratitude. We arose from the Earth, and are perfectly fitted to live in it. In recognition of this Goodenough says, "Hosannah! Not in the highest, but right here, right now, this."[10]

Reverence. Life is sacred in its mystery, and reverence is the appropriate emotion to feel towards what we designate as sacred.

A story of origin. All religions have a creation story. For Goodenough, the evolutionary process, and the emergence of complex, self-aware beings from simple non-self-aware forms of life, provides a satisfactory story of origins.

Continuation. The human genome has evolved as a self-aware, evaluating, purposeful species. It is in the continuation of the human genome, and not of the individual human being, that Goodenough finds ultimate satisfaction, and the fact that we are able to appreciate that fact:

> For me, the existence of all this complexity and awareness and intent and beauty, and my ability to appreciate it, serves as the ultimate meaning and ultimate value. The continuation of life reaches around, grabs its own tail, and forms a sacred circle that requires no further justification, no Creator, no superordinate meaning, no purpose other than that the continuation continue until the sun collapses or the final meteor collides. I confess a credo of continuation.[11]

In all this our immediate environment is paramount. We live on the Earth, in a particular biosphere, with other species, to which we are linked in a mutually dependent relationship. For Goodenough this leads to the idea that what we need today is a global ethic to regulate our existence.

A GLOBAL ETHIC

The idea of a global ethic has been taken up by a wide range of thinkers. It is a key consequence not only of Goodenough's thinking, but also of Lloyd Geering's de-mythologized and natural view of the world. Rejecting supernatural explanations of our existence involves re-thinking how we live in the world.

Geering considers that rejecting the duality of a supernatural heaven and a natural Earth that is basic to Christian theology must result in our developing a new globally-oriented ethic.

The primary focus of traditional religions such as Christianity is on the eternal afterlife. That realm is considered to be more real than this earthly realm. But if, as Geering and others maintain, there is no eternal afterlife, then the only reality we are left with is this world. A world we need to reverence rather than trash. Geering draws attention to three beliefs of traditional Christian theology that are antithetical to the notion that we should reverence the Earth. The first problematic belief is that human beings are God's greatest creation, and that God has given us license to lord it over all the other species on Earth, controlling and exploiting them to our heart's content. Second is the belief that the next world is not just more important than this world, but that only the next world is real. Third is the belief that this world is intrinsically impure and tainted, with the related expectation that God will one day consign this impure world to conflagration, making a new heaven and a new Earth.

Geering argues that collectively these beliefs have led to an attitude of disdain for the natural world. Because the natural world is seen as temporary and irredeemably impure, it doesn't matter what we do to it. And besides, even if we do spoil the natural environment God is coming along later and intends to set fire to the lot and make it all fresh and shiny again. Rejecting these supernatural notions, Geering emphasizes that we need to recognize that humanity has an obligation to keep the one world we certainly have in good shape.

Another perspective on this issue was provided by scientist James Lovelock, In the 1970s Lovelock suggested we should think of the Earth as a complex multi-faceted system. This is because in order for living organisms to come into existence, and for the diversity of life to evolve as it has, the Earth has needed to maintain certain levels of oxygen and to keep its surface temperature consistently within the limits that are viable for life over a period of two billion years. The fact this has occurred means that the Earth is a self-regulating system to which the oceans, geological processes, atmosphere, and biosphere all contribute. Lovelock called this system Gaia. He didn't mean the Earth was consciously regulating itself, but that the system as a whole did so.

Lovelock's ideas became an early harbinger of an attitude towards the Earth that Geering shares, that we should care for the natural environment in which "we live, move, and have our being." This concern has flowered into today's ecological movements, each of which share a concern for the state of the natural world. These concerns may be formulated in three observations that complement Geering's critique of Christian theology.

First, human beings, while special in some ways, are nonetheless just one species among many on this planet. This means we do not have a God-given right to exploit and plunder with impunity. So we need to divest ourselves of our self-centred, self-righteous, "it's ours to do with as we want" arrogance.

Second, this world counts. We have a responsibility to ourselves, to other species, to our descendents, and to the Earth which has nurtured us, to care for our natural environment.

Third, God isn't going to come down and clean up our mess.

Various movements have developed in the last five decades in an attempt to address this issue. Greens, environmentalists, ecologists, ecofeminists, ethical philosophers, animal rights groups, and a wide variety of scientific, social, and political researchers and activists all agree that care must be given to our shared environment. In 1973 a Norwegian philosopher, Arne Naess, invented the phrase "deep ecology" to embody these concerns. He and George Sissons proposed the following as a platform statement for the deep ecology movement:

1. The well-being and flourishing of human and non-human life on earth have value in themselves. These values are independent of the usefulness of the non-human world for human purposes.
2. Richness and diversity of life forms contribute to the realization of these values and are values in themselves.
3. Humans have no right to reduce this diversity except to satisfy vital needs.
4. The flourishing of human life and cultures is compatible with a substantial decrease of the human population. The flourishing of non-human life requires such a decrease.
5. Present human interference with the non-human world is excessive, and the situation is rapidly worsening.
6. Policies must therefore be changed. These policies affect basic economic, technological, and ideological structures. The resulting state of affairs will be deeply different from the present.[12]

Other eco-conscious advocates, while supporting the intent of these statements, would prefer to emphasize other particular ideas over these. Nonetheless, what is clear is the degree to which all those concerned about our shared environment place responsibility for the state of the environment, and for the continuation of all species, in our hands. The traditional religious assumption that after human beings have made things wrong God will make everything right is no longer part of their thinking. If we make things wrong, it is up to us to make them right again. Naturalism has replaced supernaturalism.

CONCLUSION

As noted earlier, there is much debate regarding how pantheism should be defined, what are its metaphysical and moral implications, and even who is or is not a pantheist. At the start of this chapter I identified two principal types of pantheism. Immanent pantheism identifies God with both matter and the laws that organize matter. It tends to be scientific and intellectual in approach. Transcendent pantheism sees the totality of reality as God, and imbues that totality with a sense that it is sacred. This has a more emotional charge to it.

What is significant is that the pantheistic outlook that Spinoza, Toland, and numerous other post-Enlightenment thinkers advocated now underpins today's non-theistic thinking about God. This is so even when the word God is avoided, and replaced by terms such as nature or the sacred. The intellectual appeal of pantheism is that it directs us towards the reality in which we clearly live, while its emotional appeal is that it enables us to sustain a feeling of sacredness or divinity about the world and our existence, and to do so without needing to attach our feelings to traditional religions or doctrines.

Yet many people who have given up theistic concepts of God find pantheism doesn't satisfy them. They acknowledge that God does embrace the fullness of the universe and of reality. But they want their God to be something more. This brings us to panentheism.

CHAPTER 12

Panentheism: Everything In God

The term panentheism was first coined in 1828 by a German philosopher, Karl Christian Friedrich Krause (1781–1832). Krause was a minor thinker in an era dominated by Hegel. However, his concept of panentheism subsequently influenced a number of twentieth century thinkers looking for a way to move beyond traditional theism.

Krause invented the idea of panentheism in order to reconcile theism with pantheism. He did so because while pantheism offered a concept of God consistent with the sciences, many felt that identifying God with the natural world removed God's transcendence and so diminished God too much. Indeed, some asserted that the removal of transcendence from God's qualities meant pantheism was just another form of atheism. Yet a problem remained, because pantheism clearly offered a better fit with the sciences than theism.

Krause offered panentheism as a solution to this dilemma. His concept of God retained the theistic sense of God transcending the universe, but also allowed for the pantheistic feeling that God is immanently present in the universe. Thus panentheism, which means *everything in God*, merges pantheism, which means *everything is God*, with the theistic concept of *everything below God*.

Krause's panentheism postulates that God includes and embraces the material universe and its embedded natural laws, but is not exhausted by that relationship. The universe exists *within* God's being and wholly consists *of* God's being, but God ultimately retains "something extra" that is separate from the universe. As Krause explained:

> Everything exists and lives in, with, and through God. No being *is* God except God alone. But what God Himself eternally created, He created in Himself, imperishable, in His own likeness. The world does not exist out

of God, for He is all that is; but neither is it God Himself; but it is in and through God. What God created in eternal sequence, without time and above all time, as a being living in an eternal subsistence, manifests and reveals in ever new forms what was originally planted in its essence by God; and God, as being before and above all time, and over all His creatures, works continuously into the life of all things ... nor does He cease to love His work, to maintain it, and to form it.[1]

In offering this vision of God it could be argued that Krause sought to have his pantheist cake and to eat it with theistic cream. That is, he saw God as immanent in everything, because everything is manifested out of God's essence and is actively maintained by God through the natural laws derived from God's own essence – the pantheistic perspective. Yet God simultaneously remains transcendent, personal, and loving, having existed before the world began and continuing to stand over the world and to guide it – the theistic perspective.

Krause's vision is consistent with Spinoza's and Hawking's idea that understanding the world's natural laws involves understanding God's mind. Yet, unlike for Spinoza, Krause's God is neither totally embedded in the universe nor is God abstract and dispassionate. Instead, God is personal, engaged, and loving.

Of course, panentheism may have been a new word, but the idea behind it was certainly not new. One of the earliest formulations of the panentheist perspective was made in the *Bhagavad Gita*.

EARLY PANENTHEISM

The meditators who wrote the Upanishads introduced the idea of God as Brahman. Brahman was thought of as consciousness that transcended the natural world, but at the same time penetrated and pervaded the natural world. In other words, Brahman was simultaneously transcendent and immanent. As such it was the Absolute, in very much the same sense as Tillich's Ground of being.

In the *Bhagavad Gita* (c. 400 BCE) the implication of this dual characteristic is described as being that all the feet walking in the cosmos, along with all the hands clasping, mouths eating, ears hearing, and eyes looking are the feet, hands, mouths, ears, and eyes of Brahman. So Brahman is present immanently, embedded in the activities and experiences of our existence. Yet, at the same time, Brahman stands aloof:

> Though perceiving sense objects, it has no senses;
> Though touching nothing, it sustains all;
> Though attributeless, it experiences natural powers.
> It is within all beings, yet also outside;
> It stands still, but is always moving;
> So subtle it can never be conceived,
> It is distant, yet always very close.
> Though undivided, it seems to exist
> Divided in all beings.[2]

Panentheistic ideas were also present in ancient Greek thought of the same period. In Plato's concept of the kosmos, the One (God) was thought of as a single living being which emanated the world out of its own being. Thus the One is simultaneously within the universe's emanated physical and ideal forms, yet at the same time the One transcends the universe. This idea culminated seven hundred years after Plato in the philosophy of Plotinus:

> All these things [physical forms] are the One and yet not the One. They are the One because they are from the One. They are not the One because the One abides within Itself in giving them existence.[3]

Plotinus' perspective may be termed emanationist panthentheism. He considered that everything that exists is an emanation of the One. The process of emanation began when the One, in a spontaneous act of over-flowing, manifested Intellect and Being out of itself. Next this triad, which consisted of Intellect, Being and the One, in another act of creative overflowing manifested Soul. And Soul, in turn, manifested all the forms existing in the world. Thus everything in the universe exists within the One. But they are part of a series of descending levels, which separate the One from its own emanation. So the One is immanent in the universe, yet simultaneously transcends it.

A more recent example of panentheism is offered by the American Transcendentalist, Ralph Waldo Emerson (1803–1882). Influenced by the *Bhagavad Gita*, Emerson gave the name Over-Soul to what the Indian meditators termed Brahman. His vision was that each individual human soul reflects, in part, the wholeness of the Over-Soul. Furthermore, we arrive at an appreciation of this as a result of contemplating the ever-changing natural world.

We live in succession, in division, in parts, in particles. Meantime within man is the soul of the whole; the wide silence; the universal beauty, to which every part and particle is equally related; the eternal ONE. ... Persons themselves acquaint us with the impersonal. In all conversation between two persons, tacit reference is made, as to a third party, to a common nature. That third party or common nature is not social; it is impersonal; it is God. ... The heart which abandons itself to the Supreme Mind finds itself related to all its works, and will travel a royal road to particular knowledges and powers.[4]

Today philosophers, scientists, and God-talkers from every religious tradition use panentheistic thinking to express their understanding of God and reality. For the remainder of this chapter I'll discuss four recent forms of panentheistic thought, starting with the process philosophy of Alfred Whitehead.

A.N. WHITEHEAD: PROCESS PHILOSOPHY

Alfred North Whitehead (1861–1947) was an English mathematician and philosopher. Initially he taught mathematics and logic at Cambridge University, a period that culminated in the publication of *Principia Mathematica* (1910-1913), a foundational text of modern logic, co-written with Bertrand Russell. Whitehead next moved to University College London where he began a new phase of his thinking, focusing on the philosophies of science and education.

Then, from 1924, he entered his third and final phase when, at the tender age of sixty-three, he moved to Harvard to teach philosophy. (It was joked at the time that the first philosophy lecture he ever attended was the inaugural philosophy lecture he himself gave at Harvard). This was the period during which he developed the ideas that came to be known as process philosophy. These ideas are embodied in his key philosophic work, *Process and Reality* (1929).

Whitehead started his thinking by proposing that because everything in the natural world is part of an ongoing process of change, this process of change itself, rather than the objects to which change occurs, should now be accepted as the basic units of existence.

It is nonsense to conceive of nature as a static fact, even for an instant devoid of duration. There is no nature apart from transition, and there is no transition apart from temporal duration. ... All philosophy is an endeavour to obtain a self-consistent understanding of things observed.[5]

Like Spinoza, Whitehead's aim was to provide a metaphysics that was consistent with the new world view revealed by the sciences. But where Spinoza saw God as consisting of infinite substance, Whitehead recognized that "there is no nature apart from transition," and so put the emphasis on those processes of change.

Whitehead began by proposing that at the microscopic level of reality the most basic building blocks of reality are what he called "actual entities." He considered that these entities are not things but are rather "actual occasions" of experience. Their experience consists of absorbing data received from other entities, processing it, being changed by it, and passing it on. In this way actual entities become actual occasions of subjective, feeling experience. As Whitehead himself wrote: "Each actual entity is a throb of experience including the actual world within its scope. It is a process of 'feeling' the many data, so as to absorb them into the unity of one individual 'satisfaction.'"[6]

The key to Whitehead's concept of an actual entity is that entities are at their core subjects which experience other entities in the world. As such, entities are not substantial things. Rather, they are processes. Processes of subjective experiencing. But what of entities that we do perceive as actual existing things, such as ants and trees?

Whitehead considers that all organisms in the world, including ants, trees, and human beings, consist of a *nexus* or *society* of individual actual entities. Thus the nexus that is a tree transmutes all the individual actual entities of which it is constituted into a new actual entity. Accordingly, each entity is an organism that consists of the concrescence (coming together) of all the feelings of its constitutive actual entities. So, as organisms, human beings exist as a concrescence of the feelings that arise out of the subjective experiencing of our constituent entities. This concrescence of feelings makes each of us the entity that we are. For this reason Whitehead called his a philosophy of organism.

Another of Whitehead's key ideas was that entities existing in the natural world do not consist just of mindless matter. Instead, the fact that there is order, pattern, creativity and purpose in the universe, and that these are apprehended conceptually, means that everything in nature partakes of mental-conceptual processes as well as material processes. Stated baldly, everything has a mind.

This doesn't mean that an atom thinks like we think, or is conscious of itself as we are of ourselves. Nor does a tree think as we do. What Whitehead means by saying that everything has a mental-conceptual aspect is that order, pattern, and creativity are innate in natural entities, being inherently part of them.

In one sense this is a reformulation of Spinoza's solution to Decartes mind-body split. Like Spinoza, Whitehead sees mind and body, mental and physical, as different aspects of the one thing. But unlike Spinoza Whitehead sees mind as purposive. That is, each actual entity possesses a "subjective aim." And that aim is provided by God. God creatively makes possible the coming into existence and experiencing of all the entities in the universe.

> God is in the universe, or nowhere, creating continually in us and around us. This creative principle is everywhere, in animate and so-called inanimate matter, in the ether, water, earth, human hearts. But this creation is a continuing process, and "the process is itself the actuality," since no sooner do you arrive than you start on a fresh journey. Insofar as we partake of this creative process we partake of the divine, of God.[7]

For Whitehead God has two natures, primordial and consequent. God in its primordial nature comprehends all the infinite possibilities of all entities. In fact, God actually provides all the possibilities that each individual entity may realize. But these possibilities are conceptual, not actual.

> Viewed as primordial, [God] is the unlimited conceptual realization of the absolute wealth of potentiality. In this aspect, he is not before all creation, but with all creation. But, as primordial, so far is he from "eminent reality" that in this abstraction he is "deficiently actual"– and this in two ways. His feelings are only conceptual and so lack the fullness of actuality. Secondly, conceptual feelings, apart from complex integration with physical feelings, are devoid of consciousness in their subjective forms.[8]

So God's primordial nature offers the creative potentialities of all actual entities. But what God in its primordial nature lacks is actuality, as well as subjective consciousness that provides the basis for each entity's experience. It is in the collective subjective consciousness of each entity that God achieves the realization of its own primordial nature and of all the possibilities inherent in it.

> The completion of God's nature into a fullness of physical feeling is derived from the objectification of the world in God. He shares with every new creation its actual world; and the concrescent creature is objectified in God as a novel element in God's objectification of that actual world. ... God's conceptual nature is unchanged, by reason of its final completeness. But His derivative nature is consequent upon the creative advance of the world.[9]

God's two-fold nature leads Whitehead to claim that we are co-creators with God. This is because God only realizes the creative possibilities inherent in its primordial nature in the concretization of all the universe's manifold entities, including us. So God's creative possibilities are our possibilities, and visa versa. And in making our possibilities concrete we contribute to God's completion. Whitehead calls the subjective experience of completion satisfaction. Accordingly we, through the creative process of our entity existence, contribute not only to our own satisfaction but also to God's.

A number of interesting ideas about God derive from this. First, God is dipolar. That is, God is equally potential and actuality, equally possible concept and concretized feeling. Second, the process of transforming potential into actual involves uncertainty and creativity. Nothing that occurs is pre-known or pre-arranged. This also means that some possibilities will never be realized. Third, transformation is an ongoing process. The possibilities in God are infinite. So the process by which conceptual potential is transformed into concrete actual is infinite. Fourth, God is not complete in its primordial self. The process of transforming potential into actual enables God to actualize its potential to its own satisfaction. Fifth, in exactly the same way, each entity's satisfaction results from actualizing the possibilities provided by God. So, sixth, the universe is necessary to God in order to achieve satisfaction, and God is necessary to all entities in the universe so they may achieve their satisfaction. Finally, this all means that, because no possibilities are pre-ordained, because all is open and in flux, even God doesn't know how things are going to turn out. Novelty is inherent in the process of the potential becoming actual. God and the universe proceed, hand-in-hand, in the creative revelation of novelty.

> [God] does not create the world, He saves it; or, more accurately, He is the poet of the world, with tender patience leading it by His vision of truth, beauty, and goodness.[10]

Whitehead's thoughts have stimulated a great deal of thinking about God among those who seek a non-mythological concept of God that respects scientific advances. I'll next examine two of Whitehead's ideas that have become the most influential. The first is Whitehead's concept of God as dipolar. The second is his idea of reality as process linked to evolution.

JOHN MACQUARRIE: DIALECTICAL THEISM

Scottish philosopher and Anglican theologian, John Macquarrie (1919–2007) was a ship pattern-maker's son. After studying philosophy and theology at university he was ordained a minister in the Scottish Church. During World War Two he was a military chaplain and one of his duties was to tend to German prisoners of war. This led him to learn the German language. After the war he went on to study German philosophy, and particularly the work of philosopher Martin Heidegger and theologian Rudolph Bultman.

Stongly influenced by existential thought, Macquarrie was a systematic theologian in the mould of Paul Tillich. Like Tillich, Macquarrie developed a form of panentheism, although he disliked the word, preferring to call his theology dialectical theism. Throughout his work he sought to reconcile traditional Christian God-talk with contemporary culture and its concerns.

Macquarrie's thinking started from the inadequacies he saw in the classical theism of Christianity, such as formulated by Aquinas. Macquarrie considered that the idea of God as wholly transcendent, existing separate from the world, above it like a king, did not allow for God's immanence and humility. Like many others he also had a problem with the proposition that God can intervene in human existence by miraculously setting aside the laws of nature. He was troubled by the idea that God created the world out of nothing, as this sets God and the world into a dualistic relationship, in which the created world is external to God, to which God exists as wholly other. He considered that this means the world is dispensable, and is even irrelevant to God, because whether the world is there is not God remains impassive, ever the same.

This implication of God's lack of sympathy was a key concern for Macquarrie, because it meant that God acts on and affects the world, but the world does not act on or affect God. God remains untouched by what occurs in the world, including all its struggles and suffering. As noted earlier, in the aftermath of WW2 the idea that God is remote and indifferent to human suffering became a central concern for God-talkers of all persuasions. It was in a dialectical approach to God, strongly influenced by Whitehead's concept of a dipolar God, that Macquarrie sought solutions to this problem.

Having decided classical theism was too one-sided in its emphasis on God as transcendent, separate, unchanging, unsympathetic, kingly, and other, Macquarrie sought to balance these with their opposites, such as immanence, closeness, change, and sympathy. In his Gifford Lectures, published as *In Search of Deity* (1984), he indicated God's nature using a series of linked opposites.

Being and nothing. God is both being and nothing. God as the primordial source of being gives being to everything else. But we usually think of being as something existing in the world, whereas God doesn't exist in the world as an thing in it. Macquarrie argues that we could use the language of the mystics and say that God is nothing. This is because God is not a being like other beings, and does not exist in the same way that beings in the world do. Accordingly, God may be to said not to exist and to be nothing. Yet God has primordial being and as primordial being definitely does exist.

One and many. Macquarrie proposes that God has three modes of being. In its primordial mode God is a mystery that exists beyond existence. Out of his primordial nature, in an event of giving, God then expresses his being as the universe. This is the expressive mode, in which God gives existence to the manifold beings that are other than his primordial mystery. Macquarrie likens this second mode to the Logos or Intellect that functions as an agent in the creation of the universe, and which simultaneously expresses and hides from us God's mysterious primordial being. The third mode of being is unitary. It is the urge beings feel to turn towards God and to return to God's primordial mysterious being. Macquarrie likens this mode of God's being to the Spirit of God which seeks to fulfil its own being. It is at the heart of human quest for God.

Knowability and incomprehensibility. God in his primordial mode is incomprehensible to us. However, because God has expressed his own being in and through the created universe it has become possible to gain some knowledge of God. In addition, human beings are finite images of the infinite God, a likeness that further enables us to know something of God. However, for Macquarrie this knowing is not deductive and rational. We cannot know God through reasoning our way from the created universe to the mysterious primordial mode of God's being. Rather, we can only intuit this knowledge through images and symbols, and through a sense of God's presence and unity.

Transcendence and immanence. God is transcendent in his mode of primordial being. This is God as separate from, and other than, the universe. God thus precedes the created universe and possesses a different order of existence from it. God is transcendent. Immanence refers to God as dwelling in the universe, a presence and agency that provides the universe with order and purpose. So immanence is a function of the expressive and unitary modes of God's being. As such, God is simultaneously wholly transcendent and wholly immanent.

God's impassibility and passibility. Passibility is a theological term that is used to refer to God's capacity to feel emotion. In classical theism God is wholly transcendent and perfect, and as we have already seen the perfect God cannot change. This means that God can't emotionally feel our suffering, because feeling an emotion that God wasn't already feeling would be an alteration to God's perfection. So the God of classical theism is necessarily unmoved by whatever happens to his creation. In contrast, the immanent God is present in and involved in his creation. So he is able to be affected by what happens in the universe. He becomes passible. Macquarrie proposes that God be considered to be both passible and impassible simultaneously. This means that God feels our suffering and joy and shares in it. But we can be overcome by our suffering and sorrow, whereas God can never be overcome by it. He mysteriously absorbs and transforms our suffering in himself.

Eternity and temporality. Macquarrie argues that for God to be God he must be eternal. This means he transcends time and therefore is not affected by the change that affects all temporal things. However, God is also immanent in the universe, and so shares in the existence of created beings. We experience temporality as loss and as a passing away. So God must also be involved in the universe's temporality, in the struggle and pain beings experience as they strive to grow and achieve. Further, Macquarrie points to the feeling people have that God has helped them in their struggles, that somehow God's presence was involved in their overcoming difficulties or achieving goals. So God is involved in temporality, and not just a transcendent observer of it. Accordingly, Macquarrie agrees with Whitehead that God in his consequent nature is making the temporal world, and is making himself in doing so.

Thus we see that in his dialectical approach to God, influenced by Whitehead's dipolar concept of God, Macquarrie offers an inclusive, all-encompassing vision of God that avoids either-or thinking, and in the process eliminates many of the problems of classical theism.

Having established six dialectical criteria by which God may be conceived, Macquarrie next wondered how we might obtain knowledge of God.

MACQUARRIE ON SPIRITUAL KNOWING

Macquarrie considered there are two fundamental ways of knowing. The first is the intellectual knowing of theology and philosophy, in which assertions are made using carefully defined words and backed up using equally carefully designed logical arguments. The second is spiritual knowing, which is personal and experiential. Spiritual knowing is close to the knowing we develop when we come to know another person, or when we come to know a piece of music, or when we come to know an area of countryside. But, of course, the difference is that God is not an object to be known like other objects in the world.

Accordingly, Macquarrie proposed that experiential spiritual knowledge of God involves a form of intuitive knowing, a vision even, of God as unity and presence. Macquarrie approvingly quoted Whitehead's emphasis on the significance of this vision: "The fact of the religious vision, and its history of persistent expansion, is our one ground for optimism. Apart from it, human life is a flash of occasional enjoyments lighting up a mass of pain and suffering."[11] So where theology and analytic philosophy seek knowledge, spirituality hinges on a quest for experiential knowing.

How may we achieve experiential knowledge of God? Macquarrie considered that God's primordial being is beyond the limits of our perceptions due to our being embedded in the universe which God's mysterious fullness transcends. So the only aspect of God we can gain knowledge of is God's expressive mode of being, which we experience as God's immanence in the world. God is immanently disclosed in and through the events of the world, events that we experience personally and that we intuitively perceive God as being or acting within.

It is in mystical spirituality that Macquarrie found the completest and most profound form of spiritual knowing. While acknowledging that spirituality in general, and mystical spirituality in particular, involves thought that often leaps ahead of language and as a result attracts censure from theological thinkers who want statements made about God to fit into tidy, logical boxes, Macquarrie argued that the "truths of faith are intuitively discerned before they are formulated as doctrines and incorporated into theology."[12] Thus, in the context of spirituality, direct discernment precedes intellectual truth claims and not the other way around.

What drives the mystic is the unitive impulse, which manifests as a search for God, even an attempt to return to God. For some this return involves looking at nature and seeing God in the natural world. However, Macquarrie contended that mysticism more typically "turns inward, to the very centre or ground of the self, and finds that this is not an isolated self-contained entity but is continuous with a universal spirit pervading all things."[13] In this we come back to Tillich's assertion that God is the Ground of being. It is this Ground of being that Macquarrie proposes mystics experience.

The mystic drive for a unitive experience takes different forms in different religious and spiritual contexts. There are emotive forms, apparent in the *Song of Songs*, which uses imagery drawn from sexual relations and marriage to capture the intimate relationship of the individual with God. Other forms are intellectual, being philosophic or theological. Macquarrie focused on the writings of the medieval mystic Meister Eckhart to explore this latter form.

Eckhart began by emphasizing the need for detachment, which involves standing back from the distress and flux of daily life. This then provides the conditions for two stages of a journey back to God. The first stage involves what Eckhart called the birth of God in the form of the Son or of the Logos in the soul. This is an ongoing process of birth, moment by moment, by which God is discerned in the activities of daily existence. The second step is termed the break-through and involves transcending all our concepts of God, breaking through to what exists beyond God as Trinity. In Tillich's terms, this experience consists of discovering the God beyond God. Indeed, Eckhart himself influenced Tillich's language when he asserted that this experience involves "man's last and highest parting, when for God's sake he takes leave of God."[14]

JOHN F. HAUGHT: GOD AFTER DARWIN

John F. Haught is a Catholic theologian who focuses on the intersection of religion with cosmology, evolution, and ecology. He is particularly drawn to the implications of evolution in relation to Whitehead's process concept of God.

The project Haught has set himself is to face up to the implications of neo-Darwinian evolution without avoiding those that are awkward from a religious perspective, and seeing where they lead in relation to God. Like Macquarrie he considers that the God of classical theism is inadequate for today's spiritual explorations. Instead, Haught works from the assumption that our ideas about God need to be adapted to accommodate a process outlook. The idea of God he has arrived at is presented in his book *God After Darwin* (2000).

Haught's starting point is that of evolutionary theology, which accepts the premises of the neo-Darwinian doctrine of evolution. However, he seeks to place evolution not just in a terrestrial biological context but in the context of the entire universe, because it is in the universe that biological life on Earth has arisen. In addition, evolutionary theology assumes that the universe itself is growing, developing, and evolving towards whatever its final state will be, if there is such a thing. This means that the universe is still involved in an ongoing creative process, is unfinished, and is definitely not perfected.

Equally, we live in an imperfect world. We experience suffering, struggle, conflict, and evil in addition to good, joy, happiness, and fulfilment. Life for us is messy, often destructive, sometimes apparently purposeless and senseless. In Haught's view salvation for this world, and the resolution of these negative qualities, is not just a human or earthly event, but is cosmic in scale. So as we face up to and overcome imperfections in the world, our human spiritual growth and evolution contribute to the evolution of the universe as a whole.

This means, for Haught, that God comes to us from the future. That is, we meet God in the future realization of today's still developing possibilities. In a sense this is a rethinking in more personal terms of Whitehead's idea regarding God's primordial nature, because Haught envisions that the entire universe is evolving out of its current state into a future state of physical and spiritual realization.

In addition, divine revelation in this context is not centred on the propositional statements of knowledge (i.e. commandments and threats) that are the revelations of the God of theism. Instead, Haught's idea of revelation involves an on-going disclosure of "God's own selfhood in the world."[15] This leads to the concept of kenosis.

God's giving of himself into the world involves the idea that God is humble and vulnerable, and so is not the judging, invulnerable God of classical theism. Whitehead called God tender and loving, while Macquarrie talked in terms of passibility. Haught uses the term kenosis (out-pouring, an idea Christian theologians adapted from the Neoplatonic proposition that the One overflowed from itself to create the cosmos) to indicate how God created the universe through an out-pouring from and of its own being. This is an activity of loving self-emptying, in which God, by humbly sharing his own infinitude with the finite universe, becomes vulnerable to the suffering that occurs in it. Furthermore, this act of kenosis is not a one-time activity. Rather, it is on-going, being a process by which God contributes to the continuous evolution of the universe and all in it. God gives of itself, by degrees, moment by moment.

The final point about this relationship between God and the universe is that God allows the universe to make its own way, in accordance with the laws and processes embedded in it. The universe is thus self-ordering and self-creative. God doesn't interfere in any of it, and definitely doesn't act like the omniscient and omnipotent God of classical theism. God is engaged, because the universe is in and of God. But, as Whitehead proposed, God doesn't have a pre-arranged plan for how the universe will turn out. God provides the possibilities but doesn't design or order those possibilities. So creativity is given free reign, novelty is allowed for, and even God has the freedom to be surprised by what occurs.

All this takes the concept of immanence to a personal level. God is loving, generous, and involved in what is. As Haught describes it:

> God's empathy enfolds not just the human sphere but the whole of creation, and this can mean only that the vast evolutionary odyssey, with all of its travail, enjoyment, and creativity, is also God's own travail, enjoyment, and creativity. Nothing that occurs in evolution can appropriately be understood by faith and theology as taking place outside of God's own experience.[16]

Hence, contrary to physicist Steven Weinberg's claim that the universe has no point, Haught's contention is that the universe certainly does have a point, the point being that the universe is God's creative expression. This innate creativity is visible to us in the complex biological forms that have emerged out of simpler forms. Thus, on this planet, mammals and reptiles have emerged out of amoeba and slimes. And over the fifteen billion years since the big bang the universe has similarly evolved from the much simpler state of a quark soup measuring just a few kilometers across to the immeasurable complexity that it is today.

The drive behind this movement from simple to complex Haught calls the aesthetic cosmological principle, an idea derived from Whitehead and other philosophers. This is the idea that the point of the universe may be defined in aesthetic as well as evolutionary and theological terms. So "God longs for the well-being, self-coherence, and aesthetic adventurousness of the cosmos."[17] This is the new being that Tillich and Spong drew attention to, the revelation in the world of God's own primordial being.

All this means that nature and its evolution is part of God's self-revelation. Haught, with Lloyd Gerring, acknowledges that Earth-hating supernaturalism that sees heaven as more important than our planet has tainted our relationship with our physical environment. Accordingly, he considers that an ecological commitment needs to be included in our spiritual outlook.

However, rather than examine Haught's thoughts on ecology, I will now move on to consider the ecological ideas of Sallie McFague.

SALLIE MCFAGUE: THE BODY OF GOD

Sallie McFague (b. 1933) is a feminist Christian theologian. Her starting point is an acknowledgement that God-talk is a human construct. Accordingly, she agrees with others that statements we make about God need to be recognized as metaphors rather than as literal truths. One of the metaphors McFague has explored at length is that of viewing the world as God's body.

This is actually an ancient concept. For example, the medieval Indian God-talker, Ramanuja, argued that the physical universe is Brahman's body. His rationale for proposing this hinged on the established Indian doctrine of reincarnation. Fundamental to Indian spirituality is the idea that atman, our spiritual self, is not identical with our body and that during the ongoing process of reincarnation atman puts on and takes off bodies much as we put on or take off clothes. Applying this atman-body metaphor in a panentheistic sense, Ramanuja envisioned Brahman as the spiritual self of the universe and the universe as Brahman's body. Of course, where the metaphor breaks down is that clothing is separate from us, whereas the universe is an emanation of God's own self. So while the universe is not all that God is, it is not separate from God.

Sallie McFague's take on this is intriguing because, having postulated the metaphor, she then explores it in order to tease out a number of related ideas regarding God's nature and God's relationship to humanity and the world.

McFague starts by agreeing with other panentheistic thinkers that God is not the distant transcendent king of traditional theology. Rather, and here she uses Tillich's term, God is Being-itself. God is not *a* being, but *is* Being. What the metaphor of the world as God's body offers is a way of thinking about Being-Itself in an immanent sense of being present in our world and in our lives.

Next McFague considers it is necessary to replace the traditional religious split between body and spirit, on the grounds that this split denigrates the body in favor of the spirit. What she replaces this split with is a new hierarchy of values in which bodies, because they are part of God's body, are seen as possessing value in themselves. This means that ecological, social, and economic concerns, that are intrinsic to the continuance of bodies on this planet, come to the fore.

God's incarnation in and as a body also involves risk, because bodies may be damaged and hurt. So through the body of the universe God becomes vulnerable. God, like us, shares in the responsibility of what occurs in the world. We are here in the world, and God is here with us, risking what we risk, working through what we have to work through.

A central concern for McFague is that we need to develop a new relationship not only with God but also with the world in which we live. She is painfully aware of how the monarchist concept of God has been hitched to the wagons of war and of how God has been used to justify the drive to dominate. She is also conscious of the degree to which corporate and industrial interests have plundered the Earth's resources with little or no regard for the consequences. Christians, with their low regard for this world, have contributed to this exploitation, as have wealthy, white, educated consuming Americans such as herself.

Consequently, McFague locates sin and the redemption of sin within an ecological context. She notes that Augustine suggested that sin involves concupiscence, which McFague identifies with the desire to "have it all." Another traditional idea of sin is that of "living a lie." Because the world itself, when thought of as God's body, becomes God's divine milieu, in order not to sin we need to live truthfully within the world. This means living justly and equitably with our fellow human beings and respecting and sharing with the non-human creatures with whom we live in this world.

The upshot is that the sin that has been done, and is still being done, to the Earth by humanity as a result of self-centred exploitation can only be redeemed by humanity. We did it. Now we have to address our shortcomings. To do so we need to act collectively, according to what is possible in the situations in which each of us find ourselves, to redeem the Earth from our own actions. In this McFague reinforces the deep ecology movement.

Accordingly, for McFague the metaphor of the universe as the body of God brings us face to face with the concrete recognition that we share this world.

> We now know that "all that is" is vaster, more complex, more awesome, more interdependent, than any other people have ever known. The new theologies that emerge from such a context have the opportunity to view divine transcendence in deeper, more awesome and more intimate ways than ever before. They also have the obligation to understand human beings and all other forms of life as radically interrelated and interdependent as well as to understand our special responsibility for the planet's well-being.[18]

GRASSROOTS SPIRITUALITY

So far I have examined panentheism from philosophic and Christian theological perspectives. However, we live in a secular age, in which church attendance is declining and belief in the dogmas of institutional religions is evaporating. Yet the flipside of this decline is that exploration of alternative forms of spirituality has blossomed, and belief in God remains alive.

In relation to this, Australian Anglican theologian Nigel Leaves observes in *The God Problem* (2006), "The 'death of God' and the resulting secularization of society have not reduced the number of spiritual options, but rather resulted in their proliferation."[19] Leaves sees this as having created a smorgasbord of possibilities in which people pick and choose from the range on offer, selecting what best suits their spiritual needs. This has resulted in the dismantling of traditional differences, so that a Catholic may practice Tai Chi, a Buddhist learn Reiki, and a feminist may throw the I Ching, attend wicca ceremonies, and do yoga on Saturday mornings.

While the extent of this proliferation of outlooks and practices is clear, the detail is not. In an attempt to ascertain what is going on Robert Forman initiated a survey to create a snapshot of what he calls "grassroots spirituality" in the United States the early twenty-first century. Among his findings:

- 59% of Americans in 2001 described themselves as both religious and spiritual, while 20% viewed themselves as solely spiritual.
- Roughly 40% of those who called themselves religious were not members of any particular church, mosque, or synagogue.

- Over a third of Americans believe that they have had a spiritual experience that has had a significant impact on their lives.
- There are approximately three million active small spiritual groups in America, involving around 70 million Americans, some 40% of the total population.
- If this [above] number were spread out evenly over the country, in a typical town of 50,000 there would be at least 600 small groups; in a city of two million, 25,000.[20]

Besides clarifying the actual numbers of people involved in alternative spirituality, Foreman identified their spirituality as embracing spiritual pluralism, which involves an openness to imbibing from different traditions and disciplines, along with a desire to move away from dogmatism, from a judgemental mentality, and from tired religious justifications.

Instead, Foreman sees grassroots spirituality as growing on the margins of the mainstream, largely out of sight of media. It is popularist in the widest sense, without central leadership or any overarching organisztion. In terms of goals it "is attempting to integrate consciousness, soul, and spirit into our societal dialogues."[21] All this is occurring in the context of peoples' lives, in relation to the work they do, within family life, and in public decision-making.

Sallie MacFague's exploration of the world as God's body has been met with disapproval in some Christian circles on the grounds that she is theologically unorthodox. But her ideas very much fit into Foreman's concept of grassroots spirituality. In a sense grassroots spirituality is a democratization of spirituality, taking spiritual beliefs and practices away from institutions that still operate on the feudal hierarchical model of a judging king (God), ruling aristocracy (clergy), and obedient serfs (laity), replacing it with a flat structure in which no single person has priority and everyone has the opportunity to decide for themselves what is best for them.

The other interesting aspect of Forman's study is that he considers the beliefs behind grassroots spirituality are largely panentheist. Out of the patchwork quilt of attitudes, practices, and beliefs he and his team investigated Forman has derived the following tentative definition:

> Grassroots spirituality involves a vaguely panentheistic ultimate that is indwelling, sometimes bodily, as the deepest self and accessed through not-strictly-rational means of self transformation and group process that

becomes the holistic organization for all life.[22]

During his research Forman was fascinated to hear mainstream religious believers endorsing a panentheistic outlook, and not just those with a more radical perspective. The feeling that God as a power, force, or presence permeates the universe, and that everything existing is part of a larger whole, are increasingly common positions for all.

However, Forman found that the articulation of this panentheistic outlook varied. He thought this is because grassroots spirituality tends to be practice-based, with ideas coming out of experiences and texts providing secondary sources of validation. Thus grassroots panentheism emerges out of a bottom-up "let's see what works best" exploratory approach, as opposed to a top-down "this is how it is" command structure.

PANTHEISM OR PANENTHEISM?

Panenthism is an evolving concept, with its implications still being worked through. Nonetheless, it is an interesting exercise to consider it in relation to pantheism.

Given the way both emphasize God's immanence, pantheism and panentheism have a lot in common. In fact, at times they blur into each other. For example, while Spinoza is called a pantheist, he nonetheless asserted God's qualities are infinite. Hence because his God is not limited to the physical universe he can be considered to be a panentheist. And while Meister Eckhart is undoubtedly a panentheist, at times his language reads as pantheism.

Further complicating this blurring is that pantheism is condemned as heretical by classical theists but panentheism is not. The reason is that theists consider God cannot be identified with the universe in the way that pantheism proposes. Panentheism avoids this charge because it asserts that part of God is beyond the universe. Yet it could be argued that the distinction between pantheism and panentheism is only a problem for theists. And given that the God of theism has largely been replaced by an immanent God there is no need for the rest of us to automatically take on the theistic dismissal of pantheism.

So what happens if we look at pantheism and panentheism with fresh eyes? Two points come to the fore, one experiential, the other conceptual.

First, let's consider God from the perspective of our experience of the world.

If we think of God as immanent we see God in all things, and we view the world as a sacred expression of God. Both pantheism and panentheism equally embrace this interpretation of experience. So whether we are a pantheist or a panentheist, we can comfortably agree that we exist in, of, and from God. This is why the panenthist Eckhart can be seen as a pantheist and the pantheistic Spinoza as a panentheist. From inside our experience of God as immanent in the world, while pantheism and panentheism embody different concepts of God, experientially both are the same.

Now let's consider God as encompassing the entirety of what is. In the context of our experience of the universe it makes no practical difference whether we say with pantheism that God encompasses the whole of the universe, or whether we say with panentheism that God encompasses the whole universe but remains something more than the universe. This is because we can have no experience, no concept, and no verification regarding what that "something more" is experientially. Whether God pantheistically encompasses the universe, or whether God is "more" than the universe, we can't experience either; both are beyond the limits of human perception. So whether we adopt a pantheistic perspective or a panentheistic stance, in the context of our experience of being in the world there remains only a slight difference in concept. Experientially, they denote the same experience.

Finally, let's look a little more closely at this phrase "something more." For panentheists "something more" refers to the transcendent aspect of God that exists beyond the physical universe. But pantheism also has a "something more." This equates to the whole of what is. Yet this whole includes much of which we can have absolutely no concept. The fact is that we don't have clearly understand the natures of gravity or consciousness; currently 97% of the energy and mass in the universe is unaccounted for. So while panentheism includes the concept of God as "something more" than we are able to conceive, the pantheistic conception of the whole of the universe is similarly beyond our comprehension. Hence both pantheistic and panentheistic concepts of God equally represent a reality that we are incapable of fully comprehending.

Accordingly, I suggest that while there are some conceptual niceties that distinguish pantheism from panentheism, when we consider the difference between them from our experiential perspective of looking out into the universe and wondering where or what God is in relationship to it all, there is little to distinguish them. Furthermore, as noted in the discussion of God-talk, both pantheism and panentheism are provisional positions. They are concepts we only hold while on our way to greater, more enveloping understanding. In time we will let both go, just as we are letting go of theism today, as we engage in a developmental process of seeking more appropriate concepts of reality and of God.

THE QUESTION OF SPIRITUAL KNOWING

Before moving on there remains one last issue that has risen out of the foregoing panentheistic thoughts about God. This is that a point was made by John Macquarrie when he asserted that there are two modes of knowing God. The first is an intellectual mode, as exemplified in the discussion of pantheism and panentheism. The second is an experiential mode, exemplified in the experiences of mystics. Macquarrie asserted that experiential spiritual knowing reveals the self as "continuous with a universal spirit pervading all things." He proposed that this experience brings about intuitive knowledge of God.

Interestingly, Spong maintained the same position when he wrote: "I live this moment inside a powerful experience of the divine, the holy. I call the content of that experience God. I trust its reality."[23]

However, this leads to the obvious question: Are spiritual experiences real in the ways that those who undergo them claim? And do they really give us knowledge of God?

It is important to ask this because in order for God-talk to be more than just talk there needs to be an experience of reality behind the words. The following chapter considers this issue of spiritual experiences.

CHAPTER 13

Are Spiritual Experiences Real?

Spiritual experiences are a fascinating sub-category of human experience. For those who experience them they initiate fundamental shifts in outlook or behavior. And they are reasonably common. For example, researcher David Hay discovered that up to forty percent of people surveyed in the USA, UK, and Australia claimed to have had a spiritual experience, while Robert Forman found that twelve per cent of the his team people questioned in the USA said they had had an experience involving the appearance of a spiritual figure such as God, Jesus, Elijah, or Buddha.[1] Other types of spiritual experiences include ecstatic states, out-of-body feelings, near death experiences, visions of angels or deceased saints, feelings of being one with the divine in the natural world, and experiences of God.

But for many scientists and philosophers the claims made about such experiences are problematic, leading them to ask a number of intriguing questions. For example: Why is it that Christians have visions of the Virgin Mary, Buddhists have visions of Buddha, and Indians have visions of Krishna or Rama? Why don't Christians have visions of Buddha, and Buddhists have visions of Krishna? This leads them to wonder if such experiences are cultural constructs, experienced by believers conditioned by their religious upbringing not only to expect such visions but that also dictates the particular form they take.

Another problem is that mystics frequently say that their experiences are ineffable, yet they have written extensively about those supposedly ineffable experiences. Why do they keep trying to describe experiences that, by their very definition, cannot be described? What are they really writing about?

Even more problematic, if such experiences can't be described, how can others verify they are real in the way that is being claimed? Clearly, such intensely private experiences cannot be verified in any normal, objective way.

Finally, a number of mystics were epileptics (i.e. the prophet of Islam, Mohammed), while others had spiritual experiences as a result of fasting, sleep deprivation, or being imprisoned. Accordingly, could it be that mystical experiences are no more than psychological projections that occur as the result of abnormal living conditions? More exactly, are mystical experiences just neurological epiphenomena resulting from stressed psychological states?

On the other hand, many people assume that spiritual and mystical experiences involve non-everyday perceptions of reality. One position adopted during the first half of the twentieth century was that there is a perennial philosophy that lies behind and unites all the disparate kinds of mystical experiences. The perennialist outlook underpins Evelyn Underhill's *Mysticism* (1911), which surveys accounts of mystics from various cultures and eras and proposes that they share the same experiences and goal of unity with God, however God may be named and defined. In *The Perennial Philosophy* (1945) Aldous Huxley brought together mystical texts from a wide range of spiritual traditions. Like Underhill, he proposed that all religious and spiritual expressions, from the most primitive to the most sophisticated, are of the same divine reality.

However, in recent years a number of scholars have found this lumping together of all mystical experiences under one perennialist banner questionable. They ask whether there is a really existing divine reality underlying all spiritual experiences. And they question how much such experiences are culturally constructed responses to the world around us.

This questioning has led to the realization that all spiritual experiences are not of the same order, and that hearing voices is not of the same order of experience as being one with God. In response to this W.T. Stace has proposed that mystical experiences range from extraverted, involving visions, clairaudience, and ecstatic states, to introverted, which are quiescent and inwardly directed. Neurologists have also considered this issue. Neurologically, extraverted experiences are called ergotrophic. They involve increases in heartbeat, body temperature, and neural activity and tend to be associated with visions and ecstasies. Conversely, introverted states are termed trophotropic, and are associated with the calmness of deep meditative states, or the body closing down during near death experiences.

In addition, some divide spiritual experiences into dualistic and non-dual. Dualistic experiences involve a separation between the experiencer and whatever is being experienced, as occurs during visions of ghosts or divine beings, or the hearing of voices. Non-dual experiences are unitive in nature. Examples include the experience of being one with nature, or when, during prayer or meditation, a feeling arises of being at one with, to use Tillich's term, the Ground of being. This last is the type of experience that interested John Maquarrie.

The difficulty with examining spiritual experiences is that despite there having been a great deal of scholarly attention given to mystical states in recent decades, no taxonomy of spiritual experiences currently exists. That is, there is no agreed list of definitions of spiritual experiences, no agreed descriptions, and no categorization of such experiences. So while there are studies such as William James' *The Varieties of Religious Experiences* (1902), Rudolph Otto's *The Idea of the Holy* (1923) and *Mysticism East and West* (1932), and more recent works such as *Mysticism and Philosophy* (1960) by W. T. Stace, any discussion is handicapped by the fact that even the simple question of what constitutes a mystical experience has not been fully addressed. Accordingly, our collective inquiry into the nature of mystical experiences remains at an early stage.

It is beyond the scope of this study to solve this lack. Instead, I will examine just one particular type of spiritual experience. This has drawn the attention of researchers because it offers an excellent focus for discussion regarding whether or not spiritual experiences are constructed. The particular experience is termed a pure consciousness event.

PURE CONSCIOUSNESS EVENTS

A pure consciousness event (PCE) may most simply be characterized as an experience in which our awareness is turned back on itself. Generally, no thinking, emotion, or sense experience is involved. With eyes closed, normal spatial awareness vanishes, awareness of the body diminishes or even disappears, and the dominant feeling is of calmness, stillness, peace. In its most extreme form all sense of individual identity completely vanishes.

One of the most important characteristics of this experience is it dissolves the subject-object dichotomy that underpins our everyday experience. Normally our awareness is intentional, directing our attention outside us, towards objects in the world, or towards our own bodily functions and sense experiences, which become the objects of our awareness. However, during a PCE our awareness is simultaneously both the subject (the experiencer) and the object (what is experienced). So everyday intentionality doesn't apply.

In general, PCEs are experienced during silent meditation because this is when awareness is withdrawn from active engagement with sensory and mental objects. Prayer, whether spoken out loud or repeated silently within, tends towards dualism, because it addresses what is other than the self, such as God, a saint, or some kind of spiritual power. But it is also possible for intense prayer to fall silent and lead to a PCE. The mystical literature of all the world's spiritual traditions contain accounts of such experiences.

The *Bhagavad Gita* describes the conditions for experiencing a PCE. In Discourse Six it outlines the preparations undertaken by ancient Indian meditators to practice their yoga (spiritual disciplines) which involved turning their attention inwards and concentrating on their own atman (self as consciousness).

> When the disciplined mind rests in atman alone,
> and desire for objects no longer exists,
> it is said that one is settled in yoga.
> When his thought, stilled by yoga, wholly ceases,
> and the self exults in atman perceiving atman;
> when, beyond the senses, his purified
> intellect apprehends endless bliss
> and, fixed in this state, does not move from it ...
> restraining his senses which would grab all around,
> mind controlled by the power of his will,
> by degrees, he resolutely quietens within.
> Supreme bliss arrives for that stainless yogi
> whose mind is tranquil and passions subdued,
> for he becomes one with Brahman.[2]

This passage describes a state of non-thinking, devoid of active sense experiences, which is experienced as tranquil bliss. As such, this account may be taken as a straight forward phenomenological description of a particular type of meditation experience – unless it is claimed that whoever wrote it was just making it up. (In fact, as we'll soon see, some constructivists do claim this.) However, for now let's accept this description at face value as an actual account of a pure consciousness event.

Zen Buddhist Daikaku (1213-1279), in his *Treatise on Meditation*, described this same experience of turning awareness back on itself. In Chinese mysticism this process is referred to poetically as "turning the light back on itself," the light symbolizing awareness. Zen Buddhists call the awareness that turns back on itself original essence. It is also known as Buddha nature.

> When the mind and thoughts do not range over things but are turned toward the original nature, this is called "turning the light around to shine back." ... The non-production of a single thought is what is known as the original essence of mind. ... If you merge with this original essence, this is called the realization of the thusness of the reality of things.[3]

This is an experience beyond thinking, beyond concepts, beyond language, beyond even sense of self. In attempting to describe his experience of this state, St John of the Cross (1542-1591) used paradoxical statements.

> I entered a place none know
> and remained there not knowing,
> transcending all knowledge.
> It was the perfect knowledge
> of peace and piety,
> profoundly solitary,
> entered narrowly;
> and it contained such secrets
> it surprised me, snatching my words,
> transcending all knowledge.
> I was so embedded,
> so absorbed and apart,
> that my senses departed
> from personal feelings;
> for my mind found another path
> of knowing without knowing,
> transcending all knowledge.[4]

The paradox of knowing without knowing was first offered in the Christian tradition in the sixth century by Dionysius the Areopagite. The idea behind it is that ordinary forms of knowing and knowledge don't apply to these profound types of spiritual experiences. Negative theology (discussed in Chapter Nine) may be used not only in relation to God but also to PCEs. Thus just as the reality of God is beyond all words and thoughts and so may only be described as "not that, not this," it was similarly asserted that a pure consciousness event is experienced by the "not-self" existing in a state as a state of "not-knowing."

This negative approach to describing spiritual experiences was also adopted in a commentary on one of the most famous Sufi poems, *Gulshani-i Raz* (*The Rose Garden of Mystery*) by Mahmud Shabistari (1288-1340). The poem was written as a response to questions regarding the nature of reality. The poem's first interpreter, Muhammad Bin Yahya Lahiji, wrote in his commentary:

> The perfection of contingent being [i.e. created creatures] is to regress to its basic negativity, and to come to know through its own unknowingness. It means to know with the certainty of experience that the *summum* of knowledge is unknowingness, for here there is infinite disproportion. This mystical station is that of bedazzlement, of immersion of the object in the subject. It is the revelation of the non-being that has never been.[5]

Here the process by which subjective awareness becomes merged with itself as object is described by Lahiji as "regressing to basic negativity." The experience is also called knowing through unknowingness and "the revelation of non-being" because knowledge of things in the world is not involved. Lahiji goes on to assert that "other than God does not exist."[6] That is, the end result of this experience is the realization that because all sense of the individual self is dissolved in such a state, God is left as the sole existent. This position of God being the only existent is known as non-dualism.

The perennialist claim is that this non-dual outlook is equally behind the perspectives of *Bhagavda Gita*, Daikaku, and Lahiji. Even in Christianity, which holds that there is a distinction between creature and God, mystics have written of experiences in which their sense of selfhood dissolves, leaving only God. A final example of this non-dual view of reality, experienced via a pure consciousness event, is provided by John of Ruysbroeck (1294-1381), a Flemish Christian mystic. In *The Book of Supreme Truth* he wrote:

> The enlightened have found within themselves an essential contemplation which is above reason ... through which they immerse themselves in a wayless abyss of fathomless beatitude. ... This beatitude is so onefold and so

wayless that in it every essential gazing, tendency, and creaturely distinction ceases and passes away. For by this fruition, all uplifted spirits are melted and noughted in the Essence of God, which is the Super-Essence of all essence. There they fall from themselves into a solitude and an ignorance which is fathomless; there all light is turned to darkness; there the three Persons give place to the Essential Unity, and abide without distinction in fruition of essential blessedness.[7]

Here Ruysbroeck is stating that a pure consciousness event not only dissolves personal identity, but also involves going beyond any sense of the personhood of God. For the Christian even knowledge of the Trinity is dissolved, leaving the Super-Essence of reality, which is God, as the sole existent.

The perennialist view is that such accounts are uniform across different spiritual traditions because they describe the same experience. Fundamental to this experience is the sense that our everyday sense of self has been transcended, usual processes of feeling, thinking , and sense experience cease, and all ideas about God are no longer seen as relevant.

This perennialist view, of spiritual experiences as non-dual and involving non-ordinary state of consciousness that transcend the usual distinctions of selfhood, is widely accepted in spiritual circles today. However, constructivists have big problems with this perspective.

SPIRITUAL EXPERIENCE AS CONSTRUCTION

In recent decades a number of writers have critiqued mystical experiences from a constructivist perspective. The most influential contributor to this critique has been Steven T. Katz. In his essay *Language, Epistemology, and Mysticism* (1978)[8] Katz summarized the problems constructivsts have with the claims made by perennialists regarding the experiences of mystics.

Before presenting his critique it is necessary to contextualize constructivism itself. In the same way that Aquinas' theology provided the intellectual blueprint for European intellectual culture from the twelfth century to the Renaissance, so postmodern constructivism provides one of the dominant intellectual frameworks for scholars and academics working in today's universities. Indeed, postmodern constructivism is so widely accepted that in his essay Katz doesn't outline its basic tenets. He just assumes it as a given.

Postmodern thinking assumes that all our knowledge about the world is socially conditioned and culturally constructed. Philosophically this perspective goes back to Kant, who argued that we don't directly experience things in the world, rather we experience our perception of things in the world. To put it technically, a noumenon exists "out there," in the natural world, as a thing-in-itself. But we do not experience the thing-in-itself. Instead we experience the phenomena, this being our perception of the thing-in-itself. And, Kant realized, the phenomena itself is constructed in our own mind.

Kant's insight has led to the understanding today that, to a profound degree, we construct the reality in which we live. Reality is not just "out there," waiting for us to perceive it. Rather, the reality which appears to be "out there" is actually entangled in what we are "in here," within us. So when we perceive the world, what we are actually perceiving is our own perception. And we construct our understanding of the world on the basis of that perception.

This constructivist view has blossomed into a raft of contemporary disciplines, including social constructivism, constructivist psychology, constructivist learning theory, and constructivist epistemology (how we obtain knowledge of the world). In general, constructivism maintains that all our perceptions and knowledge are socially constructed, and that ultimately we don't live in the physical world. Instead, we live in an internal world of mental, emotional, and social constructs that mediate our perceptions of the world.

There are soft and extreme postmodern interpretations of this constructivist position. The soft version concedes that there is a world "out there" but that our knowledge of the world is necessarily mediated by our mental, emotional, and social constructs. The extreme postmodern interpretation is that there is nothing "out there." All that exists are our mental constructs. And because these mental constructs function on the level of language, all that exists is language. Everything is language. This is the context Katz works in, and the reason why his essay is titled *Language, Epistemology, and Mysticism*.

Katz begins his critique by offering a soft postmodern interpretation of mystical experiences:

> *There are NO pure (i.e. unmediated) experiences.* Neither mystical experiences nor more ordinary forms of experience give any indication, or any grounds for believing, that they are unmediated. That is to say, all experience is processed through, organized by, and makes itself available to us in

extremely complex epistemological ways. The notion of unmediated experience seems, if not self-contradictory, at best empty.[9]

Katz is asserting here that there are no unmediated pure consciousness events in the way that perennialists have claimed. On the contrary, he maintains every single one of our experiences is mediated. And where does the mediation in mystical experiences come from? Katz explains:

> The experience itself as well as the form in which it is reported is shaped by concepts which the mystic brings to, and which shape, his experience. To flesh this out straight forwardly, what is being argued is that, for example, the Hindu mystic does not have an experience of *x* which he then describes in the, to him, familiar language and symbols of Hinduism, but rather he has a Hindu experience, i.e. his experience is not an unmediated experience of *x* but is itself the, at least partially, pre-formed prefigured anticipated experience of Brahman.[10]

Accordingly, the spiritual experiences of Hindus, Jews, Buddhists, etc, are shaped by their religious conditioning. So what mystics experience is not God but rather "pre-formed, prefigured" concepts that have been mixed into their experiences. What they perceive as the object of their experience, i.e. God, is "at least partially" an idea conditioned into them long before they experienced anything.

A principal implication of this is that the perennialist claim that mystics from different eras and different spiritual traditions experience the same underlying reality is simply not true. No experience is unmediated. All experiences, including mystics experiences, have socially constructed concepts embedded in them. And these constructed concepts are provided by the mystic's religious conditioning, each of which exist in separate cultural eras, which form the potential mystic's consciousness and dictate the mystic's subsequent experiences.

> Thus, for example, the nature of the Christian mystic's pre-mystical consciousness informs the mystical consciousness such that he experiences the mystic reality in terms of Jesus, the Trinity, or a personal God, etc, rather than in terms of the non-personal, non-everything, to be precise, Buddhist doctrine of nirvana.[11]

Katz further argues that language is a another problem for perennialist claims that mystics have the same experiences, because technical words used in different languages during different eras and in different cultural contexts are too vague and too packed with meaning to satisfactorily be compared. He considers that words are too vague because the same words are used in very different ways: Marxists use the word *reality* in relation to economics, while Freudians use *reality* in a psychological context. And words are too packed to be adequately understood because when, for example, Plotinus used the term *One* it was freighted with his own metaphysical, cultural, and mathematical concepts and associations, to the extinct that when we read the word *One* today it cannot convey to us the same meaning as Plotinus intended.

Finally, Katz argues that the unitive states claimed by mystics as being the end result of their practices are, in fact, creations of their conditioned consciousness.

> The different states of experience which go by the names of *nirvana, devekut, fana,* etc, are not the ground but the *outcome* of the complex epistemological activity which is set in motion by the integrating character of self-consciousness employed in the specifically mystical modality. These synthetic operations of the mind are in fact the fundamental conditions under which, and under which alone, mystical experience, as all experience, takes place. These constructive conditions of consciousness produce the grounds on which mystical experience is possible at all.[12]

By the end of his essay Katz has switched from the soft to the hard postmodern position. Where he began by asserting that mystical experiences are *mediated* by religious conditioning, by the end he claims that mystical experiences are the *outcome* of that conditioning. The "constructive conditions of consciousness" are what produce the mystic experience. This view is itself contentious.

CRITIQUING THE CONSTRUCTIVIST INTERPRETATION

American perennial psychologist Robert Forman has initiated a close examination of the constructivist critique of mystical experiences. In *Mysticism, Mind, Consciousness* (1999) he edited a collection of scholarly responses to Katz's constructivist position. Forman's crittique is detailed, and I won't present all his rejoinders. Instead, I'll focus on just four points.

Our lives are socially constructed. Forman begins by acknowledging the basic validity of the constructivist thesis. Our lives are certainly very much socially constructed and historically determined. And religious rituals, beliefs, prayers, clothing, and moral proscriptions are also certainly socially constructs, put together over time and organized into different sets of religious beliefs.

Pure consciousness events are a special category of experience. Where Forman has a problem with Katz' position is that Katz doesn't provide any evidence as to why the category of pure consciousness events should be classified with other experiences that are undeniably socially constructed. Everyday experiences involve subject and object, experiencer and experienced, which are connected by intentionality and described by shared language. However, Forman points out that in PCEs subject and object are one, and neither intentionality nor language are involved. So how does social construction apply to PCEs?

Not all spiritual experiences result from conditioning. Forman also questions the proposition that all spiritual experiences are necessarily shaped by religious indoctrination. He recounts an experience of John Daido Sensei Loori, the abbot of a Zen monastery in the USA. Long before he had even heard about Buddhism, Loori was outside one day, taking part in a photography workshop, when he set up his camera in front of a tree he planned to photograph. He sat down to contemplate on the tree as the photographer running the workshop had suggested. He then entered a state of intense concentration in which he ceased to be aware of the tree or of himself. He emerged from this state four hours later. He knew four hours had passed because it was mid-afternoon he had sat in front of the tree, and it was dusk when he again became self-aware. In an effort to make sense of what had happened Loori started Zen meditation classes. Before this Loori had not been exposed to Buddhist thought. So, Forman concludes, here is an instance in which indoctrination did not precede the experience, let alone create it.[13]

Mystics from different cultures have the same experiences. Finally, in response to Katz' contention that the spiritual experiences of those involved in different traditions must necessarily be different, Forman recounts one of his own experiences. A daily meditator, Forman has for years practiced a form of meditation advocated by the Indian Advaita tradition. He had occasion to meet with Piya Tissa, an abbot of the American Sri Lankan Buddhist Society and a teacher in the Vipassyana Theravada tradition. During an interview Forman detailed his own meditation experiences, which Tissa recognized and then described in Buddhist terms. Tissa went so far as to ask if Forman had ever seen a white light during meditation. When Forman confirmed he had, Tissa also described this in Buddhist terms. So here, Forman, claims, is an instance in which the same experience was recognized by practitioners from two different traditions. Clearly, indoctrination had not prevented them from recognizing commonalities in their experiences, nor in having similar, if not identical, experiences.[14]

The issue of experience is the litmus test here. It doesn't matter what one thinker's *theory* about another's experience may be, it is in *praxis* that the true nature of experience is revealed. This is why our current lack of a taxonomy of spiritual experiences is so significant. Only with a list of the full range of spiritual experiences, and accepted descriptions and definitions of these experiences, will it be possible to enquire into the ways that indoctrination actually informs and shapes experiences, and to discriminate between conditioned and unconditioned responses. This is doubly significant because the data Katz, other constructivists, and even perennialists all draw on are predominantly accounts written by mystics hundreds of years ago. What is needed today is what Forman has begun to provide: contemporary data.

This leads to the work of two men who have grappled with the nature of spiritual experiences from a contemporary neurological perspective.

THE BIOLOGY OF MYSTICAL EXPERIENCE

In *The Mystical Mind* (1999) research psychiatrist Eugene d'Aquili and neuroscientist Andrew Newberg present a view of the contribution our brain makes to our religious beliefs and spiritual experiences.

They begin by acknowledging that among today's academia the idea of "religion" has been rejected in favor of "the religions." That is, the constructivist critique dominates to the extent that academics recognize the wide range of particular instances of religious experiences and expressions, but the concept of "religion," as a universalization of all religions' shared qualities, is no longer considered viable. Interestingly, d'Aquili and Newman argue that a neuropsychological approach to spiritual experiences and concepts can reveal universal core elements that can be disentangled from particular religious expressions.

The premise driving d'Aquili and Newman's research is that given the way our brain is structured, and given the way it processes perceptions and generates experiences and meaning, the development of religious beliefs and spiritual experiences was inevitable. They are structured into our biology. Our brain receives all the information perceived by our senses, processes it, decides how to respond to it, and initiates that response. No experience by-passes our brain. So even if we have an individual soul or spirit (d'Aquili and Newman are neutral on that possibility), the reality is that everything we experience religiously and spiritually still has to go through our brain.

Our central nervous system connects our brain to our body. It maintains the basic functions our body needs in order to respond to the world around us. Our nervous system contains two basic subsystems, the sympathetic and the parasympathetic. The sympathetic system includes an arousal function that gives rise to ergotropic qualities. The parasympathetic subsystem is the opposite, having a quiescent function that gives rise to trophotropic qualities. These two subsystems balance each other, so if the sympathetic system becomes too aroused it creates a spillover of energy and the parasympathetic system kicks in, slowing down the whole system. Similarly, if the parasympathetic system becomes too quiescent it reaches spillover, and the arousal system kicks in and gets us going again.

Five states derive from this balance. The first is *the hyperquiescent state*. We experience this during sleep, but also during meditation, chanting and prayer. The second is *the hyperarousal state*. This occurs in extreme physical exercise, in high adrenaline activities, and gives rise to a high sense of alertness and concentration and that we are floating in energy. The third is *the hyperquiescent state with eruption of arousal system*. This occurs when we become so quiescent that the arousal system kicks in and a person meditating, chanting, or dancing feels a surge of ecstasy or a sense of absorption in a higher force or being. Fourth is *the hyperarousal state with eruption of the quiescent system*. This occurs when a hyperaroused person experiences an orgasmic, ecstatic, or rapturous rush. The fifth state involves *the simultaneous maximal discharge of both the arousal and quiescent systems*. When this occurs there is evidence of "a complete breakdown of any discrete boundaries between objects, a sense of the absence of time, and the elimination of the self-other dichtomy. In other words, it may be related to the *unio mystica*, the perfect experience of the void or Nirvana, or other unitary states."[15] So the five states derived from the nervous system's arousal and quiescent subsystems provide a basic template for spiritual experiences.

The brain's other parts, particularly the limbic system and the cerebral cortex, add significant layers of complexity to these states.

The limbic system generates emotions in response to sensory inputs. So if we perceive a speeding car, a policeman, a family member, or our favorite pet, our limbic system generates excitement, fear, happiness, or love in response to that perception. The limbic system is also connected to the neocortex and so additionally generates emotions in relation to abstract thoughts.

The mind is the result of the individual parts of the brain functioning together as a whole. However, it isn't clear exactly where the brain finishes and the mind starts. They are a pair, two complementary sides of the one coin. Our sense of selfhood arises in our mind, along with art, logic, thought, and intentions. Yet without our physical brain we wouldn't have a mind at all.

The mind's complexity derives from seven cognitive operators that provide it with its primary components. *The holistic operator* places our experiences into a global context, giving us the big picture. In religion, it gives rise to our sense of God and ultimate reality. *The reductionist operator* separates individual components from the whole. *The causal operator* puts events into sequences, and also leads us to consider ultimate cause. *The abstractive operator* generates general principles from specific events and facts. *The binary operator* divides experiences and concepts into opposites, such as good and evil, happy and sad, self and non-self, heaven and hell, and also generates higher concepts that unite opposites, such as justice and community. *The quantitative operator* enables us to extract quantity from our perceptions, whether in the form of numbers, time, distance, or people. The sciences utilize this operator to powerful effect. Where all the other operators help us order the complexities of the world as we perceive them, *the emotional value operator* allows us to ascribe emotional values to that ordering. Our emotions are generated in our limbic system, but the emotional value operator connects our limbic system with our neocortex. Our religious, social, and cultural values are all shaped by this operator.

Collectively, these cognitive operators provide us with the functions we use to respond to our environment, make sense of it, act in it, and adapt to what is happening around us. But these seven operators also enable us to "see into" the world, to organize it conceptually and emotionally, and to create complex meanings in relation to it. All the religious, spiritual, moral, legal, social, cultural, intellectual, and economic frameworks we use to make sense of the world are generated by the mind's cognitive operators. Similarly, all the explanations we create to explain the world to ourselves, including our religions, philosophies and sciences, are generated by these operators.

The final significant point d'Aquili and Newman make in relation to spiritual experiences has to do with deafferentation. This occurs when the brain's information flow is interrupted, partially or totally. This is a physiological process in which neuronal activity is repressed. Epileptic seizures cause this, as may brain tumors. In normal brain functioning the brain's individual parts work together so that the mind, which draws on all the brain's functions and parts, can carry out its daily business of processing sensory information and using it to generate interpretations, responses, and behavior. Deaffrentation stops the flow of information and cuts off some parts of the brain from others. So if, for example, the orientation association area, which is responsible for our sense that our body exists in physical space, is affected by deafferentation, all sense of our physical orientation in the external world ceases, and our mind's sense of space and time vanishes. However, the orientation association area continues trying to generate a sense of time and space. But with no awareness of a physical reality to connect to it generates a sense of no space and no time, or of infinite space and infinite time.

Deafferentation, involving the by-passing of parts of the brain, is identified by d'Aquili and Newberg as a key contributor to all the heightened and unusual states of awareness that occur during mystical experiences. The most intense of these is an experience they call "absolute unitary being" (AUB), in which a subject feels that he or she is one either with God or, in the case of non-theists, with ultimate reality. Because the areas of the brain that generate a sense of individual self are cut off from one another the subject's sense of being an individual self dissolves, replaced by a sense of being one with the universal reality.

Significantly, it also appears that the brain's language centre is frequently by-passed during such experiences. The result is that the subject has a very intense experience but is unable to articulate what was experienced. Indeed, if the experience is centred in the brain's non-dominant right hemisphere, the functions in the left hemisphere may not even be aware that it has occurred. It is only afterwards, when the subject attempts to articulate the experience, that the verbal-conceptual parts of the brain kick in and assemble a description and rationale regarding what happened, using whatever language and concepts that are at hand. Yet while the conceptual and verbal expression of those expressions differ, d'Aquili and Newberg argue that all experiences of absolute unitary being are necessarily the same in all cultures.

> Clearly, in AUB experiences there can be no distinction between what is experienced by different individuals, even from totally different cultures. ... The actual experience of AUB in itself is necessarily the same for any individual who experiences it. This is necessary from a neurophysical as well as a physical perspective. It is necessarily experienced as an infinite, unified, and totally undifferentiated state.[16]

In response to Katz's constructivist interpretation of mystical experiences, d'Aquili and Newberg assert that because the brain's parts and functions are identical across cultures, religious and spiritual experiences are inevitably similar because we all use the same cognitive operators. In the case of AUB (as a pure consciousness event), the experience is identical for different people living in different cultures and eras because their brain's neurological structure and functions are the same.

This brings us to a point where we need to evaluate the perennialist and constructivist perspectives on spiritual experiences.

IS SPIRITUALITY A CONSTRUCTED PARTICULAR OR A PERENNIAL UNIVERSAL?

The claims made by a constructivist such as Katz and a psychological perennialist such as Foreman both have validity. Yet both also have to make allowances for the opposing perspective.

To begin with the perennialists, Forman acknowledges that cultural conceptual and linguistic features are undeniably embedded in religious and spiritual concepts and experiences. Indeed, the words Buddha, Krishna, Jesus Christ, Tao, Yahweh, Ein Sof, Allah, and God are cultural constructs. And clearly we learn about spirituality in specific cultural contexts. So all religious and many spiritual experiences undoubtedly are cultural constructs.

On the other hand, constructivists have to give up their claim that there are no universals, only particulars. As d'Aquili and Newberg point out, all human beings share the same brain structure and the same cognitive operators. So our creation of causal and holistic explanations, our ability to abstract universal propositions from particular instances, and our tendency to attach emotional values to ideas, provide us with neuro-psychological universals.

In addition, pure consciousness events cannot be naively treated like any other everyday experience. They are a special category of experience in which language, thought, sense perceptions, and intentionality are not present in the way they are present in our everyday experiences. Accordingly, more work needs to be done in exploring the implications of these types of experiences, and less simplistic assumptions need to be made with respect to them.

The upshot is that while we need to accommodate both constructivist and perennialist claims regarding spiritual experiences, we cannot be simplistic or naive in the way we affirm or deny either. Human experience is more varied, more complex, and far less cut and dried than either the perspectives of naive constructivists or naive perennialists allow.

What is required is that both perspectives be deconstructed, then reconstructed using new sets of operating assumptions. Robert Forman has made a start in doing so. Reflecting the modern rejection of metaphysical concepts in favor of phenomenological experience, Forman situates his foundational spiritual universals in our experience of our own consciousness.[9]

Forman begins by arguing that our subjectively experiencing consciousness, by which we are aware at all, is equally present in all human beings. As such he considers that our capacity to subjectively experience the world and ourselves is a universal experiential given and not a social construct. On the other hand, he agrees that the activity of our subjective consciousness does involve socially constructed concepts and behaviors. So the ways our subjective consciousness expresses itself is socially and culturally constructed, but our innate capacity to subjectively experience is universal.

Forman then goes on to consider the nature of our knowledge of things. He begins by drawing on the distinction psychologist William James made between knowledge-by-acquaintance and knowledge-about. Knowledge-by-acquaintance consists of direct sensory experience, while knowledge-about adds concepts and feelings to our sensory experiences, transforming them into recognizable objects, creatures, and events. Without knowledge-about our sensory experiences remain inchoate perceptions, such as of redness and of texture. With knowledge-about our perception of redness and texture is transformed into, say, a red curtain.

In neurological terms, knowledge-by-acquaintance consists of the raw data that our senses experiences produce while knowledge-about consists of the processing of that raw sensory data by our cognitive operators and limbic system. In terms of constructed particulars and perennial universals, we may say that raw sensory data is largely the same for everyone (allowing that some people are deaf or color blind, etc) and so consist of a neurological universal, while the processing reflects socially constructed concepts and feelings.

This distinction is clear. But to these two complementary ways of knowing Forman adds a third category of knowing, which he calls knowledge-by-identity. Forman argues for this third category of knowing on the basis that our knowledge that we are consciousness is not gained either via knowledge-about or knowledge-by-acquaintance. Knowledge-about involves learning, but we don't need anyone else to tell us we are conscious, nor do we learn to be conscious from others. Similarly, knowledge-by-acquaintance consists of our coming to know objects and processes that are separate from our self. But knowledge-by-identity involves our experiencing our own subjective consciousness. That is, we know we are conscious because we *are* conscious. Consciousness is innate in our awareness of ourself as an experiencing "I." As a result, Forman proposes that knowledge-by-identity should be added to our analysis of experiential knowing in general, and of spiritual experiences in particular.

This leads to a consideration of what we learn via knowledge-by-identity. Mystics commonly claim that PCEs lead to knowledge of God. Is this the case?

DO PURE CONSCIOUSNESS EVENTS DISCLOSE GOD?

A common perennialist position is that mystics experience God. Certainly, when mystics undergo a PCE and enter into the depths of their own consciousness they enter a non-ordinary state of consciousness. But does this mean they are experiencing God? Or, in the case of non-theists, ultimate reality?

For example, the ancient Indian meditators proposed that individual consciousness is identical with Brahman, the Absolute, which they also called purusha (cosmic consciousness). Accordingly, they claimed that in a PCE the meditator didn't just experience his or her own consciousness, but also experiences the cosmic consciousness that is Brahman:

> Supreme bliss arrives for that stainless yogi
> whose mind is tranquil and passions subdued,
> for he becomes one with Brahman.
> The purified yogi, merged with atman,
> then feels the endless bliss of bonding with Brahman.[17]

Similarly, Christian mystics frequently claimed that their PCEs involved a direct experience of God in which all sense of an independent conditioned self was dissolved. As John of Ruysbroeck described it:

> The enlightened have found within themselves an essential contemplation which is above reason. ... By this fruition, all uplifted spirits are melted and noughted in the Essence of God.[18]

However, there are significant differences in the assumptions made by Indian meditators and Christian mystics, which in turn lead to differences in the ways they described what occurs during pure consciousness events.

The ancient Indian meditators proposed that the individual atman (consciousness) is made of the same stuff (cosmic consciousnss) as Brahman, the Absolute. So their position was that when meditators experience their atman they necessarily simultaneously experience Brahman.

In contrast, the orthodox Christian theological position is that there is a distinction between creature and God. For the orthodox Christian creatures and God do not consist of the same substance, so orthodox worshippers cannot conceive of a direct experience of God; the intrinsic difference between the substances of God and creature prevents it. However, the Christian mystic asserts that if the worshipper loses all sense of creaturely selfhood (today we would say all conditioned sense of self), then it *is* possible to experience God. But in order to conform to the strictures orthodoxy many mystics wrote not of experiencing God but of experiencing God's Essence or, as Meister Eckhart put it, God beyond God. Thus in a PCE mystics enter their own subjectively experiencing consciousness, transcend their sense of conditioned creaturehood, pass beyond the metaphysical God of theology, and experience a unity in which the orthodox distinction between creature and God no longer exists. What exists is neither creature nor God, but that which transcends both.

Accordingly, while the Indian assumption of the identity of individual consciousness with Brahman and the Christian assumption of separation between creature and God are opposed, in the transcendence of selfhood that they both describe, and in the sense of non-conditioned unity that is experienced, they may be said to be describing the same experience.

Nonetheless, the question remains: Is what they describe an experience of God or of the Absolute? Clearly, we may agree that Christian and Indian mystics describe powerful experiences involving a transformative inwardly-felt sense of unity. But are these *experiences of God*? How we answer this question depends on how we define the relationship between God and individual consciousness.

Looking at this question from a panentheist perspective, which assumes that God is immanent in the world but also transcends it, such an experience can at most be only of a part of God. This is because the whole of what God is transcends the universe. But each of us, as a subjectively experiencing consciousness, exist within and are limited to the universe. Therefore the totality of God is intrinsically beyond us. So while a PCE may involve an experience of being immersed in God, or of becoming one with God, such an experience can actually only at most involve an aspect of the totality of what God is.

Alternatively, from a pantheistic perspective, such an experience must be with the immanent aspect of God which underlies physical reality. But does a PCE result in the disclosure of the totality of God's immanent aspect? Given the vastness of the universe, and therefore the vastness of God's immanence, and the necessarily limited nature of human consciousness, that is unlikely.

Accordingly, the traditional mystic claim that PCEs disclose God need to be set aside for now, as unproven at best, and as over-reaching at least.

However, there is one final perspective on this issue of mystic experience to consider. This is the claim made by Don Cupitt that there are no such experiences at all.

LANGUAGE GOES ALL THE WAY DOWN

Don Cupitt (b. 1934) is formerly an Anglican minister and theologian who today is one of the most interesting God-talking philosophers. Like Lloyd Geering Cupitt has adopted a non-realist position. Rejecting metaphysics, Cupitt considers that we need to face the world and recognize it as our sole reality.

In a postmodern perspective he calls Energetic Spinozism, Cupitt postulates that the basic features of human reality involve language (which we use to communicate), temporality (everything occurs in a succession), and scattering energy (language needs a body to broadcast it). The result is that:

> There is at least, then, an outpouring and scattering stream of language-formed events. And we do best to picture the world at large as a beginning-

less, endless and outsideless stream of language-formed events that continually pours forth and passes away. The stream of events becomes real and determinate, or "formed," in being read as language by us.[19]

So we live in a "stream of language-formed events." All our sense of possessing a purpose and of comprehending meaning derives from our interaction with the world as a stream of language. Cupitt additionally proposes that there is no private sub-world of consciousness within each of us. So we have no individual subjective consciousness in the way that Robert Forman proposes. Instead, we exist only within a succession of constructed linguist signs.

This is an extreme form of postmodernism, which when applied to mystical experiences, as Cupitt has done in *Mysticism After Modernity* (1995), leads to an interesting conclusion:

> There is no such thing as "experience," outside of and prior to language. ... Language goes all the way down. Language doesn't copy or convey experience; language determines or forms experience as such. Language "forms" certain events, and thereby makes them into conscious experiences. Language is mind: I mean, what we call "the mind" is secondary; it is an effect of language. St John of the Cross did not first have a language-transcending experience and then subsequently try to put it into words. On the contrary, the very composition of the poem was *itself* the mystical experience.[20]

This position may be seen as running counter to the brain research outlined by d'Aquili and Newberg that shows that language and concepts occur in just one part of the brain, and that while they play a significant role in human meaning-making they are not all-encompassing. In fact, it possible for us to bypass our brain's own conceptual-linguistic functions and to experience non-verbally and non-conceptually. So Cupitt's emphasis on language, which is characteristic of academic postmodernism in general, like Katz's constructivism does not address the full breadth and complexity of human experiencing.

Nonetheless, postmodern perspectives continue to be influential. Therefore it is necessary next to examine the postmodern perspective and to discover what it tells us about God.

CHAPTER 14

God After Metaphysics

The rise of postmodernism is commonly interpreted as a reaction against modernity and its subsequent cultural form, modernism. Modernity encompasses the broad sweep of intellectual and social developments that began in the seventeenth century outlined in Part One. The principal features of modernity include the fall of feudalism and the rise of democracy, the replacement of religiously derived values with secular values, the normalizing of liberal social freedoms, the adoption of rational thought and science as the principal means of understanding reality, and the political, economic, and cultural institutionalizing of capitalism and industrialization.

In contrast, modernism signals a dissatisfaction with modernity, which by 1860 was increasingly being seen as class-bound, rigidly devoted to rational thought, mired in realism, and as not having gone far enough to shrug off the cultural limitations of the past. Impressionism, Marxism, and Freudianism were the harbingers of modernism because they offered fresh ways of looking at the world and more profound ways of understanding human beings.

American poet Ezra Pound offered modernism's clarion call when he exuberantly declared, "Make it new!" By the early 1900s this exuberance had become modernism's hallmark and was firmly identified with the artistic avant-garde. To be modern involved embracing technology and appreciating new art, theatre, literature, and ideas. While World War One put a serious dent in modernism's exuberance, it returned during the Jazz Age of the 1920s when modernism shifted out of artistic circles and onto the wider culture. Then came the Great Depression, followed by World War Two. When the world emerged from these two overwhelming shocks European culture had lost its enthusiasm for modernism and the call to the new became limited to the sciences and space-age technologies.

Now with a much diminished audience, the modern avant-garde took its leave from the cultural main stage and returned to the artist studios and garrets from which it had emerged during the Victorian era. It only re-emerged in the 1960s, when youth culture, embodied in popular music, cinema, and the visual arts, once again echoed Ezra Pound's call to "Make it new!" and challenged the establishment with a new bout of exuberance. It was during this post-war period that postmodernism emerged.

THE POSTMODERN MOVE

Some see postmodernism as a reaction against modernism, others as a continuation of modernism's reaction against modernity, while yet others view it as just another phase of the post-Enlightenment inquiry into the nature of reality.

Postmodernism does not embody a single set of ideas. It doesn't have a central creed to which believers sign up. Instead, it is an intellectual attitude that adopts a range of related analytic tools – deconstruction, poststructuralism, semantics, linguist analysis – to critique our experience of the world. Because postmodern thinkers emphasize those aspects of postmodern practice that most appeal to them, it is more correct to refer to multiple postmodernisms rather than to any single postmodernism. Nonetheless, postmodernism displays a number of key characteristics.

First, modernity evolved over a period of three hundred years out of far-reaching cultural and intellectual changes across a wide range of disciplines. In contrast, modernism initially developed in artistic circles and among thinkers such as Marx, Freud, and Jung over a period of several decades. So both modernity and modernism emerged out of general culture. In contrast, postmodernism is an intellectual practice that developed among academics working in university contexts. And while the term postmodernism is used today to describe many different activities, from music, to fashion, to art, to hair styles, in its strict sense it applies to ways of thinking critically. So where modernity resulted from the Enlightenment project to transform Western culture, and where modernism was a multi-disciplinary movement within modernity, postmodernism is a move made by intellectuals to critique human knowledge and interactions.

As an intellectual outlook postmodernism emerged from predominantly continental universities and was driven by a weariness (hand-in-hand with a wariness) of the ways power is wielded by political and economic elites, and cynicism over how cultural hegemonies are produced and sustained. Thus Michel Foucault (who notably denied he was a postmodernist) critiqued notions of political power, the role of institutions, the nature of cultural discourse, sexuality, madness, and sanity, while Jacques Derrida interrogated the nature of texts, proposing that every text contains hidden cultural prejudices and assumptions that the techniques of deconstruction help us bring to light.

One criticism commonly made about postmodern writing is that it is frequently difficult to understand exactly what is being stated. Nonetheless, a number of themes may be identified as distinctly postmodern.

Reality is not a given. Science assumes that there is a real world "out there" with which we directly interact. However, since Kant it has been realized that this form of naive empiricism is incorrect, and that in fact we don't interact with reality. Instead we interact with our *perception* of reality. Some postmodern thinkers go so far as to assert that there is no "real world" at all, there are only signs, gestures, words, all of which need to be interpreted. So what we actually live in is not the world, but rather a world of interpretation. In this context the sciences are seen as offering just another set of interpretations among many.

Rational thought is suspect. The Enlightenment emphasis on rational thought has created intellectual straightjackets. Rational thought is suspect.

Anti-foundationalism. There are no foundations on which religions, philosophies, metaphysics, and morality may validly be based. There is no final truth, no fundamental idea, or being, or entity that illuminates all else. Some include the sciences and their discoveries in this rejection.

Anti-universalism. There are no universally valid statements. Each statement applies only to the circumstances in which it is uttered. So we cannot talk about religion in a universal sense, we can only discuss specific religions.

Anti-authoritarianism. There is no single authority in whom truth is embodied. Those who do set themselves up either as authoritative or as an authority must be critiqued and, if required, stood up to. This position has led some postmodern thinkers into political activism.

Relativism. Rather than a central foundation of truth, there are a multiplicity of perspectives, each of which are valid. This view is applied in strong and weak senses. The weak sense is that assertions are true within their particular social or conceptual frameworks. The strong sense is that nothing is true in any context. Postmodern thinkers range along the continuum that stretches between these poles of interpretation.

Contextualism. Knowledge is context-specific. It is only by coming to know something in its particular context that we can know it at all. Outside that context things make no sense – because they possess no universal qualities.

Reality consists of texts. Everything may be read as a text, including a dinner party, a game of football, a political rally, a sculpture, and a poem. Because authority is not recognized, the status of the author of any text is diminished in favor of the text itself and the reader's reading of that text. Because texts possess no intrinsic authority, they do not convey knowledge. Instead, they offer an experience. And because there are no foundational truths or values, a reader's misreading of a text is valid. However, there is controversy in academic circles over how far a text may validly be misread.

What this adds up to is a view of the world as contingent. There is no truth to be discovered. There are only individual instances of floating interpretation with which we may engage. There are no grand narratives, no metaphysical explanations, no transcendental realities existing beyond the immediacy of our experience. Some postmodernists say there isn't even a self, there isn't a subject which experiences. There is only a continuous stream of interpretation.

Today extreme postmodernism is increasingly being viewed as no longer viable. Logically, it leads to nihilism and the abandonment of values – which, in reality few actually practice (particularly when even postmodernists engage in the socially constructed exchange of working for pay). Further, postmodern relativism is circular: if nothing is authoritative, then nothing has final validity, including statements made by postmodernists denying authority and foundationalism and asserting contingency and contextualism. Certainly, postmodern thinkers such as Foucault and Derrida do not embrace the extreme conclusions of radical postmodern thought. Consequently, extreme postmodernism may be seen as a cultural phenomena that has served its purpose of challenging modernity but that has now run its course. Nonetheless, in its wake it has opened up intriguing conceptual territories for continued exploration.

It is in this context, after postmodernism, that God-talkers grapple with the notion of God today. The impact of postmodern thought has already been seen in Chapters Nine and Ten, in the way that God-talkers accept that theology can no longer validly be anchored to the metaphysics of transcendence, and that mythological texts may not be naively read as simple truths. The remainder of this chapter will explore ways that various thinkers have approached God without metaphysics. I'll start with Martin Heidegger.

MARTIN HEIDEGGER: THE END OF METAPHYSICS

The German philosopher Martin Heidegger (1889-1976) has had a huge impact on twentieth century thought. Paul Tillich was a colleague of Heidegger's at the University of Marburg in Germany in 1924, during which period he had intense discussions with Heidegger. Tillich's concept of God as Being-Itself, the Ground of all being, was influenced by Heidegger's philosophy of Being. Thus through Tillich Heidegger's ideas have influenced many Christian God-talkers, including John Macquarrie, who translated Heidegger's masterwork, *Being and Time* (1927), into English.

Heidegger's central concern was with Being. He considered that Western philosophy from Plato onwards had erred in focusing on particular beings rather than on Being itself. Much of his thinking involves exploring selected aspects of Western philosophy and tracing this historical misunderstanding of Being. Heidegger agreed with Neitzsche that the old metaphysics of God as *a* being had come to an end. Not only this, but metaphysics as a way of thinking was also dead. And because, for Heidegger, metaphysics beat at the heart of philosophy, this meant that philosophy too had come to an end.

But this didn't mean there would be no more philosophy and no more metaphysics. That would have meant the end of the work of philosophers completely, which would have put Heidegger out into the streets. Rather Heidegger asserted that "the end of metaphysics" actually constituted a new beginning for metaphysics. Heidegger found this new beginning in his concept of Being.

A key idea that drives Heidgger's thought is that Being manifests in time. This means Being becomes transitory, mortal. Heidegger called this form of temporal Being *Dasein*. Dasein is usually translated as being-in-the-world, although Heidegger found this unsatisfactory. Dasein is our existential reality as we exist in the midst of temporality. The problem for Dasein is that it lives in dread. Dasein needs to escape this dread and live an authentic existence.

Accordingly, Heidegger interpreted Neitzsche's proclaimation that God was dead as a call to find new weight and new meaning in our lives. Previously, the transcendent God of theism had given the lives of our forebears weight and meaning, because everything in their lives was related to God. But for us this is no longer possible. We are cast back onto ourselves, onto our existential existence as Dasein. What gives our life weight and meaning, what enables us to live authentically, is what Heidegger called "the fourfold."

The fourfold consists of earth, sky, mortals, and the divinities. The earth is the physical world in which we live, including the land, mountains, trees, and rivers. The sky is the sky over our heads, and includes the sun, moon and stars, as well as the rhythms of the seasons that rule our existence. The mortals are us, who live a temporal existence. And the divinities are "the beckoning messages of the godhead."[1] Influenced by Greek concepts of the ancient gods as immanent in the world, Heidegger maintained a non-religious sense of the sacred. So the divinities are not gods or actual divinities, but are instead our sense of the disclosure of Being as we dwell in mutual relations with the earth, sky, divinities, and our own mortality. In an authentic existence all four exist in oneness.

There is a whiff of German folk peasantry in all this, an association that Heidegger denied. He maintained that dwelling in the fourfold was meant in a pre-scientific sense, and that it involves a simple phenomenological relationship to things in the world. However, he argued that the arrival of a sense of the divinities, which would be followed by awareness of Godhead, can't be forced by us. We can only wait, and it will arrive – or not.

Many other thinkers, finding the idea of divinities too much of a reversion to outmoded metaphysics, ignore this aspect of Heidegger's thought. So why did Heidegger offer it? Why were the divinities important to him? The answer is that he sought in human existence some kind of deep connection with reality, and only the concept of divinities carried sufficient weight and significance to him personally in his quest for this deep connection.

Among the many thinkers influenced by Heidegger, I'll consider the thinking of just one, Jacques Derrida.

JACQUES DERRIDA: WHAT'S THE DIFFÉRANCE?

French-Algerian historian and thinker, Jacques Derrida (1930-2004), was the instigator of deconstruction. As a form of critical thinking it developed out of Derrida's concern that since Plato Western thinking has been dominated by metaphysics, especially by what he termed the "metaphysics of presence."

Derrida adopted the term "presence" from Heidegger, who considered it that traditional Western metaphysics fill our minds with concepts that take us away from focusing on our direct existential experience of being in the world. Derrida took this critique another step by arguing that the metaphysics of presence operates according to binary oppositions, such as God and man, being and becoming, eternity and time, body and soul, good and evil. The problem with this dualistic approach is that we privilege one over the other. We approve of good and disapprove of evil. Good therefore becomes a permanent presence in our thinking and evil an absence (or, at least, a desired absence). Similarly, we privilege God over humanity. Hence God has always been the creator and humanity the created; God commands and humanity obeys. Metaphysically, God is always present and humanity is, in comparison, a spiritual absence – an absence because we are mired in ignorance and sin. In the same way, all world religions have historically privileged the soul over the body and eternity over time, and Western philosophy has privileged being (permanent, spiritual, transcendent) over becoming (transitory and embedded in created matter). Even if today we consider that humanity is present and God is absent, or foreground our humanist existence in time over the spiritual existence of our soul in eternity, or feel that evil has more impact in the world than does good, we are still thinking in terms of binary opposites. So, in Derrida's view, whichever extreme we emphasize, we are dominated by the metaphysics of presence.

Derrida's response to this dominance was not to do what Western thinkers have always done and emphasize one binary opposite over the other. Instead, he chose to enter into the margins between the two, his purpose being to destabilize and question their apparently fixed relationship. This led him to the practice of différance.

Différance is not about arriving at a basic irreducible truth. What différance seeks is to explore the slippage between concepts and words. When examined through the lens of différance, a text becomes unstable, and reading becomes a play, a dance around and through the text's words and ideas. The aim is to discover what exists between sign and signified, between speech and writing, between word and concept. So where Heidegger strove to discover some higher sense of reality within our experience of the world, Derrida sought no such metaphysical foundation. Instead, he found his delight in the play between between presence and absence. However, in all this deconstructing Derrida nonetheless admitted, if not to an end point of arrival, at least to an arrival at a more profound appreciation than was apparent before any inquiry began.

> Deconstruction is not negative. It is not destructive, not having the purpose of dissolving, distracting or subtracting elements in order to reveal an internal essence. ... "Deconstruction," which in my mind is intended to

translate a word such as *Abbau* in Heidegger ... is a matter of gaining access to the mode in which a system or structure, or ensemble, is constructed or constituted, historically speaking. Not to destroy it, or demolish it, nor to purify it, but in order to accede to its possibilities and its meaning; to its construction and its history.[2]

So deconstruction is not an endless process of slice and dice. What it offers is an opportunity to arrive at an open understanding of how systems, processes, ideas, and institutions are historically constructed, how they interact with each other, and what that means at the time we consider them – given that at another time, in another context, with different questions to the forefront of our thinking, other aspects will likely capture our attention.

Morally, deconstruction is not open slather. Heidegger was a member of the Nazi party from 1933 to 1945. This has generated considerable controversy because Heidegger proposed that Dasein should maintain an authentic existence by not limiting itself to the contingencies of everyday existence. So, the question was asked, how was it that Heidegger was morally, politically, intellectually, and philosophically able to go along with Nazi politics when so many others in the 1930s saw that Nazism embodied violent totalitarianism and choose to leave Germany rather than support it? A post-war investigation decreed that Heidegger had succumbed to "herd mentality" in going along with Germany's general populace, and that although he was a member of the Nazi party, he was not guilty of collaboration. But this left answered the question of how Heidegger's concept of Dasein living an authentic existence accorded with Heidegger himself succumbing to "herd mentality." And when further evidence about Heidegger's support of the Nazi party came to light during the 1970s, debate over Heidegger's moral choices was reignited. Derrida joined this debate. So in deconstructive thinking moral choice matters, and the openness implicit in Derrida's différance cannot be identified with moral non-commitment or arbitrary moral values.

Another significant aspect of Derrida's thought is how he refused to be limited by assumptions regarding what constitutes the proper bounds of intellectual inquiry. Hence religion, the bête noir of twentieth century intellectuals, drew Derrida's attention, even if, in a typical gesture, his interest was in "religion without religion," that is, in concepts to do with religiousness and the religious rather than in the dogmatic positions of any particular religion.

In his exploration of the religious Derrida was particularly attracted to negative theology. As noted earlier, negative theology is based on the premise that God cannot be known in positive terms and that any experience of God is either ineffable or can only be described in negative terms, as "not this, not that." In other words, spiritual knowledge has a fundamental indeterminate quality. This quality of indetermination attracted Derrida because différance similarly explores indications and traces without arriving at final assignations.

In God-talk our inability to finally determine God's nature results in God being called a mystery. Derrida considered that deconstruction involved a play with and a wait for "the impossible." For Derrida, interrogating reality involves interrogating the impossible, exploring and embracing it in the hope that it may become part of the human possible. As we have seen, St John of the Cross described this embrace of God as mystery, as knowing without knowing, while Plotinus wrote of going beyond knowledge and being. Derrida acknowledged:

> What there is in Plotinus of the movement beyond being ... is something that interests me greatly. I think that deconstruction is also a means of carrying out this going beyond being, beyond being as presence, at least.[3]

This recognition in Derrida's thought of what cannot be finally determined echoes Heidegger's intent of seeking beyond a superficial experience of things to a weightier experience of reality. However, where Heidegger was overwhelmingly serious there is a refreshing humor in the way that Derrida names this indeterminateness "the impossible."

Ultimately, we are striving to understand the manifold complexities that overlap, intertwine, and are mutually embedded not just in the texts we read but in our experience of reality. Our experience of reality is extremely complex, involving phenomenological, sub-atomic, biological, neurological, technological, cultural, historical, psychological, emotional, and intellectual factors. Will we ever untangle, are we capable of deconstructing, all those factors? It's impossible. So, as Derrida gleefully points out, "the impossible" is our goal!

Underpinning Derrida's thinking about the impossible is an openness to the religious. But, as in all Derrida's thinking, he approaches the religious with hesitation, poking and prodding the margins, weighing it up, rather than naively embracing any particular religion. So Derrida embraces faith, but considers that faith helps sustain us during our on-going investigation of the impossible.

Post-Enlightenment thinkers have opposed faith to reason on the grounds that religious faith is directed towards insubstantial metaphysical illusions whereas reason enables us to engage with reality. So faith must be rejected in favor of reason. Derrida's view is that, on the contrary, faith and reason walk hand-in-hand towards the impossible. Reason provides us with the intellectual capacity to deconstruct reality, while faith pushes us onwards, towards what we don't yet know, into what reason can't yet access, towards the goal of understanding "the other." Religions yoke this faith to particular dogmas, but for Derrida faith, in itself, cannot be limited to any particular religion:

> So this faith is not religious, strictly speaking; at least it cannot be totally determined by a particular religion. That is why this faith is absolutely universal. ... This does not mean that in any particular religion you do not find a reference to this pure faith which is neither Chrsitian nor Jewish nor Islamic nor Buddhist, etc. Now I would say the same thing about the messianic. ... As soon as you address the other, as soon as you are open to the experience of waiting for the future, of waiting for someone to come: that is the opening of experience.[4]

So faith consists of opening ourselves up to the possibility that the impossible may arrive. This arrival Derrida calls the messianic. And just as faith takes specific forms in particular religions, so the messianic may exist as a particular messiah. Yet, without denying the validity of historical messiahs, Derrida sees the messianic as a universal promise or secret or gift that we feel is there, just beyond our reach, ever promising to arrive ...

Does this sound a lot like waiting for God? Another philosopher thinks so.

JOHN D. CAPUTO: EMBRACING THE IMPOSSIBLE

John Caputo (b. 1940) is an American humanist thinker whose work explores contemporary philosophy and theology. He is drawn to the ideas of Heidegger and Derrida, and has sought particularly to make Derrida's ideas clear to English-speaking readers – a welcome task given that the elliptical style of Derrida's thinking and writing frequently transforms the impossible into the impenetrable (a tendency he unfortunately shares with too many other philosophers, including Heidegger).

Caputo's book, *On Religion* (2001), offers an intriguing play with Derrida's concept of the impossible in relation to God, while his essay, *The Experience of God and the Axiology of the Impossible* (2003),[5] is a briefer exposition of the same ideas. I'll draw on this to summarize Caputo's ideas about God.

Caputo agrees with other post-religious thinkers that modernity's foundational philosophic and religious metaphysical explanations no longer intellectually or emotionally satisfy us. Traditional Western metaphysics is over. This leaves us needing to evaluate the reality of our existence not in terms of a supernatural super-reality, but in the context of our experience of daily living. With the metaphysical notion of a supernatural God no longer available, he situates God at the heart of our experience.

> Let me pose a risky hypothesis: I will venture the idea that the very idea of "experience" drives us to the idea of God ... that the very idea of "God" is of something that (or of someone who) sustains and sharpens what we mean by experience, with the result that "the experience of God" requires a "God of experience." On this hypothesis, then, "God" and "experience" are intersecting, pre-fitted notions that fit together hand in glove. This is all possible, I will hypothesize, only in virtue of the impossible, of what I call, after Derrida, "*the* impossible." The impossible will be the bridge, the crucial middle term in my logic, that links "God" and "experience."[6]

Caputo iterates that he doesn't mean "the impossible" in the sense of something that we absolutely cannot think, say, or do. Rather, he thinks of "the impossible" in Derrida's sense of a quest that takes us beyond the merely possible – which is also the pragmatic, the reasonable, the predictable stuff of living. Our passion as seekers of God within our experience becomes one of rejecting the merely possible and of seeking what we can't conceive, what we can't really get to grips with. This means that in our quest to understand God "only the impossible will do."[7]

To explain what is involved in this move into the impossible Caputo offers Derrida's idea of the "horizon of the possible." Everyday living is about living within the limits of the commonsense, the reasonable, the possible, whereas seeking God involves going beyond the limits, the horizon, of the possible.

Caputo asserts that the Western metaphysical embrace of "the horizon of the possible," and the limitation it places on our concept of God, goes back to

Kant. Kant argued that we couldn't have any perception of God because God isn't a thing to be perceived. Further, because metaphysical ideas about God cannot be verified empirically – we can't experience the eternal or the transcendent – they should be discarded. What he proposed instead was that God should be located in the moral sphere of our actions, that only in the good of our actions we may reflect the good that is God.

Caputo's critique of this position is that Kant, whether deliberately or not, became the apostle of the possible. Morality was defined by Aquinas as hinging on living according to the four cardinal virtues of practical wisdom, justice, courage, and moderation. Caputo calls the person who practices these moral virtues "the well-hinged fellow." This fellow is an exemplar of the pragmatic, the commonsense, and the reasonable. He is an expert in the possible. And when the well-hinged fellow opens the well-hinged door of reasonableness, what does he find? Nothing more than what he already knows.

But those who seek God have to go beyond the limits of what we consider commonsense and possible, beyond what we already know. Seeking God involves opening the door and entering entirely new ways of experiencing. Accordingly, Caputo asserts that in comparison to the well-hinged fellow a seeker of God is unhinged. The term "unhinged" is not an invitation to moral licentiousness. Rather, being unhinged involves embracing the impossible that resides within our experience, seeing it as a marker pointing towards God. Caputo considers that the unhinged possess the three virtues of faith, hope, and love, which he contrasts to the faith, hope, and love of the well-hinged.

The faith of the well-hinged is in what is safely known and believed. In comparison, the faith of the unhinged involves believing it is possible to go beyond what is already known, beyond what is reasonable and commonsense. The faith of the unhinged is that we can experience the impossible.

The hope of the well-hinged is in reasonable expectations, in what can be foreseen, in the hope for a future that emerges directly and understandably out of the present. In contrast, the hope of the unhinged is for what cannot be foreseen. It is hope experienced by the desperate. At those times when we feel completely hedged in, when there seems to be no future for us, when nothing can be foreseen as emerging from our present situation, in those moments all we can do is we "hope against hope" that the impossible will reveal itself. For Caputo, those are the moments when we call on God, motivated by our impossible hope.

The love of the well-hinged manifests within reasonable bounds, is limited to a circle of friends and family, and has boundaries that are never stepped over. In comparison, the love of the unhinged has no such boundaries. This love may be mad, may over-step the mark, may lack commonsense. Caputo draws attention to the Sermon on the Mount, in which Jesus says we should love our enemies and turn the other cheek to those who strike us. This is unreasonable loving that takes us past the limits of a well-hinged life.

In these formulations of unhinged faith, hope, and love Caputo is not talking in a metaphysical sense, but in terms of our phenomenological experience of living. We don't experience the impossible, we don't seek the impossible, during periods when our life plays out in an orderly fashion and when everything is under control. We do so only in moments of disorder, when our life feels like it is out of control, when we can't see our way forward, when we don't know what is going to happen next. It is in those moments that we tend to have faith in, hope for, and love of the impossible, of God.

Could we believe in and seek the impossible without calling it God? Caputo agrees we could. But in the context of our experience, he asks if there is really a difference? Quoting Augustine, he reflects on the question, "What do I love when I say I love God?" He admits this is a difficult question to answer, and that perhaps we can't answer it definitively because, ultimately, undecidability sits in the heart of our existence.

> I am simply saying, or confessing, in a kind of post-modern Augustinian confession, that we do not know who we are – to which I hasten to add: and *that* is who we are. We are not thereby left with nothing, but rather with ourselves. ... We are left holding the bag – of our passion, the passion of our non-knowing, our passion for God, of our love of God, where we do not know what we love when we love our God.[8]

Caputo concludes by observing that this experience of the impossible, to which we give the name God, can be experienced equally by those who participate or do not participate in churches. Indeed, being religious in a conventional sense is irrelevant. And that is why, following Derrida, he calls this engagement with the impossible "religion without religion."

Another approach to the question of God after metaphysics, which arrives at a similar place but via a very different trajectory, is offered by Ken Wilber.

KEN WILBER: THE EYE OF CONTEMPLATION

American integral philosopher, Ken Wilber (b. 1949), has explored the issue of spiritual experience and knowing in a series of wide-ranging and influential books. He has synthesized ancient and contemporary knowledge, including philosophy, biology, developmental psychology, cultural thinking, and much else, to create what he terms an integral approach to spirituality. The best introduction to his work is *A Brief History of Everything* (1996). In *The Marriage of Sense and Soul* (1998) Wilber presents a succinct introduction to his ideas that covers the same period of history that is being examined here. I have principally drawn on the latter work to create the following summary, which offers only a tiny taste of Wilber's multi-faceted thinking.

Wilber's analysis is that premodern, modern, and postmodern outlooks each exist side by side in contemporary approaches to reality. The premodern period, which lasted culturally up to the Renaissance, was dominated by magical thinking, religious mythologizing, and vertical social hierarchies. The period of modernity, which began after 1620, replaced the magical, religious, mythological perspective with a rational, empirical, scientific outlook. Modernity replaced the supernatural with the natural, separated church and state, dismantled social hierarchies, and introduced secular freedoms and rights.

Modernity also played a highly significant cultural role in that it created a differentiation between aesthetics-art, empiricism-science, and morality-religion, realms that Wilber calls the Big Three. Before the Renaissance these three spheres were undifferentiated. Furthermore, they were dominated by religion. So Galileo's empirical discoveries were made subservient to religion, as was Michelangelo's art. Only during the modern era were these three spheres differentiated, which in turn allowed scientists and thinkers to work without the interference of religious authority. The freedom of modernity enabled scientists and thinkers to make astounding advances in just three centuries.

Wilber calls this achievement the dignity of modernity. The dignity of modernity is reflected in the features of the world that we glory in today (however inadequately they are put into practice): social freedoms; universal education; technological advances; notions of social justice, sexual and racial equality; and the values of liberal democracy. Yet modernity has also proven to be a disaster.

The disaster of modernity is that this differentiation of the Big Three quickly turned into disassociation. Aesthetics-art, empiricism-science, and morals-religion were not just separated, they spun away from each other. The result was they were transformed into disconnected, stand-alone realms of activity. Art, science, and religion no longer talked to each other as they had during the premodern era, when they were three aspects of the one religious world view. And to clinch the disaster, the empirical sciences quickly came to dominate the modernist outlook, diminishing the significance of the other two realms.

Another way of viewing this dissociation is in terms of the Good, the True, and the Beautiful. The Good is the realm of justice, of ethics, and of how we treat one another. The True refers to objective, measurable, empirical truths of the type that the sciences deal in. And the Beautiful manifests in aesthetics and in the valuations we each make as discriminating individuals. Wilber observes that each of these three spheres has a different language. The Good involves WE language, because it focuses on the shared social realm of our communal interactivity. The True uses IT language, because it deals in objective entities. And the Beautiful uses the I language of subjective expression.

The differentiation of the Big Three of morality, sciences, and aesthetics was actually culturally useful at the start of the modern era because each came to be seen for the distinct realm that it is. The opportunity that was then on offer was to *reintegrate* the Good, the True, and the Beautiful on a new and higher level. What actually happened was *disintegration and dissociation*. And not only did a gulf open up between each of the Good, the True, and the Beautiful, but the objective scientific outlook of the True was elevated above the other two. As a result, scientific IT language has come to dominate Western culture at the expense of interior I impressions and shared WE values. This diminishment of the Good and the Beautiful in favour of Truth caused the disaster of modernity:

> Put bluntly, the I and the WE were colonized by the IT. The Good and the True were overtaken by a growth in monological Truth that, otherwise admirable, became grandiose in its own conceit and cancerous in its relations to the others. Full of itself and flush with stunning victories, empirical science became *scientism*, the belief that there is no reality save that revealed by science, and no truth save that which science delivers. The subjective and interior domains – the I and the WE – were flattened into objective, exterior, empirical processes, either atomistic or systems. ... Art and morals and contemplation and spirit were all demolished by the scientific bull in the china shop of the consciousness. And there was the disaster of modernity.[9]

Modernity's collapse of I and WE into IT Wilber calls flatland. Flatland is characterized by the way that everything in human culture is viewed in terms of sense experiences, of things, of exteriors. And whatever cannot be seen as exterior – as interpersonal values and subjectively generated meanings are not – either had to be reduced to measurable ITs, or else was rejected as possessing no true significance. This view arguably reached its apogee with the logical positivists who asserted that only statements that could be tested by empirical measurement were valid. So statements that concerned things that could not be physically measured, such as the nature of goodness or the experience of of God, were declared to be nonsensical and invalid.

Wilber contends that it has become clear that scientism's flatland view of reality is severely limited because it only tells us one aspect of the story of what our existence involves. But this situation has a plus side, in that it has created an opportunity for postmodern thinkers to generate the long-required integration of Truth, Good, and Beauty. The problem is that postmodern thinkers weren't interested in integration. Instead, their strategy became to discredit the sciences. They did so by asserting that the objective, empirically measuring sciences offer no more than one of many possible interpretations of reality. So, Wilber argues, where science had previously killed off religion and art, now postmodernism killed off science. The result was all the Big Three lay eviscerated on the highway of academic excess.

Wilber considers that there is much in postmodern thinking that is valuable and worth retaining. For example, he argues that we need to accept that reality is not entirely a given but is interpreted, that meaning is context-dependent, that no single perspective is privileged, and that we have to pay careful attention to language and to the relationship between signifiers and signified.

But, and here Wilber's critique becomes pungent, the problem with extreme postmodernism is that by emphasizing interpretation to the exclusion of all else, by arguing reality consists of nothing but sliding signifiers, by saying there are no subjects having experiences, and that there are no intersubjective realms of shared values and meaning, postmodernists are actually continuing the disaster of flatland scientism. This is because extreme postmodernists remove the subjective component from human experience when they maintain that reality contains no interiors whatsoever, that is has no within.

Wilber considers that in order to extract ourselves from the wasteland posited by extreme postmodernism, what need to re-establish the interior and the subjective, the WE and the I, as valued aspects of our reality. Wilber suggests a post-postmodernist reintegration of the Big Three will help us achieve that. And the empiricism of the sciences is a significant factor in this reintegration.

One of the principal drivers of modernity was the acquisition of evidence. Researchers, scholars, and scientists sought new data and new information about the world. It was this new data that enabled post-Enlightenment thinkers to see reality in ways that were previously inconceivable within a mythic world view. Wilber suggests that rather than ignoring that principle of basing our world view on the collection of data, what we should do is push the evidence accumulation further and deeper. We need to move beyond flatland, beyond surfaces, and start accumulating data about reality using each of the Big Three. Wilber considers that we may do this by perceiving in three different but complementary ways, utilizing the eye of the flesh, the eye of the mind, and the eye of contemplation.

The eye of the flesh observes and interacts with data generated by the physical world; the eye of the mind perceives and interacts with mental data such as logic, mathematics, and concepts; and the eye of contemplation perceives and interacts with data received during spiritual experiences. The key is experience. Experience on the different but complementary levels of the physical, the mental, and the spiritual. The spiritual offers us the means of integrating all three.

> Authentic spirituality, then, can no longer be mythic, imaginal, mythological, or mythopoetic: it must be based on falsifiable evidence. In other words, it must be, at its core, a series of direct mystical, transcendental, meditative, contemplative, or yogic experiences – *not sensory* and *not mental*, but transsensual, transmental, transpersonal, transcendental consciousness – data seen not merely with the eye of flesh or with the eye of mind, but with the eye of contemplation.[10]

These three ways of experiencing also offer complementary ways of conceiving of God. With the eye of the flesh we can glory in the presence of the immanent God in the physical world around us. With the eye of the mind we can consider God in terms of moral value, personal meaning, and in the patterns that underlie both physical phenomena and the events our lives. And with the eye of contemplation we can enter deep, self-reflexive, non-verbal and non-conceptual ways of experiencing.

But the point is *we don't have to choose between these three ways of perceiving*. It is not that one perspective is right and the other two are wrong. Rather they are three different but equally valid ways of experiencing and interacting with reality. It is only by embracing and honoring all three approaches that we are able to reintegrate the Big Three of the Good, the True, and the Beautiful and arrive at a multi-faceted concept of the world and God that allows for surface and depth, subject and object, constructed and innate.

THE CALL TO EXPERIENCE

Wilber's contention that the answers to our deepest questions about reality are best sought in the data we accumulate via multi-faceted experience is clearly not a new concept. The mystics of all the world's religions have long been technicians of the spirit, exploring their own experience in order to discover new data, that they called mystic knowledge, about reality.

But, as has been shown, today we recognize the extent to which the writings of the ancient mystics, in which they described their experiences, are interwoven with metaphysical, theological, and mythological assumptions and language that we can no longer accept on face value. We live in a world that is very different to the world those mystics occupied, which means we cannot naively adopt their conceptual and religious frameworks.

Accordingly, contemporary thinkers reject traditional religious metaphysics, theologies, and mythologies in favor of confronting and examining the existential nature of our experiencing the world. And that also means locating God in the context of our experience. This is what thinkers such as Heidegger, Tillich, Derrida, and Caputo have done, situating Being-Itself, or the impossible, or God in the existential reality of our experience as human beings.

On the other hand, it could be argued that philosophers don't go far enough in their explorations of human experience. This is because they stop at conceptual-verbal formulations of our experience. In contrast, the aim of the ancient mystics was to enter experientially into their own subjectively experiencing consciousness, using prayer and meditation as pragmatic means of plunging into their own awareness and exploring where that led them.

What adds yet another layer to this discussion of experiential knowledge is that the types of spiritual experiences described in mystic literature are actually far more common that is generally proclaimed. The fact is that none of us have to be a medieval mystic, or even a contemporary one, in order to have a spiritual experience. In his study *Religious Experience Today* (1990) David Hay reveals evidence of the frequency with which otherwise quite ordinary people have spiritual experiences. To quote some of his statistics, drawn from eleven surveys conducted from 1962 to 1987 in Britain, USA, and Australia:

- An average of 35% attested to having had a spiritual experience.
- Experiences were spread evenly across all age groups.
- Experiences included becoming aware of patterns in events, the presence of God, a guiding presence which was not God, the presence of the dead, an evil presence, a sacred presence in nature, an experience of oneness, and receiving help as a result of praying.
- 24% of atheists had had a spiritual experience, as had 23% of agnostics, and 23% of those who had no religious affiliation.
- An average of 36% had never told anyone about their experiences.[11]

Hay makes the point that while most spiritual experiences appear to occur to people when they are alone, the triggers for those experiences vary considerably. The most frequent trigger described in a 1978 survey was listening to music, followed by prayer, experiencing the beauties of nature, quiet reflection, attending a church service, listening to a sermon, watching small children, reading the Bible, and being alone in a church. However, Hay notes that triggers and circumstances actually included virtually all aspects of human experience:

> Religious experience has occurred in every conceivable human context, including the grimness of a slum, on a battlefield, in a concentration camp, in the midst of torture, during the conduct of a scientific experiment, in a business office, during radiation treatment for cancer; in fact, it is impossible to find any human situation whatsoever where such experience could not occur – indeed, has not occurred.[12]

POSTMODERNISM AND SPIRITUALITY

However, in the context of the wide range of human spiritual experiences the great lesson of postmodernism is that we cannot assume a simple relationship between our experiences and our descriptions of those experiences.

When we use words and concepts to describe an experience that was highly significant to us, we use words that already, before our experience, meant something significant to us. And we don't make up those words. We learn them. So all the words we use to describe what happens to us, and all the concepts we attach to those words, are already culturally constructed and freighted with meanings given them by our forebears and contemporaries. This includes the word God.

So God is partially a culturally pre-given construct and partly a negotiated adjustment to that construct, a negotiation that we carry out in the context of our own subjective experiences. This is why the postmodern emphasis on questioning our assumptions, of challenging what we know, and especiallly of reminding us that *what we know really only consists of what we think we know* is so important. The upshot is that because our understanding of our own subjective experiencing and knowing is open, not closed, so God, who we can only approach in the context of our experience, must also remain an open question. Ultimately, God is not a question that we are capable of fully and answering and closing.

So where has that brought us in this exploration of revolutionary concepts of God?

PART 3

GOD FOR TODAY

CHAPTER 15

The Post-God God

Nietzsche's 1882 declaration of God's death stands at a cultural turning point. The God whose death he announced was the personal God of theistic Christianity. But, as we saw in Part One, by 1882 this God had already died for innumerable thinking people. And while this death did necessarily lead thinkers to reject the idea of God outright, for others it stimulated a search for new concepts. Accordingly, from today's perspective Nietzsche's declaration may be viewed as signalling not so much the end of the God as the beginning of a new phase of thinking about God.

Before Nietzsche the God of Christianity had become a known entity who was defined by long-established dogma, celebrated through mythology, and worshipped in ritual. After Nietzsche the notion of God returned to its ancient state of an unknown before which we need to hesitate before making pronouncements regarding what God is. This unknown is the post-God God.

The term "post-God God" includes all thinking that places God beyond the God of mythology, beyond the God of metaphysics, beyond the God of religious dogma. Whether called the God beyond God, the Being beyond beings, the Ground of being, Being-Itself, or the Impossible, the post-God God is the elusive God we each have yet to discover.

Catholic God-talker Elizabeth Johnson has proposed that there are three points we need to keep in mind during our search for God. First, God is a mystery, the fullness of which we cannot express in words. Second, because words are inadequate, we can only use a metaphorical approach that likens God to things we comprehend. Therefore no statement about God is literally true. And third, because no single statement encompasses the totality of what God is, many different words and perspectives are valid. But none is definitive.

Definitive explanations are not possible because the old certainties of traditional religions are no longer sustainable. God can no longer be thought of as a being seated in the drawing room of metaphysical certainty, behind curtains of spiritual mystery theology draws back to reveal the truth. Rather, the post-God view is that any concept we propose about God is just that – a proposal.

As a consequence, what we say in our God-talk is not *the* truth, but is at best *a* truth that embodies what we have discovered. So far. The following seven points offer a broad outline of post-God thinking about God:

- *Pluralism.* There are many different culturally and historically determined ways in which people may validly express their understanding of God.
- *Exclusivity claims are invalid.* No one religion, no single form of spiritual expression, has the truth packed in a box and tied with truth's ribbon.
- *Perennialism holds.* All human beings, no matter what era or culture they live in, share the same neurological configuration and cognitive capacities. These naturally univeralize our experiences and our understanding of God (even if not everyone chooses to do so).
- *Perennialism is buffered by constructivism.* Nonetheless, shared experiences and understanding manifest in culturally constructed environments.
- *Ideas are part of our experience, not their prime shaper.* We receive and develop ideas both before and after our experiences. But spiritual experiences, as with our other types of experience, are not exclusively or even necessarily centred in the verbal-conceptual parts of our mind. We experience in other ways than the conceptual-verbal.
- *Understanding is grounded in subjectivity.* Ideas about God are inextricably bound up in our innate subjectivity, which combines perennial impulses, subjective experiencing that contains both perennial and conditioned elements, and culturally conditioned expression.
- *Subjectivity is the key.* Spiritual experiences, and the understanding that we derive from them, are just a portion of our total experience of reality. So any questions about God are intimately caught up in the mystery of our existence as subjectively experiencing beings.

This last observation leads to a consideration of the nature of knowing.

OUR KNOWING IS SUBJECTIVE

Because our consciousness is inherently subjective, objective descriptions of how we perceive and obtain knowledge (whether scientific, religious, neurological, or philosophic) have so far proved difficult, even impossible, to develop and sustain. This same problem applies when we attempt to obtain and justify knowledge of God. Only we experience what is going on inside ourselves during any experience, God-focused or otherwise. And we cannot directly and objectively communicate to others what our awareness experiences. Language only presents approximately, in allusive (and elusive) ways, the content of our subjective experience. This leads to five realizations.

1. *We live in a subjectively experienced "now."* Alfred Whitehead attempted to grapple with the subjectivity of our awareness by defining actual existing entities as occasions of subjective experiencing. In his view our awareness partakes in an ongoing flow of data processing. Our subjective awareness takes in data, processes it, and passes it out to other entities. Our memory of previously processed data gives us our sense of the past. And our appreciation that more data is arriving gives us our awareness of the future. So our awareness rides a continuous data wave, which comes at us from the "future" and passes on into the "past," on which we balance like a surfer riding the crest of a wave that never breaks. We are each aware that we are riding the wave of the present moment, but we can't stop the experience and stand back to objectively examine what is going on. Accordingly, as we balance on the wave of the present moment, we are unable to give an objective account of what occurs during any single instance of subjective awareness, because as soon as we attempt to examine a particular experience ... it has already gone.

2. *This is why pure consciousness experiences are significant.* One way of observing what is going on during the activity of subjective experiencing is to turn our awareness back on itself and make the activity of our own subjective experiencing the object of our awareness. By turning away from the objects we experience via our senses, by shucking off the everyday contents of awareness that usually fill our consciousness and instead turning our awareness back onto itself, we become open to what is at the core of us as subjectively experiencing beings. Interestingly, at our perceptual core we are subjectively experiencing awareness, yet this subjective awareness is mysterious to us. We experientially know, and we know that we know, yet we do instinctively grasp *what* knows.

3. *So our knowing needs to admit the unknown and the unknowable.* This is why Derrida's comments on the ultimate undecidableness of experience, his suggestion that we are seeking the unknowable trace, the impossible, is so pertinent.

Our knowing is a subjective process that does not, that cannot, produce objective finality. Accordingly, we can never objectively nail down, once and for all, what God is. What happens instead, if we adopt an open approach, is that our ongoing experiences of the world reveal new territories for exploration. So we need to incorporate openness into our search to understand God in any way.

4. *Rationality and the inexplicable can hold hands in a spirit of openness.* While human beings naturally possess and drive to understand reality and God using rational thought (especially the capacities of our cognitive operators), it remains necessary to leave space for what we cannot currently explain. The inexplicable deserves that space because, as human history shows us, over time we will gradually inhabit it and integrate it into what we do understand. Accordingly, if we reject outright what is currently inexplicable then we deprive ourselves of the opportunity to explore it and one day make it rationally understood. So our drive towards rationality needs to adopt a spirit of openness and accommodate the inexplicable.

5. *We can know without knowing.* Some parts of us are capable of processing apparently inexplicable experiences and adjusting our awareness to them. We can experientially *know* without necessarily being able to *say*. Yet not being able to say does not invalidate our knowing.

These five points have a serious impact on what we can know and say about God, first because God is not an object like other objects in the world, and second because there is an indefiniteness, a mystery, at the heart of our awareness that impacts on everything we can experience and know.

So what can we now say about the post-God God?

WHAT IS THE POST-GOD GOD?

If God is not a thing, not a supernatural being, not a personal being, not an object among all the other objects in the universe, what is the post-God God? By way of answering this question, I'll explore four propositions.

1. *"God" is a special type of word.* Lloyd Geering draws attention to the fact that God is a symbolic word that we each fill with content and meaning. However, because the ways we experience and gain knowledge about the world involve subjective awareness, any meaning we give to God necessarily has subjectivity built into it. This leads to the issue of projection. We each generate the interpretations, values, and meaning that we extract from our conditioning and

experiences, and subsequently project them onto the world. Just as we project motives onto others based on our understanding of our own and others' motives, so we project our personal interpretations, values, and meaning into the word God.

2. *God as dipolar.* Alfred Whitehead and John Macquarrie proposed that God includes and embraces opposite qualities. Thus rather than having to choose between God as transcendent or immanent, prior or consequent, loving or detached, they proposed that God includes each opposite. The implication of this is that while dipolar concepts offer us a way of thinking objectively about God, nonetheless, because God cannot be reduced to any single quality, God ultimately remains objectively inexplicable, a mystery.

3. *God as a fulcrum.* In the context of our subjective experiencing of the world, and in relation to the values and meanings we generate to explain our experiences, God functions as a fulcrum. By this I mean we naturally place God at the very centre of what is most significant and meaningful to us. Paul Tillich attempted to capture this sense of God as fulcrum when he described God as ultimate concern. God as fulcrum embodies what we human beings consider to be ultimate in our lives and in the universe, and what attracts our deepest and most profound concern. So God as fulcrum becomes the centre of our deepest concerns, an indeterminacy at the heart of our experience that we cannot fully articulate, but that we nonetheless know is there.

4. *God as negotiation.* However we conceive of God, in the end the notion of God cannot be wholly captured in any single statement, whether dipolar or otherwise. Our thinking may only ever tentatively approaches, but never fully captures, God as God. Accordingly, God is perhaps most appropriately thought of as a negotiation. Through the course of our lives we generate ideas regarding what is going on (or take on board ideas others have generated to explain their experiences). These ideas form an ongoing negotiation we have with the world and ourselves. Any idea we have about God necessarily arises out of that negotiation. God is the focus of our ongoing negotiation with reality, via which, by degrees, we approach an understanding of what is happening to us and others as we surf the data wave of the now.

Yet perhaps there is a way to be a little more definite than this. I'll attempt to do so by offering my personal thinking on God.

CHAPTER 16

A Pertinent Proposal?

During the eleventh century Anselm of Canterbury offered a definition of God as "that than which nothing greater can be conceived." Anselm captured in this proposition a key aspect that we continue to associate with God: ultimacy. Whatever God might be to itself, for us God represents that which is greatest, most powerful, most knowing, and so on.

But any notion of God as ultimate is necessarily tied to our ideas of reality. When we assert that God is the greatest, most powerful, and most knowing, what we are doing is describing God in relation to qualities, objects, and processes that make sense to us in the context of our human experience.

Until the Renaissance the Western concept of reality was underpinned by Ptolemaic cosmology. Ptolemy was a second century Greek astronomer who created a geocentric model of the universe that was accepted as fact into the modern era. The Ptolemic model placed the Earth at the centre of the universe, with God's heaven stationed just beyond the fixed stars that circled the Earth. Christian theologians conceived of God as a super-being living in His heaven just beyond the stars, in a handy position to intervene in human affairs whenever He decided to do so.

But in the early 1600s Brahe, Kepler, and Galileo, building on ideas proposed a few decades earlier by Copernicus, showed that the Ptolemaic model was wrong and that the Earth actually circles the Sun. In the 1920s Edwin Hubble added to this heliocentric model by showing that the Milky Way is merely one among innumerable galaxies. Suddenly reality, as perceived in the physical form of the universe, effectively became infinite to us.

Accordingly, any consideration of God as ultimate must accept that the infinite physical universe is the reality in which we live, and that any ideas about God must be shaped in relation to the effectively infinite universe.

However, complicating this is that we perceive only a tiny portion of the physical universe. And cosmologists keep discovering new features that expand our knowledge of what constitutes the universe. Accordingly, all that we can definitely state about the universe is that it is vaster than we can possibly imagine, that we know hardly anything about it and, unsurprisingly, that it keeps surprising us.

A further consideration is that, on the basis of probability, the universe is so vast that it is certain to contain non-terrestrial forms of life. To assert that during the fourteen billion years or so that have passed since the big bang *no* other form of self-conscious life besides human beings has developed anywhere in billions of galaxies seems to be more a form of geocentric narcissism than a reasonable likelihood. In fact, given that as I write this scientists have just discovered a new biology of life on Earth (in which arsenic takes the place of phosphorus), there may very well be forms of life in the universe that are so different from terrestrial biology that even if we were staring right at them we wouldn't recognize them as living beings. Clearly, given how little we actually know about the universe, let alone about other beings in it, even for us to tie self-conscious awareness to a carbon-based physical body is just an assumption. Over time human beings may very well discover other ways of being conscious, alternative to walking around in a body. We need to remain open to any possibility.

Accordingly, to adopt Anselm's proposition, given the limits of our knowledge, and given that the entirety of the universe constitutes a reality that is vaster than anything we could possibly conceive, I propose that the universe itself constitutes "that than which nothing greater can be conceived." I name this totality The Whole Of What Is.

THE WHOLE OF WHAT IS

As a name for reality, I propose that The Whole Of What Is encompasses not only everything that we are certain exists in the universe, but also everything that we know nothing about, in whichever dimension, including everything existing that we human beings will certainly never experience or comprehend.

In harmony with Spinoza's thinking, the Whole Of What Is is not only the ultimate existent, it is also the *only* existent. Because nothing can exist separate from the totality of reality, (if it isn't part of reality it doesn't exist, and if it doesn't exist it can't be real) everything that exists is necessarily a part of The

Whole Of What Is. Therefore nothing exists but The Whole Of What Is. This makes The Whole Of What Is the only existent. It is the totality of all that is. Apart from The Whole Of What Is nothing can, does, or ever will exist.

So where does God exist in relation to The Whole Of What Is?

GOD AND THE WHOLE OF WHAT IS

Anselm defined God as "that than which nothing greater can be conceived." However, because this definition equally applies to The Whole Of What Is, I propose that The Whole Of What Is also a name for God.

Of course, we could just as easily talk about The Whole Of What Is and leave God out of it altogether. In fact, avoiding using the name God would be no bad option given all the strange ideas and activities human beings have generated around the word over the millennia. But whichever term we use, we are still talking about the totality of what is as the ultimate existent.

One of the implications of accepting The Whole Of What Is as God is that it may equally be used in relation to pantheistic, panentheistic, and theistic concepts of God.

With respect to pantheism, because only The Whole Of What Is exists, everything that exists is part of, is infused by, and participates in The Whole Of What is. Therefore it may validly be viewed from a pantheistic perspective.

With respect to panentheism, because so much of The Whole Of What Is remains unknown to us, and because so much will always remain beyond human experience and conception, God as the Whole Of What Is is not limited to what we may perceive and conceive. By its very nature The Whole Of What Is transcends our comprehension.

Conversely, if we desire a personal God to worship then The Whole Of What Is provides both a visible God, in its manifestation as the entire universe, and a panentheistic deity that includes both the visible universe and everything else that is in it yet exists beyond our comprehension.

So, in a very real sense, it doesn't matter whether we conceive of The Whole Of What Is in personal, pantheistic, or panentheistic terms – because the fact is that whatever we say about it is inherently partial, limited and, in an ultimate sense, wrong. Yet no matter what we correctly or erroneously assert, it is within The Whole Of What Is that we continue to live, move, and have our being. We are a part of The Whole Of What Is no matter what we think, feel, or do.

IS THE WHOLE OF WHAT IS CONSCIOUS?

Is The Whole Of What Is, which I am also calling God, conscious as we are conscious? Does The Whole Of What Is subjectively experience reality in anything like the way that we subjectively experience reality?

In order to address this question I need to introduce the notion of scale. If The Whole Of What Is does possess a capacity to subjectively experience, given the vast difference in scale between us and The Whole Of What Is, the nature and process of its subjective experiencing and feeling is necessarily of a completely different order to what we human beings experience and feel.

Thinking about the scale of The Whole Of What Is in physical terms, when we look out from the Earth the nearest star, Proxima Centauri, is 4.22 light years (40 trillion kilometres) away. It is a similar distance from our Milky Way Galaxy to our nearest galaxy, Alpha Centauri.

In turn, the Milky Way is part of the Local Group of galaxies. The Local Group contains 30 galaxies, made up of around 700 billion stars, and is 5 light years across. Star nurseries exist within these galaxies, consisting of swirling clouds of molecular gas which collapse under gravitational force to form the stellar plasma from which new stars are born.

The Local Group is part of the Local Supercluster. It contains around 100 groups of galaxies, 2000 galaxies in all, and is approximately 110 million light years across. In its entirety the Local Supercluster is 100 billion times the size of the Milky Way, yet is small compared to other superclusters.

A discovery made in recent decades is that our Local Supercluster is being drawn gravitationally towards a region called the Great Attractor. This has a mass equivalent to tens of thousands of galaxies and is attracting galaxies hundreds of millions of light years away from it. As yet we know little about it.

On the next scale up superclusters join together to form sheets or walls of galaxies. The largest yet discovered is the Sloan Great Wall. Around 1.37 billion light years in length, it contains millions of galaxies. There are likely millions of these sheets or walls. Together they form filaments that look like immense fingers stretching through the void of galactic space. So on this scale the universe is laced with filaments of light emanated by immense sheets or walls of superclusters of galaxies.

At the next scale up a feature astronomers call the End of Greatness occurs. On this scale the universe becomes a homogeneous blend, in which the individual filaments of superclusters disappear, leaving a smoothed out texture of light rippling across the background darkness of interclustural space.[1]

In the context of this unimaginable immensity, questions such as whether God, as The Whole Of What Is, is conscious as we are, or subjectively experiences and feels as we do, simply fades away. Indeed, we cannot say much at all, given that we are far smaller in relation to the End of Greatness than a bacteria is minute in relation to us. And just as bacteria can have no inkling of the nature of our subjective consciousness and cannot appreciate the complexity of our experiencing, so we can have no appreciation of what occurs at these highest scales of the universe.

Accordingly, the claim that human beings are the pinnacle of conscious beings existing in the universe is clearly untenable. To continue with the bacteria analogy, we know that bacteria exist on a scale physically "below" us. Yet while they are not conscious as we are, they are born, reproduce, and die, and so have their own bacterial level of consciousness. They are, in Whitehead's terms, subjectively experiencing actual entities. Logic says that we need to extrapolate beyond our human existence and assume that just as we exist as complex subjective experiencing beings existing on a level "above" bacteria, so other beings existing at an even more complex level of experiencing exist beyond us. To think otherwise, to assert that living beings exist on a lower scale than us but none exist on a higher scale, that conscious life in the universe has reached its peak with human beings, is unreasonable.

Indeed, it is interesting to speculate that The Whole Of What Is is a living conscious being, with us existing in it as cells exist within our bodies. Of course, we have no way of knowing whether this is so, or how it might be so. Nonetheless, given the limits of our experiential and conceptual reach we need to be careful not to deny real possibilities. Openness remains a necessary strategy.

GOD AND EVOLUTION

Evolution offers further fascinating possibilities in relation to The Whole Of What Is. As just noted, the assumption that biological life on Earth is a cosmic anomaly, never repeated anywhere else, is untenable. This means that it is very possible that evolution applies across the universe, and that there is no reason to assume that other forms of life are carbon-based and breath oxygen like us. They may not even exist in bodies at all.

As noted in Part Two, both Alfred Whitehead and John Haught considered God and the universe in relation to creativity and evolution.

For Whitehead, the universe is involved in an endless process of creativity. God provides the creative possibilities, while living entities choose from those possibilities and subsequently actualize what they have chosen in physical reality. So the universe is endlessly creative. And nothing is preordained. Rather, reality consists of a moment-by-moment revelation of what is to be. Even God doesn't know how things will turn out until they do so.

For Haught the universe exists as *kenosis*, an out-pouring from God's own being. Like Whitehead, Haught proposes that God has no pre-determined plan regarding what the universe will become. Rather God is involved, along with all the universe's conscious beings, in a creative process of growing, developing, and evolving into what is to become.

For both Whitehead and Haught we human beings, as actual existing entities, perform a vital function within The Whole Of What Is by actively and creatively contributing to its evolution. As Whitehead put it, we are co-creators of reality with God, even if we are so with every other conscious entity in the universe.

Where it will all end up, who knows. But we can live knowing we may be tiny parts, but that our existence contributes, however minutely, to the evolving reality of The Whole Of What Is.

CHAPTER 17

God As Quest

Why does God remain significant in an era when there have been such radical changes to the ways we human beings view reality? Today it is possible (many would say desirable) to live a satisfying, creative life without reference to God. So why is God still important to us?

Complexifying this question is that unlike, say, a table, God is not available to our senses. The word "God" is just a sound, a sprinkling of letters written on a page. As a sound, as a cipher, "God" only has the meaning that we give it. It is a meaning we could very well choose not to explore. Yet in the context of today's post-religious grassroots spirituality, and despite the problems so many have with religious dogma, rules, and institutions, ideas of a transcendent, immanent, or personal God continue to be meaningful to many of us.

The concept of the transcendent God remains meaningful because it symbolizes our desire for self-transcendence. This applies whether we view self-transcendence in terms of rising above the limitations and frustrations of daily life, or of overcoming our personal limitations and failings, or of our individual continuance after our body dies. The transcendent God is also significant to us during those times when we become aware of participating in a reality that transcends all that we are. This gives rise to emotions we class as religious or spiritual, including a sense of smallness, gratitude, amazement, wonder, and awe. At such moments we have a natural inclination to direct our feelings towards God, which we identify with the transcendent totality of all that is.

The immanent God remains meaningful to us today because it symbolizes the perplexing fact of our own consciousness, and encompasses our unfathomable experience of being self-conscious and aware entities living in a present moment that overflows with the layered complexity of subjective experiencing. The profound mysteriousness of our subjective experiencing gives rise to our sense that there is "something" deeper than we are immediately aware of hidden within our moment-by-moment existence. We call this hidden immanent "something" God. Yet God is really just a symbolic word that references all that we sense exists in our experience but that we are unable to identify. The mystery of the immanent God thus reflects the mystery of our own existence as self-conscious beings, the mystery that anything aware exists at all.

The notion of God as personal remains meaningful because life is personal. Our perceptions, feelings, and thoughts are all centred on our personal experiences as self-conscious beings. From these personal perceptions, feelings, and thoughts we construct notions of the sacred, notions that we subsequently project onto other beings, objects, and processes around us. Examples include when we look at the stars in the night sky and feel an astounded reverence at the unimaginable immensity of which we form a tiny part, or when we look at the Earth and perceive its beautiful and dazzling landscapes and forms as manifestations of the sacred, or when we see the activities of our fellow living things as somehow embodying the sacred. In the past human beings saw animals, plants, objects, or natural processes such as fire or the dawn, as God or as sacred manifestations of God. Today these animistic and totemistic attitudes are less common. Instead (and putting aside notions of God as a particular being), thinking about God as personal tends to hinge around ourselves as personal beings, or involve heightened personal experiences, in which we feel that we are personally interacting with the immanent or transcendent God.

What each of these transcendent, immanent, and personal approaches to God share is that they equally express the enigma that reality is to us, an enigma that human beings have long sought to penetrate and understand. Our drive to understand reality has led to the development of the religions, sciences, and philosophies that we use to examine the world, to peer into its depths, and to make sense of what we experience. Our forebears used the notion of God to embody the understanding that they arrived at. And God continues to be a useful notion when we contemplate the mystery of what is.

This is reflected in Stephen Hawking's view, shared by Thomas Aquinas, that looking into the world and discerning its patterns is like looking into the mind of God. In this sense our continued fascination with the idea of God is tied up with our desire to understand the reality in which we live. "God" gives us a word that embodies our experience of reality as the ultimate mystery. As Albert Einstein elegantly put it:

> The most beautiful emotion that we can experience is the mysterious. It is the fundamental emotion that stands at the cradle of all true art and science. He to whom this emotion is a stranger, who can no longer wonder and stand rapt in awe, is as good as dead, a snuffed-out candle. To sense that behind anything that can be experienced there is something that our minds cannot grasp, whose beauty and sublimity reaches us only indirectly: this is religiousness.[1]

Whether we call our striving to "see behind" what occurs in the world religious, or spiritual, or scientific, or philosophic, or plain and simple curiosity, it involves a quest. A quest to penetrate the mysterious and to make it, one increment at a time, a little more familiar, a little less strange. This mystery that tantalizes us we may call God.

Embracing the fullness of every subjective experience, incorporating all that is to be understood, embodied in all beings who have the power to understand, God is the mystery that we have emerged out of, the mystery we live our lives in the midst of, the mystery that both embraces and that beats at the heart of The Whole Of What Is.

Sapere aude!
(Dare to know!)

BIBLIOGRAPHY

Armstrong, Karen (1999). *A History of God*, London: Vintage.
Bacon, Francis (1620). *Novum Organum*.
Barnes, Jonathan (1987). *Early Greek Philosophy*, NY and London: Penguin.
Bosch, Lourens Peter van den. *Theosophy or Pantheism? Max Müller's Gifford Lectures on Natural Religion*, Public Domain: www.here-now4u.de/eng/theosophy_or_pantheism_friedr.htm
Bulfinch, Thomas (1881). *The Age of Fables*.
Campbell, Joseph (1962). *The Masks of God: Oriental Mythology*, NY: Penguin.
_____ (1964). *The Masks of God: Occidental Mythology*, NY: Arkana.
Caputo, John D. (2001). *On Religion*, London: Routledge.
_____ (ed) (1997). *Deconstruction in a Nutshell: A Conversation with Jacques Derrida*, NY: Fordham University Press.
Clayton, Philip and Peacocke, Arthur (2004). *In Whom We Live and Move and Have Our Being: Panentheistic Reflections on God's Presence in a Scientific World*, Grand Rapids and Cambridge: William B. Eerdmans Publishing Company.
Cleary, Thomas (1998). *The Essential Tao*, NY: Castle Books.
Cooper, John W. (2006) *Panentheism: The Other God of the Philosophers*, Grand Rapids: Baker Academic.
Corbin, Henry (1971). *The Man of Light in Iranian Sufism*, NY: Omega Publications.
Cupitt, Don (1995). *After God: The Future of Religion*, London: Phoenix.
_____ (1998). *Mysticism After Modernity*, London: Blackwell Publishers.
D'Aquili, Eugene and Newberg, Andrew B. (1999). *The Mystical Mind: Probing the Biology of Religious Experience*, Minneapolis: Fortress Press.
Darwin, Charles (1859). *On the Origin of the Species by Means of Natural Selection, Or the Preservation of Favoured Species in the Struggle for Life*, London: John Murray.
Dawkins, Richard (2006). *The God Delusion*, London: Black Swan.
Derrida, Jacques (1995). *On the Name*, edited by Thomas Dutoit, California: Stanford University Press.
Emerson, Ralph Waldo (1836). *Nature*, Boston: James Munroe Company.
_____ (1847). *Essays*, Boston: James Munroe Company.
Feuerbach, Ludwig (1841). *The Essence of Christianity*, translated by Marion Evans, NY: Calvin Blanchard, 2nd edition, 1855.
_____ (1843). *Principles of the Philosophy of the Future*, from *The Fiery Brook: Selected Writings of Ludwig Feuerbach* translated by Zawar Hanfir, NY: Doubleday.
Forman, Robert K. C. (ed) (1990). *The Problem of Pure Consciousness: Mysticism and Philosophy*, Oxford University Press.
_____ (1998). *The Innate Capacity: Mysticism, Psychology, and Philosophy*, OUP.

_____ (1999). *Mysticism, Mind, Consciousness*, State University of New York Press.
_____ (2004). *Grassroots Spirituality*, Imprint Academica.
Frazer, James George (1922). *The Golden Bough: A Study in Magic and Religion*, London: Macmillan, abridged edition, originally published in two volumes 1890.
Freud, Sigmund (1927). *The Future of an Illusion*, translated by James Grey. NY: W.W. Nortion & Co (re-pub. 1961).
Geering, Lloyd (1994). *Tomorrow's God: How We Create Our Worlds*, Wellington: Bridget Williams Books.
_____ (2002). *Christianity Without God*, Wellington: Bridget Williams Books.
Goldstein, Rebecca (2006). *Betraying Spinoza*, NY: Schocken Books.
Goodenough, Ursula (1998). *The Sacred Depths of Nature*, Oxford University Press.
Gregory, John (1991). *The Neoplatonists*, London: Kyle Cathie.
Griffin, David Ray (2001). *Reenchantment Without Supernaturalism: A Process Philosophy of Religion*, Cornell University Press.
Gura, Philip F. (2007). *American Transcendentalism: A History*, NY: Hill and Wang.
Haldane, Elizabeth S., and Ross, G.R.T, (1973). *The Philosophical Works of Descartes*, Volume 1, Cambridge University Press.
Hampshire, Stuart (2005). *Spinoza and Spinozism*, Clarendon Press
Hartshorne, Charles (1984). *Omnipotence and Other Theological Mistakes*, State University of New York Press.
Haught, John F. (2000). *God After Darwin: A Theory of Evolution*, Westview Press.
Hawking, Stephen (1988). *A Brief History of Time*, London: Bantam Books.
Hay, David (1990). *Religious Experience Today*, London: Mowbray.
_____ (2007). *Why Spirituality is Difficult for Westerners*, Societas.
Hegel, G.W.F. (1807). *The Phenomenology of the Spirit*, translated by J.B Baillie, NY: Harper & Row, (1967).
_____ (1817). *Encyclopaedia of the Philosophical Sciences*, translated by Steven A. Taubeneck, Continuum, (reprinted 1990).
_____ (1837). *Lectures on the Philosophy of World History*, translated H.B. Nesbit, Cambridge University Press, 1875.
Hick, John. (1964). *The Existence of God*, Macmillan Publishing Company.
Hill, Keith (2009). *The Bhagavad Gita: A New Poetic Version*, Auckland: Attar Books.
Isaacson, Walter (2008). *Einstein: His Life and Universe*, NY: Simon and Schuster.
James, William (1897). *The Will to Believe and other Essays*, Dover (reprint 1956).
_____ (1902). *The Varieties of Religious Experience*, Touchstone (reprint 1997).
Johnson, Elizabeth A. (2007). *Quest for the Living God*, NY: Continuum.
Kant, Immanuel (1784). *An Answer to the Question: What is Enlightenment?*
Kaplan, Aryeh (1989). *The Bihar Illumination*. NY: Samuel Weiser.
_____ (1985). *Meditation and Kabbalah*. Samuel Weiser.
Katz, Steven T. (ed) (1978). *Mysticism and Philosophic Analysis*, NY: Sheldon Press.
Kaufman, Walter (1976). *The Portable Nietzsche*, Penguin Books, (originally pub. 1954).
Keller, Catherine ((2008). *On the Mystery: Discerning Divinity in Process*, Fortress Press.

Körner, S. (1955). *Kant*, London and Penguin Books.
Krause, K.C.F (1900). *The Ideal of Humanity and Universal Federation*, translated by W. Hastie, T. & T. Clark (reprinted by BiblioLife).
Leaves, Nigel (2006). *The God Problem: Alternatives to Fundamentalism*, San Francisco: Polebridge Press.
McFague, Sallie (1993). *The Body of God: An Ecological Theology*, Fortress Press.
McGrath, Alister (2004). *The Twilight of Atheism*, Doubleday, Galilee.
Macquarrie, John (1985). *In Search of Deity: An Essay in Dialectical Theism*, London: Crossroad Publishing Company.
Mascarò, Juan (1965), *The Upanishads*, London: Penguin.
Mavrodes, George I. (1970). *The Rationality of Belief in God*, NY: Prentice-Hall.
Miller, Ed L. (1972). *God and Reason: A Historical Approach to Philosophic Theology*, MacMillan Publishing Co.
Mortley, Raoul (1991). *French Philosophers in Conversation*, London: Routledge.
Nadler, Steven (1999). *Spinoza: A Life*, Cambridge University Press.
Nikhilananda, Swami (1975). *Vivekananda: A Biography*, Calcutta: Advaita Ashrama.
O'Brien, Elmer (1964). *The Essential Plotinus*, New American Library.
Osbourne, Arthur (1987). *The Teachings of Ramana Maharshi*, London: Century.
Otto, Rudolf (1958). *The Idea of the Holy*, translated by John W. Harvey, Oxford University Press (originally pub. 1917).
Paine, Thomas (1852). *The Age of Reason: Being an Investigation of True and Fabulous Theology*, Boston, Josiah P. Mendum
_____ (1791-92). *The Rights of Man*, (ed) Henry Collins, Penguin (1976).
Peacocke, Arthur ((1993). *Theology For a Scientific Age*, Fortress Press.
Pereira, José, editor (1976). *Hindu Theology: A Reader*, Image Books.
Plato (1976). *Timaeus and Critias*, translated by Desmond Lee, London: Penguin.
Polo, Marco (1854). *The Travels of Marco Polo*, translated by John Marsden, (ed) Thomas Wright, London: Henry G. Bohn.
Redding, Paul (2006). *Georg Wilhelm Friedrich Hegel*, article in The Stanford Encyclopedia of Philosophy (Fall 2006 Edition), Edward N. Zalta (ed.), URL = <http://plato.stanford.edu/archives/fall2006/entries/hegel/>.
Rees, Martin (1997). *Before the Beginning: Our Universe and Others*, London: Touchstone.
_____ (1999). *Just Six Numbers: The Deep Forces that Shape the Universe*, NY: Basic Books.
Rescher, Nicholas (1996). *Process Metaphysics: An Introduction*, NY: SUNY.
Rolt, C. E. (1979). *Dionysius the Areopagite: The Divine Names and The Mystical Theology*, London: SPCK.
Ruysbroeck, John of (2010). *The Spiritual Espousals*, translated by Wim van den Dungen, Antwerp. Public domain: www.sofiatopia.org/equiaeon/3thlife.htm
_____ (1916). *The Adornment of the Spiritual Marriage; The Sparkling Stone; The Book of the Supreme Truth*. Translation by C. A. Wynschenk. Introduction and notes by Evelyn Underhill. London: J. M. Dent.

Shah-Kazemi, Reza (2006). *Paths to Transcendence According to Shankara, Ibn Arabi and Meister Eckhart*, Bloomington: World Wisdom.
Shankara (1975). *Self Knowledge (Atma-Bodha)*, translated by T.M.P. Mahadevan, Delhi: Arnold-Heinemann.
Shelburne, Donald W. (ed) (1966). *A Key to Whitehead's Process and Reality*, University of Chicago Press.
Smart, Ninian (1971). *The Religious Experience of Mankind*, Glasgow: Collins.
Spinoza, Baruch (1995). *The Ethics of Spinoza*, Dagobert D. Runes (editor), NY: Citadel Press.
Spinoza, Benedictus de (1677). *Ethics*, translated by Edwin Curley, NY: Penguin (2005)
Spong, John Shelby (2001). *A New Christianity for a New World*, HarperCollins.
Strauss, David (1860). *The Life of Jesus Critically Examined*, translated by Marian Evans, NY: Calvin Blanchard (4th edition).
_____ (1865). *A New Life of Jesus* (2 vols), London/Edinburgh: Williams and Norgate.
Suzuki, Beatrice Lane (1969). *Mahayana Buddhism*, NY: The Macmillan Company.
Tanner, Norman, SJ. (ed). *Decrees of the Ecumenical Councils*, Public domain: http://www.dailycatholic.org/history/20ecume1.htm
Tillich, Paul (1952). *The Courage To Be*, London: Collins Fontana Library (1962 ed)
Tiner, J.H. (1975). *Isaac Newton: Inventor, Scientist and Teacher*. Michigan: Mott Media.
Toland, John (1995). *Christianity Not Mysterious*, edited by Peter Browne, reprinted in *History of British Deism*, 8 vols, Routledge/Thoemmes Press, (originally pub. 1696).
Underhill, Evelyn. (1961). *Mysticism*, E.P. Dutton & Co.
Vivekananda, Swami (1952). *Advaita Vedanta: The Scientific Religion*, Calcutta: Advaita Ashrama.
Voltaire, F.M.A. de (1756). *Poèmes sur le Dèsastre de Lisbonne*. From *Selected Works of Voltaire*, edited and translated by Joseph McCabe, London: Watts and Co (1911).
White, Morton Gabriel (ed) (1961). *The Age of Analysis*, NY: New American Library.
Whitehead, A.N. (1926). *Science in the Modern World*, Cambridge University Press.
_____ (1927). *Religion in the Making*, Cambridge University Press.
Wilber, Ken (1996). *A Brief History of Everything*, Boston and London: Shambala.
_____ (1998). *The Marriage of Science and Soul: Integrating Science and Religion*, NY: Broadway Books.
Wilson, A.N. (2000). *God's Funeral*, London: Abacus.
Wrathall, Mark A. (ed) (2003). *Religion After Metaphysics*, Cambridge University Press.

REFERENCES

CHAPTER 1. AN IMPERTINENT PROPOSAL
1   Kaufman, *The Portable Nietzsche*, p 95.
2   1911 *Encyclopedia Britannica*, "Buckle, Henry Thomas."

CHAPTER 2. THE CHALLENGE OF SCIENCE
1   Bacon, *Novum Organum*, Aphorism I.
2   Ibid, Aphorisms CV and CVI.
3   Ibid, Aphorism XCIII.
4   Ibid, Aphorism LXXXIX.
5   Haldane and Ross, *The Philosophical Works of Descartes* pp 230-231.
6   Blake, from *The Song of Los* in *Collected Works*, p 246.
7   Quoted in Tiner, *Isaac Newton*, p 107.
8   This has become a famous quote, repeated in a wide variety of contexts.
9   Reprinted in Hick, *The Existence of God*, p 100.
10 Quoted by Wilson, *God's Funeral*, p 240.
11 Darwin, *On the Origin of the Species*, Conclusion.
12 Ibid, p 490.
13 Quoted by Wilson, *God's Funeral*, p 235.
14 Quoted by McGrath, *The Twilight of Atheism*, p 30.
15 D'Holbach, *Système de la nature (System of Nature)*. Quoted in Stanford Encyclopedia of Philosphy in article: http://plato.stanford.edu/entries/holbach/

CHAPTER THREE. THE BIBLE, CRITICALLY EXAMINED
1   Renan, *Life of Jesus*, p 215.
2   Strauss, *A New Life of Jesus*, Vol 2, p 434.

CHAPTER FOUR. LET'S COMPARE GODS
1   Frazer, *The Golden Bough* chapter 51.
2   Campbell, *The Masks of God: Occidental Mythology*, p 27.

CHAPTER FIVE. SIGNS OF THE TIMES
1   Voltaire, *Poèmes sur le Dèsastre de Lisbonne*.
2   Ibid.
3   Ibid.
4   Ibid.
5   Ibid.
6   Gibbon, chapter 15, Introduction.

7   Ibid, chapter 16, Conclusion.
8   Paine, *The Age of Reason*, Part One, p 5.
9   Ibid, p 6.
10 Ibid, p 10.

CHAPTER 6. DOUBTS OF THE PHILOSOPHERS
1   Haldane and Ross, *The Philosophical Works of Descartes*, p 144.
2   Ibid, pp150-152.
3   Kant, *An Answer to the Question: What is Enlightenment?*
4   Quoted in Körner, *Kant*, p 27.
5   Hegel, *The Phenomenology of the Spirit*, Preface.
6   Hegel, *Lectures on the Philosophy of World History*, #553, 554, 557.
7   Hegel, *The Phenomenology of the Spirit*, Preface.
8   Hegel *Lectures on the Philosophy of World History*, #40.
9   Redding, *Georg Wilhelm Friedrich Hegel*.
10 Feuerbach, *The Essence of Christianity*, p 10.
11 Feuerbach, *Principles of the Philosophy of the Future*, Part 1, #17.
12 Ibid, Part 2, #23.
13 Feuerbach, *The Essence of Christianity*, p 24.
14 Ibid, p 352.
15 Ibid, pp 36 and 41.

CHAPTER 7. THE FORK IN THE ROAD
1   Tanner, *Decrees of the Ecumenical Councils*, Day 1, Session 3:5–7.
2   Quoted in McGrath, *The Twilight of Atheism*, pg 129.
3   Quoted in Wilson, *God's Funeral*, pg 184.
4   Ibid p 133.
5   Ibid p 39.
6   Nikhilanada, *Vivekanda*, p 24.
7   From Vivekananda's closing address, September 27, 1893.
8   Paine, *The Age of Reason*, Part One, p 6.

CHAPTER 8. WORLD WAR AND ITS DISCONTENTS
1   Freud, *The Future of an Illusion*, p 70.

CHAPTER 9. GOD-TALK IS A HUMAN INVENTION
1   Quoted in Peacocke, *Theology for A Scientific Age*, p 48.
2   Quoted in Shah-Kezami, *Paths to Transcendence*, p 4.
3   Ruysbroeck, *The Spiritual Espousals*, Sermon, 117, 3, 5.
4   All quotes in this paragraph from Johnson, *Quest for the Living God*, p 21.
5   Keller, *On the Mystery*, p 18.
6   Ibid, pp 20, 21.

CHAPTER 10. BEYOND THE MYTHOLOGICAL GOD
1. Quoted in Leaves, *The God Problem*, p 24.
2. Tillich, *The Courage To Be*, p 49.
3. Ibid, pp178-179.
4. Ibid, p 181.
5. Geering, *Tomorrow's God*, p 114.
6. Ibid, p 145.
7. Ibid, p 236.
8. Spong, *A New Christianity for a New World*, p p 45, 52.
9. Ibid, p 63.
10. Ibid, pp 70-73.
11. Ibid, pp 237-238.
12. Ibid, p 214.

CHAPTER 11. PANTHEISM: GOD IS EVERYTHING
1. Toland, *Christianity Not Mysterious*, pp 4, 6.
2. Spinoza, *The Ethics of Spinoza*, pg 118. Section 4, Proposition 63.
3. Ibid, p 167. Section 1, Propositions 11, 14, 15, 18.
4. Ibid, p 171. Section 1, Appendix.
5. Ibid, pp 153, 198, 152, 180. Section 5, Prop 25; Section 2, Prop 47; Section 5, Prop 24; Section 1, Appendix.
6. Hawking, *A Brief History of Time*, p 184.
7. Quoted in Dawkins, *The God Delusion*, p 36.
8. Quoted in Goodenough, *The Sacred Depths of Nature*, p 10.
9. Ibid, pg 11.
10. Ibid, p 169.
11. Ibid, p 171.
12. See http://www.deepecology.org/platform.htm

CHAPTER 12. PANENTHEISM: EVERYTHING IN GOD
1. Krause, *The Ideal of Humanity and Universal Federation*, pp 5-6.
2. Hill, *The Bhagavad Gita*, Discourse 13: 14-16.
3. O'Brien, *Ennead V 2*, p 108.
4. Emerson, *Essays*, pp 224-245, 252, 251.
5. Quoted in White, *Age of Analysis*, p 88.
6. Sherburne (ed), *A Key to Whitehead's Process and Reality*, p 8.
7. Whitehead, *Science and the Modern World*.
8. Sherburne, p 179.
9. Ibid, p181.
10. Ibid p 182.
11. Whitehead, *Science in the Modern World*, p 275.
12. Macquarrie, *In Search of Deity*, p 192.

13 Ibid, p 193.
14 Quoted in Macquarrie, p 196.
15 Haught, *God After Darwin*, p 39.
16 Ibid, p 51.
17 Ibid, p 136.
18 From an article originally published in *The Christian Century*, January 2-9, 1991, pp. 12-15. Reprinted in public domain: http://www.religion-online.org/showarticle.asp?title=54. Copyright by The Christian Century Foundation.
19 Leaves, *The God Problem*, p 46.
20 Forman, *Grassroots Spirituality*, pp 8-9.
21 Ibid, p 4.
22 Ibid, p 51.
23 Spong, p 238.

CHAPTER 13. ARE SPIRITUAL EXPERIENCES REAL?
1 Forman, *Grassroots Spirituality*, p3.
2 Hill, *The Bhagavad Gita*, Discourse Six: selected verses from 18 to 27.
3 Cleary, *The Original Face*, p 30-31.
4 Author's translation.
5 Corbin, *The Man of Light in Iranian Sufism*, p 117-118.
6 Ibid, p 118.
7 Ruysbroek, *The Book of Supreme Truth*, chapter 12. Translated by Wynschenk.
8 Published in Katz (ed) *Mysticism and Philosophic Analysis*, pp 22-74.
9 Ibid, p 26.
10 Ibid, p 26.
11 Ibid, p 27.
12 Ibid, p 63.
13 The full account is in Foreman, *Mysticism, Mind, Consciousness*, pp 21-24.
14 See ibid, pp 48-50.
15 D'Aquili and Newberg, *The Mystical Mind*, p 26.
16 Ibid, p 117.
17 Hill, ibid.
18 Ruysbroek, ibid.
17 From *Appendix, The Last Philosophy* (1995). The whole *Appendix* is available on Don Cupitt's website: http://www.doncupitt.com/doncupitt.html
18 Cupitt, *Mysticism After Modernity*, p 74.

CHAPTER 14. GOD WITHOUT METAPHYSICS
1 Heidegger appears to have drawn on the writings of the German Romantic poet Hölderlin in this concept of Godhead.
2 Mortley, *French Philosophers in Conversation*, pp 96-97.
3 Ibid, p 97.

4   Caputo, *Deconstruction in a Nutshell*, p 22.
5   Published in Wrathall (ed), *Religion After Metaphysics*, pp 123-145.
6   Ibid, p 123.
7   Ibid, p 124.
8   Caputo, *On Religion*, p 128.
9   Wilber, *The Marriage of Sense and Soul*, p 56.
10   Ibid, p 166.
11   Hay, *Religious Experience Today*, pp 79-85.
12   Ibid, p 74.

CHAPTER 17. GOD AS QUEST
1   Quoted in Isaacson, *Einstein*, p 387.

INDEX

A
Advaita Vedanta 87
Aesthetic cosmological principle 150
Age of Enlightenment 8, 68
Age of Reason 35
The Age of Reason See Paine, Thomas
Agnostic 32
Al-Hallaj 212
Ancien régime 59-60
Anthropology 49
Anselm of Canterbury 206-208
Aquinas, Thomas 17-22, 62, 79, 96, 103-104, 143, 163, 189, 213
Aristotle 17, 19, 21, 30, 69
Astric, Jean 36
Atheism 8, 32, 36, 53, 61, 62, 64, 75, 81, 83, 86, 95, 125, 126, 136
Avant-garde 93, 178-179
Ayer, A.J. 95

B
Bacon, Francis 7, 19-20, 23, 81, 88
Balzac, Honoré de 27
Bauer, F.C. 37-39, 42, 74-75
Being 18, 54, 61, 67, 70, 76, 110-113, 117-119, 130, 138, 144, 151, 182-183, 195, 204
Being-Itself 112, 113, 117-119
Bhagavad Gita 47, 85, 137, 138, 160
Bible 5, 8, 15, 17-22, 25, 30, 33-38, 41, 42, 45, 46, 54, 68, 80-84, 89, 93, 100-101, 119, 196
  Affirms geocentric world view 21
  Battle over 35
  Date of creation 15
Biblical criticism 34-42
  Critique of *Pentateuch* 35
  Documentary hypothesis 37
  Search for historical Jesus 38
  Two-source hypothesis 40
Blake, William 8, 24

Blavatsky, Madam 86
Bohr, Niels 98, 99
Book of the Dead (Egyptian) 85
Brahe, Tycho 21
Brahman 54, 105, 137, 138, 150, 160, 165, 174, 175
Bruno, Giordano 123
Buckle, Thomas Henry 15
Buddhism 9, 52, 85, 107, 108, 114, 160, 167, 195
Bulfinch, Thomas 48
Burton, Richard 47

C
Campbell, Joseph 51
Caputo, John 187-190, 195, 202, 215, 223
  On Religion (2001) 187
Catholic Church 17-18, 21, 59-61, 63, 80-81, 103
  First Vatican Council (1869) 80
  Index of Forbidden Books 23, 81
Champollion, Jean-François 45
Christianity 9, 31, 33, 49-51, 53, 54, 72, 73, 79-84, 85, 87, 96, 101, 113-115, 117, 119, 122, 133, 143, 162, 195, 201
  And the New Testament 37-42
  As a mystery 122-123
  Criticism of 56-64
  Toland's criticism of 122
  See also Theism
Classical theism *See* Theism
Clifford, William 25
Cognitive operators 170, 172-173, 204, 213
Columbus, Christopher 43
Comparative religion 51-53
Concepts of reality *See* Worldviews
Conscious beings (probability of) 207, 210
Constructionism 99, 108, 163-166, 168, 172-173, 202
Copenhagen interpretation 98

INDEX 225

Copernicus, Nicolaus 21, 25
Cupitt, Don 176, 177
  Mysticism After Modernity (1995) 177
Cuvier, Georges 27, 28

D
Daikaku 160, 162
Dao 124
D'Aquili, Eugene 168-172, 177
  The Mystical Mind (1999) 168, 215, 223
Darwin, Charles 8, 17, 25-35, 81, 99, 100, 148
  The Origin of Species 17, 31
Darwin, Erasmus 26
Dasein (Heidegger) 182, 185
Data wave of the now 203, 205
Dawkins, Richard 9
Deconstruction 99, 101, 179, 180, 183, 185-186
Deep ecology movement 134, 152
Deism 29, 30, 31, 218
Derrida, Jacques 180, 181, 183, 184, 185, 186, 187, 188, 190, 195, 203
Descartes, René 20, 65-70, 77, 81, 126-128
  Meditations of First Philosophy (1641) 65-66
  Principles of Philosophy (1644) 20
Dhammapada 47
D'Holbach, Baron 32, 95
Diderot, Denis 60
Dionysius the Areopagite 51, 105, 106, 161
Dionysus (Greek mystery god) 50-51
Dipolar (concept of God) 142-145, 204, 205
Discovery of dinosaurs 27
Discovery of fossils 96
Duality 116, 143, 158

E
Earth 8, 15, 21-25, 27, 34, 49, 52, 58, 94, 113, 116, 120-121, 132-134, 148, 150-152, 206-210, 213
East Indian Companies 44
Eckhart, Meister 147, 154, 155, 175, 212

Eddington, Arthur 97
Eddy, Mary Baker 86
Egypt 15, 40, 44, 45, 94, 100
Eighty Years' War 18
Einstein, Albert 8, 68, 96-99, 125, 130, 214
Eliot, George. *See* Evans, Marian
Ellwood, Robert 114
Emerson 85, 122, 138, 215, 222
Emerson, Ralph Waldo 138
End of Greatness 210
Evans, Marian 82-83
Evolution 8, 17, 26-28, 31, 35, 99, 114, 147-150, 210-211
  Larmarck's theory 26
  Mendel's "hereditary particle" 29
  "Survival of the fittest" 28, 31
Existentialism 95, 113
Experience *See* Spiritual experiences *and* Subjectivity
Ezra (as redactor of *Pentateuch*) 36-37, 125, 178-179

F
Feuerbach, Ludwig Andreas 71, 74-78, 83, 95
  The Essence of Christianity (1841) 75-76, 83
Forman, Robert 152, 153, 154, 157, 166, 167, 168, 172, 173, 174
Foucault, Michel 180, 181
Frazer, James George 48-50
  The Golden Bough (1890) 48-50
Freethinkers 25, 35
French Revolution 60, 61, 63
Freud, Sigmund 89, 94, 95, 102, 118, 179
Friedman, Alexander 97
Fundamentalism 82, 84

G
Gaia 133
Galilei, Galileo 20–25, 30, 81, 191, 206
Gama, Vasco de 44
Geering, Lloyd 113-118, 120, 124, 132-134, 176, 204
  Tomorrow's God (1994) 114

Geocentric narcissism 207
George Eliot. *See Evans, Marian*
Gibbon, Edward 58-64, 81
   The History of the Decline and Fall of the Roman Empire (1776-1788) 58
Global ethic 132
Globalization 116
God
   Absence of 94
   And the impossible 187-190, 203
   Aquinas' definition 17, 31
   As absentee landlord (Deism) 29
   As Being-Itself 112-113, 117-119, 201
   As conceived in 1800 14
   As conceived in 1900 89
   As conceived in 2000 102
   As concept 13, 25, 50, 53, 54, 166, 182, 206, 212, 213
   As divine watchmaker 26
   As evolving 147-150, 211
   As fulcrum 205
   As Ground of being 112, 117, 147, 158, 201, 204
   As immanent 121, 143-146, 149, 154, 176, 205, 208, 212-213
   As mystery 106, 119, 131, 132, 144, 186, 201, 204, 205, 213-214
   As negotiation 205
   As passible 145, 148-149, 151, 205
   As presence 7, 71, 86, 101, 144-146, 154, 183-184, 186, 194, 196
   As projection 76, 204
   As symbolic word 115, 204, 213
   As The Whole Of What Is 207-211
   As transcendent 121, 136, 152, 175, 181, 205, 208, 212, 213
   As Trinity 123, 147, 163, 165
   As ultimate 104, 105, 112, 113, 118, 131, 136, 153, 206-209, 214
   Beyond concept of 161, 201
   Consequent nature of 141, 142, 145
   Darwinist evolutionary position 31
   Deist concept of 29, 31
   Descartes' meditations on 66
   D'Holbach's dismissal of 32
   Dialectical theism 143
   Dionysius the Areopagite's idea of 105
   Dipolar nature of 142-145, 205
   Freud's critique of 95
   Geering's view of 115
   God above God (Tillich) 113, 119, 161
   God without religion (Spong) 117
   Hegel's concept of 71-74
   Intuitive knowing 119, 129, 156
   Kant's concept of 70
   Kenosis 149, 211
   Lahiji's concept of 162
   Marx's critique of 95
   Nineteenth century conclusions 53
   Plotinus' concept of 138
   Post-God God 201-205
   Primordial nature of (Whitehead) 141, 142, 144, 145, 146, 148
   And pure consciousness events 174
   Rejection of supernatural concept of 32, 89, 121, 123, 201
   Ruysbroeck's concept of 162
   Scientific doubt of 32
   Spinoza's concept of 127
   Spong's definition of 118
   Theistic (personal) concept of 89, 102, 109, 112, 113, 117, 118, 136, 143-145, 148, 149, 154, 156, 182, 208, 213
   Tillich's concept of 112
   Twentieth century cynicism of 94
   Universe as God's body 150-153
   Vulnerability of 148-149, 151
   Whitehead's concept of 141
   See also Panentheism, Pantheism *and* The impossible
God-talk 103-111, 118, 143, 150, 156, 186, 201-202
   See also Theology
Goodenough, Ursula 131, 132, 216, 221
Grand narratives 99, 100, 181
Ground of being 112, 117, 147, 158, 204

H

Haught, John F. 147-150, 211
   God After Darwin (2000) 148

INDEX

Hawking, Stephen 8, 213
Hay, David 157, 195, 196
Hébert, Jacques 60
Hegel, G.W.F. 71-78, 83, 85, 86, 125, 136
   The Phenomenology of the Spirit (1807) 71
Heidegger, Martin 143, 181-187, 195
   Being and Time (1927) 182
Heisenberg uncertainty principle 98
Heisenberg, Werrner 98-99
Hennell, Charles 82
Henry the Eighth 18
Hobbes, Thomas 35, 36
Holtzman, Heinrich Julius 40
Hubble, Edwin 97, 206
Hume, David 32, 61, 62, 81
Huxley, Aldous 158
Huxley, Thomas 32

I
Immanence 121, 143-146, 149, 154, 176, 205, 208
Impossible, The *See* The impossible
Index of Forbidden Books 23, 81
Indian religion 9, 52
Indo-European languages 46, 54
Industrial Revolution 14
Inquisition 22, 23
Intuitive knowledge 129, 156
Islam 47, 52, 54, 106, 114, 195, 212

J
Japhetic language and culture 46
Jesus 15, 25, 34, 35, 37, 38, 39, 40, 41, 42, 45, 49, 50, 51, 62, 73, 82, 83, 103, 112, 113, 117, 157, 165, 172, 189
Judaism 9, 15, 30, 35, 37, 38, 40, 63, 83, 90, 103, 106, 111, 125, 154, 187, 212
Johnson, Elizabeth 106, 201

K
Kant, Immanuel 68, 69, 70, 71, 72, 75, 76, 77, 81, 163, 164, 180, 188, 189
   Critique of Pure Reason 69
Karl Marx 94
Kama Sutra (1883) 47

Katz, Steven T. 163-166, 172, 177
   Forman's response to 166-168
   Language, Epistemology, and Mysticism (1978) 163-164
Keller, Catherine 106, 109
Kenosis 149, 211
Kepler, Johannes 21, 23
Knowledge-by-identity 173-174
Krause, Karl Christian Friedrich 136-137

L
Lahiji, Muhammad Bin Yahya 162
Lamarck, Jean-Baptiste 26
Language 163-165, 177
Laotze 124
Leaves, Nigel 152
Lemaître, Georges 97
Lisbon earthquake (1755) 56, 99
   Poem on the Lisbon Disaster (1756) 56
Locke, John 24, 32
Lovelock, James 133
Luther, Martin 18, 81, 110, 114
Lyell, Charles 28, 30

M
Macquarrie, John 143-149, 156, 182, 205
   In Search of Deity (1984) 144
Marx, Karl 73, 89, 94, 95, 179
McFague, Sallie 150-152
Mediterranean mysteries 50-51
Mendel, Gregor 8, 29
Metaphysics 9, 15, 29, 69, 125, 140, 176, 180-184, 188, 190, 195, 201, 204
   End of metaphysics 182-184
   Beyond metaphysical God 110-120
Milky Way Galaxy 69, 209
Mirabai 212
Modernism 178-179, 191-192
Moses 8, 15, 35, 36, 41, 94, 125, 212
Moses de León 212
Müller, Max 52, 53, 85
   Sacred Books of the East (1879) 52
Mysticism 71, 144-147, 157, 158, 162-166, 174, 175, 195, 212
Mythological God 8, 123

Mythology 8, 9, 13, 46, 48-50, 79, 81, 93, 201, 204

N
Naess, Arne 134
Naturalism 135
Negative theology 161
New being (Tillich, Spong) 112, 119, 150
Newberg, Andrew 168-172, 177
   The Mystical Mind (1999) 168
Newton, Isaac 8, 23-25, 30, 68, 96-98
   Belief in God 24
   Philosophiae Naturalis Principia Mathematica (1687) 23
Nietzsche, Frederick 8, 13-14, 73, 79, 85, 113, 201
   "God is dead" 13, 201
   Thus Spake Zarathustra (1882) 13
Noah 8, 15, 46
Non-dualism 158, 162
Non-realism 113

O
Openness (as intellectual attitude) 48, 89, 153, 185, 186, 204, 210
Origin of the Species (Darwin) 31
Otto, Rudolph 159

P
Paine, Thomas 9, 61-64, 89-90
   The Age of Reason (1795-1807) 60, 62-64, 89
Paley, William 26
Panentheism 102, 120, 135, 136-156, 208
   Forman's definition 153
   Vs pantheism 154-156
Pantheism 5, 102, 120, 121-135, 139, 150, 151, 208
   Vs panentheism 154-156
Papal Infallibility 81
Passible *See* God
Pentateuch 35
Perennialism 158, 162-165, 172-174, 202
Peron, Francois 49
Phenomenon (Kant) 49, 69, 71, 76

Philology 45, 52
Planck, Max 98
Plato 69, 138, 182, 183
Plotinus 138, 166, 186
Pluralism 202
Polo, Marco 43
Postmoderism 99, 100, 163, 177-181, 193, 196
   Radical postmodernism 181
   Relationship to Enlightenment 100
   Wilber's critique of 193
Pound, Ezra 178, 179
Process philosophy 139-143
Ptolemaic worldview 21-22, 206
Pure consciousness events 159-163, 171-176, 203
Pusey, Edward 83

Q
Quakers 62
Quantum physics 98-99
Quetzalcoatl 44
Qu'ran 30

R
Ramakrishna 86, 87
Ramanuja 150
Rationality 16, 204
Reason 18-21, 24, 25, 30, 32, 53, 57, 61, 64, 67-72, 79, 122-126, 129-130, 144, 154, 162, 175, 187
   The Goddess of Reason 61
   The reasonable (Caputo) 188-190
Reformation 15, 18, 110, 114
Religion 9, 43, 47, 49-55, 61, 89, 95, 100, 106, 133, 147, 170
   As God's will in the world 17, 20
   And world mythologies 47-51
   Blake's view of 24
   Caputo on 187-190
   Clash with the sciences 25, 30, 80-82,
   Comparative religion 8, 16, 51-55
   Creating alienation 82-84
   Ellwood's five stages 114
   God without religion (Spong) 117-119

Hegel on 72-74
Invented by humanity 75-76
Neurological view 170
Non-realism 113-117
Religion without God (Geering) 113-117
Religion without religion (Derrida) 185-187, 190
Religious naturalism 131-132
Problems with 58, 60, 94, 110-111, 122, 126, 152, 168, 180, 184, 202
Wilber's view 191-194
World Parliament of Religions (1893) 85-88
Renaissance 19, 123, 163, 191, 206
Renan, Ernest 34-35, 38, 39, 40-42, 81
Life of Jesus (1863) 34, 41
Robespierre, Maximilien 61
Rosetta Stone 45
Rubaiyat of Omar Khayyam (1859) 47
Ruysbroeck, John of 162-163, 174
The Book of Supreme Truth 162

S
Sapere aude (Kant) 68, 214
Sartre, Jean-Paul 95, 102
Savior gods 51
Scientific method 7, 19-20, 25, 35, 88, 116
Scientific Spinozism 129
Scientism 192-193
Secular thinking 54, 103, 110, 152, 178, 191
Shabistari, Mahmud 162
Shankara 105, 106, 218
Sin 24, 57, 115, 151, 184
Sissons, George 134
Sloan Great Wall 209
Spinoza, Baruch 36, 37, 75, 81, 124-130, 135, 137, 140-141, 154-155, 207
Ethics (1677) 126-127
Tractatus Theologico-Political (1670) 126
Spiritual experiences 156, 157-177, 194-196, 202-203
Biological basis of 158, 168, 172-173, 186, 202
Cognitive operators 170-171

Constructed or universal? 172
Cuppitt's view of 177
D'Aquili and Newman's view of 168
Deafferentation 170-171
Ergotrophic experiences 158
Trophotropic experiences 158, 169
Wilber's view of 194
See also Pure consciousness events *and* Subjective nature of experiences
Spiritual knowing 146, 156
See also Spiritual experiences
Spong, John Shelby 110, 117-120, 150, 156
A New Christianity For a New World (2001) 117
Stace, W.T. 158, 159
St John of the Cross 161, 177, 186
Strauss, David Friedrich 38-39, 41-42, 74-75, 83
The Life of Jesus (1835) 38
Subjectivity (the subjective nature of experience) 72, 74, 76, 78, 121, 140-142, 173-174, 192-193, 195, 197, 202-205, 209-210, 212
Sufism 47, 162, 212
Supernaturalism 32, 89, 117, 121-124, 135, 150
Symbols 51, 112, 115, 144, 165

T
Tao Te Ching 47
Teresa of Avila 8
The impossible (Derrida and Caputo) 186-190, 195, 201, 203
Theism 148, 149, 154, 182, 201, 208
Atheism 8, 32, 53, 62, 64, 81, 83, 136,
Classical theism 89, 136, 143-145
Dialectical theism (Macquarrie) 143-146
No longer relevant 102, 109, 111-113, 117, 118, 201
Monotheism 54
Theology 19, 41, 53, 63, 71, 72, 84, 125, 133, 134, 143, 146, 148, 149, 151, 163, 175, 187
As God-talk 103-109, 181

Development of 71-72
Exclusivity claims 87, 202
World as magical 24
Problems with Christian theology 39, 63, 75, 79, 113-117
Classical theism 143-145, 148, 149
Negative theology 106, 161, 185,
Non-realism 113
Theory of Relativity 96-97
The Whole Of What Is 207-211
Thirty Years' War 18
Tillich, Paul 111-113, 115, 117-120, 143, 147, 150, 151, 158, 182, 195
The Courage To Be (1952) 111-112
Ultimate concern 113, 205
Tissa, Piya 167
Toland, John 122-126, 135
Christianity Not Mysterious (1696) 122-123
Torah 30
Transcendence 121, 136, 152, 175, 181, 208, 213
Travels of Marco Polo (1298) 43
Trinity 123, 147, 163, 165

U
Übermensch 73
Ultimate questions
 Ultimacy 131-132, 206
 Ultimate concern (Tillich) 113, 205
 Ultimate reality 170-171, 174
 See also God as ultimate
Underhill, Evelyn 158
Unhinged (Caputo) 189-190, 202, 204-206
Unitarian beliefs 25, 35
Universe 21-24, 32, 97-102, 114, 116-117, 121, 123-124, 127-131, 135, 136-154, 204, 205, 206-211
Upanishads 52, 85, 88, 124, 137
Ussher, James 15, 27

V
Virgil 48, 49
Vivekananda 85-88

Voltaire, F.M.A. 56-58, 64, 81, 85
 Poem on the Lisbon Disaster (1756) 56

W
Weinberg, Steven 131, 149
Wellhausen, Julius 37
Whitehead, Alfred North 139- 146, 148-150, 203, 210-211
 Process and Reality (1929) 139
Wilber, Ken 190-195
World's Parliament of Religions (1893) 85-87
World views 8, 9, 49, 82, 89, 121, 210-213
 Abstract worldview 52-53
 Darwin's concept of the world 26-27
 Atheistic concept 32
 Derived from cognitive operators 170
 Experiences of world as constructed (Katz) 163-166
 Feuerbach on world as projection 74-77
 Hegel's worldview 71-74
 Kant's thinking on concepts 68-71
 Mythological worldview 48-51
 Postmodern worldview 179-181
 Twentieth century scientific worldview 96-99
 Twentieth century intellectual worldview 99-101
 Ultimacy and reality 206
 Wilber's three ways of perceiving world 190-195
 See also Pantheism, Panentheism *and* The Whole Of What Is
World War One 93-94, 178
World War Two 93-95, 143, 178, 202

Z
Zend Avesta 47

www.ingramcontent.com/pod-product-compliance
Lightning Source LLC
Chambersburg PA
CBHW021403290426
44108CB00010B/369